GUINNESS WORLD RECORDS 2012

GAMER'S EDITION

British Library Cataloguing-in-Publication Data: a catalogue record for this book is available from the British Library.

ISBN 10: 1904894768

ISBN 13: 9781904994763

Check the official **GWR Gamer's Edition** website – **www.guinnessworld records.com/ gamers** – regularly for record-breaking gaming news as it happens, plus exclusive interviews and competitions.

ACCREDITATION: Guinness World Records Limited has a very thorough accreditation system for records verification. However, while every effort is made to ensure accuracy, Guinness World Records Limited cannot be held responsible for any errors contained in this work. Feedback from our readers on any point of accuracy is always welcomed.

Guinness World Records Limited does not claim to own any right, title or interest in the trademarks of others reproduced in this book.

© 2012 Guinness World Records Ltd, a Jim Pattison Group company

GAMER'S EDITION 2012

EDITOR-IN-CHIEF
Craig Glenday

SENIOR MANAGING EDITOR
Stephen Fall

GAMING EDITOR
Gaz Deaves

LAYOUT EDITORS
Rob Cave,
Eddie de Oliveira

INDEX
Chris Bernstein

TAGLINE QUIZ
Joanna Tubbs

PROOFREADING
Matthew White

DESIGN
Lisa Garner and
Keren Turner at Itonic Design, Brighton, UK

VP PUBLISHING
Frank Chambers

DIRECTOR OF PROCUREMENT
Patricia Magill

PUBLISHING MANAGER
Jane Boatfield

PUBLISHING ASSISTANT
Charlie Peacock

PICTURE EDITOR
Michael Whitty

DEPUTY PICTURE EDITOR
Laura Nieberg

PICTURE RESEARCHER
Fran Morales

ORIGINAL PHOTOGRAPHY
Richard Bradbury,
Ranald Mackechnie,
Ryan Schude

COLOUR ORIGINATION
Resmiye Kahraman at FMG, London, UK

Printed by Courier Corporation in the USA

GAMER'S CONSULTANTS

Stuart Ashen
(Gaming Fail)
Dan Bendon
(Fighting Games)
Matthew Bradford
(Puzzle Games)
John Brown
(Racing Games)
David Crookes
(Instant Gaming)
Joseph Ewens
(Sports Games)
Ellie Gibson
(Party Games)
Robert Haxton
(Pro-Gaming Review)

Kirsten Kearney
(Shooting Games)
Richard Leadbetter
(Xbox 360 vs PS3)
Keza MacDonald
(Role-Playing Games)
Alec Meer
(MMO Games)
Chris Schilling
(Action-Adventure)
Wesley Yin-Poole
(Strategy & Simulation)
Twin Galaxies
(Scoreboards)

GUINNESS WORLD RECORDS

MANAGING DIRECTOR
Alistair Richards

SVP FINANCE
Alison Ozanne

FINANCE MANAGERS
Jason Curran,
Neelish Dawett,
Scott Paterson

ACCOUNTS PAYABLE MANAGER
Kimberley Dennis

ACCOUNTS RECEIVABLE MANAGER & CONTRACTS ADMINISTRATOR
Lisa Gibbs

HEAD OF LEGAL & BUSINESS AFFAIRS
Raymond Marshall

IT MANAGER
Graham Pullman

WEB APPLICATIONS DEVELOPERS
Imran Javed,
Anurag Jha

TELEVISION

SVP PROGRAMMING & TV SALES
Christopher Skala

DIRECTOR OF TELEVISION
Rob Molloy

TV DISTRIBUTION MANAGER
Denise Carter Steel

TELEVISION ASSISTANT
Jonny Sanders

COMMERCIAL

VP COMMERCIAL
Paul O'Neill

CREATIVE DIRECTOR
Adam Wide

LICENSING MANAGER
Chris Taday

PROJECT MANAGER
Athena Simpson

RECORDS MANAGEMENT

VP RECORDS
Marco Frigatti (Italy)

HEAD OF RECORDS MANAGEMENT (UK)
Andrea Bánfi (Hungary)

HEAD OF RECORDS MANAGEMENT (US)
Mike Janela

HEAD OF RECORDS MANAGEMENT (JAPAN)
Carlos Martínez (Spain)

RECORDS MANAGEMENT & ADJUDICATIONS
Jack Brockbank (UK),
Dong Cheng (China),
Momoko Cunneen (Japan), Shaun Cunneen (Japan),
Danny Girton Jr. (USA), Ralph Hannah (UK/Paraguay),
Johanna Hessling (USA), Freddie Hoff (Denmark), Kaoru Ishikawa (Japan),
Mike Janela (USA),
Olaf Kuchenbecker (Germany), Annabel Lawday (UK), Amanda Mochan (USA), Erika Ogawa (Japan), Talal Omar (Yemen), Anna Orford (France),
Kimberly Partrick (USA), Vin Sharma (UK), Chris Sheedy (Australia), Lucia Sinigagliesi (Italy), Elizabeth Smith (UK), Şeyda Subaşi-Gemici (Turkey), Kristian Teufel (Germany), Louise Toms (UK), Carim Valerio (Italy), Tarika Vara (UK), Lorenzo Veltri (Italy), Aleksandr Vypirailenko (Lithuania), Xiaohong Wu (China)

COMMUNICATIONS

SVP USA & GLOBAL MARKETING
Samantha Fay

MARKETING MANAGER (US)
Stuart E F Claxton

SENIOR PR EXECUTIVE (US)
Jamie Panas

SALES & PRODUCT DIRECTOR (US)
Jennifer Gilmour

LICENSING, PROMOTIONS & EVENTS (US)
David Cohen

PR & MARKETING ASSISTANT (US)
Sara Wilcox

SENIOR MARKETING MANAGER
Nicola Eyre

MARKETING MANAGER
Justine Bourdariat

SENIOR PR MANAGER
Amarilis Whitty

PR MANAGER
Claire Burgess

PR EXECUTIVE
Damian Field

DIRECTOR OF DIGITAL MEDIA
Katie Forde

VIDEO CONTENT MANAGER
Adam Moore

COMMUNITY MANAGER
Dan Barrett

ONLINE EDITOR
Kevin Lynch

DESIGNER
Neil Fitter

FRONT-END WEB DEVELOPER
Simon Bowler

PUBLISHING SALES

GLOBAL SALES DIRECTOR – PUBLISHING
Nadine Causey

SENIOR NATIONAL ACCOUNTS MANAGER
John Pilley

SALES & DISTRIBUTION EXECUTIVE
Richard Stenning

SVP JAPAN
Frank Foley

BUSINESS DEVELOPMENT MANAGER (JAPAN)
Erika Ogawa

SALES & MARKETING EXECUTIVES (JAPAN)
Momoko Cunneen,
Shaun Cunneen

HEAD OF HR
Jane Atkins

UK OFFICE MANAGER
Jennifer Robson

HR & OFFICE ADMINISTRATOR (US)
Morgan Wilber

ABBREVIATIONS & MEASUREMENTS: Guinness World Records Limited uses both metric and imperial measurements. The sole exceptions are for some scientific data where metric measurements only are universally accepted, and for some sports data. Where a specific date is given, the exchange rate is calculated according to the currency values that were in operation at the time. Where only a year date is given, the exchange rate is calculated from December of that year. "One billion" is taken to mean one thousand million.

GUINNESS WORLD RECORDS 2012

GAMER'S EDITION

CONTENTS

INTRODUCTION 006
HOW TO BE A RECORD-BREAKER 008
GAMING AWARDS ROUND-UP 010
THE *GAMER'S* AWARDS 012
GAMING ROUND-UP 016

FEATURE: ACCEPT THE CHALLENGE . .020

HARDWARE 022

BEST OF XBOX 024
BEST OF PLAYSTATION 026
BEST OF Wii .028
BEST OF PC 030
BEST OF 3DS AND DS 032
BEST OF MOBILE 034

GAZ DEAVES
Supercute in his Tanooki suit, the legendary
Mr Deaves penned our Hardware section.

FEATURE: XBOX 360 vs PS3 036

SHOOTING GAMES 038

CRITICAL HIT!: *BATTLEFIELD* 040
FIRST-PERSON SHOOTERS 042
THIRD-PERSON SHOOTERS 044
2D SHOOTERS 046
ONLINE SHOOTERS 048
RAIL SHOOTERS 050
CRITICAL HIT!: *GEARS OF WAR* 052

KIRSTEN KEARNEY
Our own Samus Aran, Kirsten aimed to please
in the Shooters section.

SPORTS GAMES 054

CRITICAL HIT!: *SSX* 056
SOCCER 058
AMERICAN SPORTS 060
EUROPEAN SPORTS 062
EXTREME SPORTS 064

JOSEPH EWENS
Clearly mad for *Madden*, if it's "in the game",
Joseph has it in our Sports section.

FEATURE: PRO-GAMING REVIEW 066

RACING GAMES 068

CRITICAL HIT!:
    FORZA MOTORSPORT 070
SIMULATION RACING 072
ARCADE RACING 074
STREET RACING 076
KART RACING 078

JOHN BROWN
Despite his *Donkey Kong* look,
there was no monkey business
from John when he wrote our
Racing section.

PARTY GAMES 080

CRITICAL HIT!: KINECT 082
LIFESTYLE & FITNESS 084
AUGMENTED REALITY 086
RHYTHM – INSTRUMENTS 088
RHYTHM – DANCING 090

ELLIE GIBSON
Rocking out as *Dance Central*'s Taye, Ellie
was the life and soul of our Party section.

FEATURE: GAMING FAIL 092

ACTION-ADVENTURE 094

CRITICAL HIT!: *ASSASSIN'S CREED* 096
SANDBOX 098
NARRATIVE ADVENTURE 100
STEALTH 102
SURVIVAL HORROR 104
2D PLATFORMERS 106
3D PLATFORMERS 108
GRAPHIC ADVENTURE 110

CHRIS SCHILLING
Cutting a fine figure as assassin
Ezio Auditore, Chris tracked down
all of our Action-Adventure needs.

THE WORLD'S BIGGEST-SELLING VIDEOGAMING ANNUAL

FIGHTING GAMES 112

CRITICAL HIT!: CAPCOM CROSSOVERS. 114
2D FIGHTERS 116
3D FIGHTERS 118
    BEAT-'EM-UPS 120
    COMBAT SPORTS. 122

DAN BENDON
A hit in the streets as Akuma, Dan made our Fighting Games section a KO.

PUZZLE GAMES 124

CRITICAL HIT!: ANGRY BIRDS 126
BLOCK PUZZLES 128
SPATIAL PUZZLES 130
PHYSICS-BASED PUZZLES 132
LOGIC PUZZLES 134

MATTHEW BRADFORD
In the guise of Professor Layton, Matt mastered the mysteries of Puzzle Games for us.

FEATURE: STAR WARS 136

ROLE-PLAYING GAMES. . . 138

CRITICAL HIT!: POKÉMON. 140
ACTION RPGs 142
JAPANESE RPGs 144
WESTERN RPGs. 146
STRATEGY RPGs 148

KEZA MacDONALD
When it came to RPG records, Pokétrainer Keza caught 'em all.

MMO GAMES. 150

CRITICAL HIT!: ULTIMA ONLINE 152
FANTASY MMORPGs 154
SCI-FI MMORPGs 156
SOCIAL NETWORK GAMING 158

ALEC MEER
Proving his allegiance to the horde, Alec got his Orc on for our MMO section.

STRATEGY & SIMULATION 160

CRITICAL HIT!: STARCRAFT 162
TURN-BASED STRATEGY 164
REAL-TIME STRATEGY 166
SIMULATION ROUND-UP. 168
LIFE SIMULATORS. 170

WESLEY YIN-POOLE
Not such an ugly zergling, Wesley guided us through the Strategy & Simulation section.

INSTANT GAMING. 172

CRITICAL HIT!: DONKEY KONG 174
CLASSIC ARCADE 176
MODERN ARCADE 178
ALTERNATE REALITY GAMES 180

DAVID CROOKES
Dressed here as Dragon's Lair's Dirk the Daring, David gave us Instant Gaming records... very quickly indeed.

TOP 50 GAME ENDINGS 182

TWIN GALAXIES SCOREBOARDS 192

FEATURE: eSPORTS LEAGUE TABLES .208

INDEX 210
TAGLINE QUIZ ANSWERS 214
PICTURE CREDITS/
ACKNOWLEDGEMENTS/STOP PRESS . 216

TROLL SOLDIER

Army of Trolls is the portfolio of London-born, videogame-obsessed artist Gary J Lucken. Working from his computer in Bournemouth, Dorset, UK – and surrounded by Japanese toys and piles of old 2D videogames – Gary produces a unique brand of colourful artwork heavily influenced by the games, toys and pop culture he loves so much. His "pixel portraits" of our section writers are shown here and on each chapter opener. www.armyoftrolls.co.uk

INTRODUCTION

FILLED WITH MORE FANTASTIC FACTS, FEATS AND PHOTOS THAN EVER BEFORE,

WELCOME TO THE 2012 *GUINNESS WORLD RECORDS GAMER'S EDITION*. WE'RE BACK AGAIN WITH A NEW BOOK PACKED WITH AMAZING GAMING RECORDS!

appear as one of our **Critical Hits!**, with its own double-page feature.

As ever, we've had applications from aspiring record-breakers in every corner of the globe this year. Wherever people are gaming, they're breaking records. If you think you have what it takes to get in on this action, turn the page and learn **How to be a Record-breaker**. There is also an exciting new way to set Guinness World Records online – turn to page 20 to discover **Guinness World Records Challengers**.

We always enjoy hearing what our readers think, and this year's reader survey showed us your **Top 50 Game Endings**. You'll find the results starting on page 182, but be warned: the list is positively packed with spoilers!

We've also had great fun with this year's features. We've recruited Richard Leadbetter of Digital Foundry, the guys who test all the games and equipment for the folk at Eurogamer.net. He's given us his take on the long-running tech rivalry between Xbox 360 and PS3 (on page 36). We've got YouTube joker Ashens to give us his take on some legendary examples of **Gaming Fail** (on page 92). We also unleashed our own Jedi-in-training Charlie Peacock to take a look back at 30 years of *Star Wars* games (on page 136).

So, get comfortable in your favourite gaming chair, sit back and enjoy *Gamer's Edition 2012*. We've had a lot of fun making it and hope that you will enjoy reading it, too.

SUPER-SIZED ACTION!

At *Gamer's Edition* we love seeing titanic tech and enormous equipment, so we were really excited to visit the Delft University of Technology in the Netherlands to play some old-school Mario on a massively scaled-up version of a NES joypad. This gaming beast was the product of student Ben Allen (UK, centre), who was assisted in this endeavour by Stephen van't Hof and Michel Verhulst (both the Netherlands, left and right, respectively). Turn to page 22 to find out the full details of this towering engineering achievement!

Now in its fifth year, *Guinness World Records Gamer's Edition* is back! There's been no shortage of gaming records broken this year, so to browse the latest facts and feats on the games you like to play, check out our **Record-breaking Games** section starting on page 38. Your favourite series might even

LOCATION SHOTS

Our pictures crew have travelled the world to capture the most spectacular images of gaming feats just for our book. Gaming Editor Gaz Deaves goes ape for good gaming pics, and to prove it he donned a gorilla suit to make like Donkey Kong in our *Mario Kart* photo shoot. He was joined by top *Mario Kart*er Sami Çetin, Guinness World Records Editor-in-Chief Craig Glenday (in a gorilla mask) and GWR adjudicator Liz Smith, our own Princess Peach. Turn to page 68 to discover what record Sami set.

748 The total number of official world records featured in this year's *Guinness World Records Gamer's Edition*.

IT'S *GAMER'S EDITION* 2012

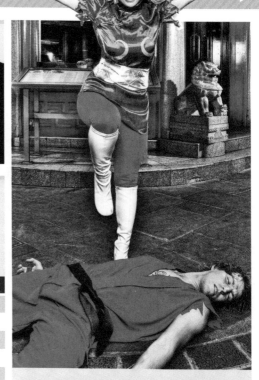

STILL GOING GLOBAL

We've been to loads of events this year, including the gaming mega-show E3, The Gadget Show Live, Eurogamer Expo, San Diego Comic Con, GAMEFest, Nottingham Games Festival and many more. One of the highlights was the Kapow! Comic Con in London, UK, where we met comics writer Mark Millar (right), who accepted the certificate for the **most popular videogame superhero** on behalf of Spider-Man, who has starred in 37 solo adventures.

MARATHON MEN

American videogames magazine *Game Informer* really caught the bug for breaking Guinness World Records this year with a successful attempt in March for the **longest marathon playing a fighting game**. This feat was soon beaten by another group – you can find out who on page 117. The *Informer* crew then resolved to set themselves an even bigger challenge, with six members of staff each attempting a different gaming marathon. Here's how they fared, from left to right:

NAME (COUNTRY)	RECORD TITLE	TIME
Dan Ryckert (USA)	Longest *Super Mario* marathon	50 hr
Jeff Cork (USA)	Longest *Grand Theft Auto* marathon	50 hr
Phil Kollar (USA)	Longest JRPG marathon	34 hr
Tim Turi (USA)	Longest survival horror marathon	27 hr 8 min
Ben Reeves (USA)	Longest stealth game marathon	48 hr
Bryan Vore (USA)	Longest RPG marathon	43 hr 21 min

KICKING IT WITH KAYANE

Best known among pro-gamers under her tag of "Kayane", Marie-Laure Norindr (France) became the **first woman to win a pro-*Street Fighter* event** at the Evolution Championship Series 2010 when she beat Sola "Burnyourbra" Adesui in the women's *Super Street Fighter IV* final. We met up with her, dressed as Chun-Li, having some fun at the expense of "Ken" (stuntman Ant Skrimshire) in London's Chinatown ahead of EVO 2011 – check out page 112 to see who else she met there.

IGN'S MILLIONS

Gaming website IGN.com accepted the Guinness World Records certificate for the **most popular videogames website**, with a massive 20,516,000 visitors in February 2011 alone. Veteran games commentator Tal Blevins (right, with our own Gaz Deaves) was on hand to accept the award.

TAGLINE QUIZ

We love a good quiz at *Gamer's*, especially if it tests our gaming knowledge. Running across the bottom of most pages of this year's edition you'll see a "tagline" that has been used to promote a videogame. Our challenge to you is to name the game from the tagline, or "pin the tag on the game". The answers can be found on pages 214–215.

HOW TO BE A RECORD-BREAKER

SO YOU'RE GOOD AT GAMING. BUT ARE YOU GOOD ENOUGH TO EARN A GUINNESS WORLD RECORDS TITLE? RECORD-BREAKING IS FUN, FREE AND OPEN TO ALL. THERE ARE LOTS OF WAYS TO PROVE YOUR SKILLS AND BE AWARDED WITH AN OFFICIAL CERTIFICATE...

STEP 1:
APPLY ONLINE AT GUINNESS WORLD RECORDS.COM
The first port of call for any record attempt should be the GWR website. Choose the "Set a Record" option. You'll need to register on our website first, then you'll be able to tell us the game you are playing, what record you want to set and how you'll measure it. Remember that Guinness World Records feats need to be measurable, breakable (unless it is a significant first) and verifiable. If your idea cannot meet these criteria, then it won't make the grade as a world record.

STEP 2:
GET THE GUIDELINES
If we like your record idea we'll send you the official rules that you must follow when attempting your chosen feat. These guidelines will detail what game settings should be used and what glitches are permitted, if any.
Everyone MUST follow the same rules so that each attempt can be judged fairly.

If we reject your record proposal, we will get in touch with you to tell you why.

STEP 3:
ATTEMPT YOUR RECORD
After plenty of practice you should be ready to show us what you've got. Be sure to video your record attempt and get at least two independent witnesses to watch you perform your feat. They will need to write witness statements as evidence that you actually did what you said you would. You should also send us anything else you think will support your claim.

STEP 4:
SEND IN YOUR EVIDENCE
Collate all your evidence, as per our guidelines, and post it to GWR HQ. Our trained team of records managers will check your footage, statements and other evidence and make their decision on whether you have broken the record. If you are successful, you will know when your Guinness World Records certificate arrives in the post. This is confirmation that you are

THE RECORD HUNT
Do you work in the games industry? Do you think a game you have worked on is truly record-breaking in some way? Did it have an amazing technical innovation or do something really different? If so, we would love to hear from you. If you get in touch with us early enough in the development process, we might be able to recognize your game's achievement in time for its launch!

OFFICIALLY AMAZING! If you are not successful, don't worry – keep practising and try again.

ON THE ROAD
Our adjudicators also attend events around the world from which gamers walk away with their very own Guinness World Records certificate. At the Gadget Show Live in Birmingham, UK, on 13 April 2011, 316 gamers took part in the **largest mobile phone gaming party.** Our own Kaoru Ishikawa is shown above with former *Hollyoaks* actors Matt Littler (left) and Darren Jeffries.

SO DO I GET INTO THE NEXT GAMER'S EDITION?
You've got yourself a world record, but do you get into the book? We have more than 25,000 records on the Guinness World Records database and only a fraction of these make it into the final book. Each year, members of our editorial team go through all of the latest entries looking for records that are truly amazing to fill the pages of our next edition. If a record is especially notable – or is particularly eye-catching – we might also send our pictures team to capture your skills in action.

TYPES OF RECORDS

Videogame records come in three varieties:
1) Technical achievements. Usually these are things that the game itself does or has achieved – from amazing sales to technological firsts.
2) *Otaku* achievements. *Otaku* is the Japanese word for an "obsessive fan" and these records relate to the activities of the fan community – typically for collecting or dressing up as videogame characters.
3) In-game achievements. Anything you can do in the game – from high scores and fastest completions to longest marathon sessions.

1. TECHNICAL ACHIEVEMENT

Our consultants contact various game makers looking for records. Some people in the industry contact us directly to tell us of their achievements that they suspect are record-worthy. This was the case with Toro Station (formerly Mainichi Issho), the **most prolific console-based gaming news service**. Produced by Sony, Toro Station ran for 1,591 episodes between 11 November 2006 and 15 May 2011. The PlayStation mascot cats, Kuro and Turo (above left and right) accepted the certificate on behalf of Toro Station at Sony's office in Japan.

2. OTAKU ACHIEVEMENT

Our talent spotters scour the internet and travel the globe in search of keen gaming fans such as Mitsugu Kikai (Japan), who is the proud owner of the **largest collection of Super Mario memorabilia**. Counted in Tokyo, Japan, on 15 July 2010, his colossal collection contains 5,400 unique items relating to the famous Italian plumber from the popular Nintendo videogame series, all kept in his apartment.

3. IN-GAME ACHIEVEMENT

Most of our record claims come from our readers and are for things they've achieved in a videogame, although some are more unusual than others. Dutch gamer Jesse Moerkerk (pictured far right with GWR's Gaz Deaves) performed the **longest gaming session in indoor freefall**, playing *Super Mario Galaxy 2* (Nintendo, 2010) for 18 min 52 sec at Indoor Skydive Roosendaal, the Netherlands, on 11 January 2011. As you can see from the inset pictures of his feat in progress, using the Wii Remote in freefall is a challenge in itself!

GAMING AWARDS ROUND-UP

BAFTA BEGAN REWARDING VIDEOGAMES IN 1998 WITH THE INTERACTIVE

AWARDS CEREMONIES PROVIDE AN OPPORTUNITY TO RECOGNIZE THE BEST GAMES AND TECHNICAL ACHIEVEMENTS THE INDUSTRY HAS TO OFFER. HERE IS OUR SELECTION OF THE HIGHLIGHTS OF THE MOST RECENT VIDEOGAME AWARDS SEASON.

GAME CRITICS AWARDS BEST OF E3 2011

Selected by commentators and journalists from across the games media, the Game Critics Awards Best of E3 aim to recognize the most promising pre-release titles at the annual E3 trade show, long before they are made available to the public.

AWARD	WINNER (DEVELOPER)
Best of Show	*BioShock Infinite* (Irrational Games, right)
Best Console Game	*The Elder Scrolls V: Skyrim* (Bethesda Softworks)
Best Handheld Game	*Sound Shapes* (Queasy Games)
Best Hardware	PlayStation Vita (Sony)
Best Action Game	*Battlefield 3* (DICE)
Best Role-Playing Game	*The Elder Scrolls V: Skyrim* (Bethesda Softworks)
Best Fighting Game	*Street Fighter X Tekken* (Capcom)
Best Racing Game	*Forza Motorsport 4* (Turn 10 Studios)
Best Motion Simulation Game	*The Legend of Zelda: Skyward Sword* (Nintendo)
Best Downloadable Game	*Bastion* (Supergiant Games)

Source: Game Critics Awards, presented in June 2011

TEARS FOR FEARS

One of the main characters in *BioShock Infinite* is Elizabeth (above), who has the power to pull objects from other places and times through holes or "tears" in reality. One E3 demo showed Elizabeth using her powers to open a tear to the 1980s.

WORLD OF MINECRAFT

Mojang, the developer of *Minecraft* (above), swept up many 2012 awards, but their next title, *Scrolls*, has already gained criticism from Bethesda Softworks. They are worried that the title is too similar to their *Elder Scrolls* series. Mojang's solution? To settle this dispute like gamers: with a videogame deathmatch!

DEVELOP INDUSTRY EXCELLENCE AWARDS 2011

Voted for by people who make games, the Develop Awards focus on technical and creative achievement, especially on new game series (Intellectual Properties, or IPs).

AWARD	WINNER (DEVELOPER)
Best New IP	*Enslaved* (Ninja Theory)
Best Licenced Game	*F1 2010* (Codemasters Birmingham)
Best Visual Arts	*Limbo* (Playdead)
Best Audio Accomplishment	*Papa Sangre* (Somethin' Else)
Publishing Hero	Valve
Best Technical Innovation	Kinect
Best New Studio	Mojang
Best In-house Studio	Media Molecule
Best Independent Studio	Crytek
Development Legend	Ian Livingstone
Grand Prize	Rovio Mobile

Source: Develop magazine, presented in July 2011

$30,000 The amount of money (equivalent to £19,000) given to the winner of the Seumas McNally Grand Prize, the top award at the Independent Games Festival.

ENTERTAINMENT AWARDS – *GOLDENEYE* WON THE FIRST "BEST GAME" GONG ▶

VIDEOGAME BAFTAS 2011

In addition to film and television, the British Academy of Film and Television Awards (BAFTA) has a set of awards to recognize excellence in videogames. These awards are among the most prestigious in gaming.

AWARD	WINNER (DEVELOPER)
Academy Fellowship	Peter Molyneux
Best Action	*Assassin's Creed: Brotherhood* (Ubisoft)
Artistic Achievement	*God of War III* (Sony)
Best Game	*Mass Effect 2* (BioWare)
Best Family	*Kinect Sports* (Rare)
Best Handheld	*Cut the Rope* (Zeptolab)
Best Multiplayer	*Need for Speed: Hot Pursuit* (EA)
Best Original Music	*Heavy Rain* (Sony)
Best Social Network Game	*My Empire* (Playfish)
Best Sports	*F1 2010* (Codemasters)

Source: BAFTA, presented in March 2011

GOD COMPLEX

A veteran of the videogames industry and pioneer of "God" games (in which players control the development of a civilization), Peter Molyneux started his career selling floppy discs with games on them and now serves as Creative Director of Microsoft Game Studios, Europe.

GAME DEVELOPERS CHOICE AWARDS 2011

As its name suggests, the Game Developers Choice Awards are voted for by an advisory panel of people who work in the games industry and reflect the achievements that have impressed people who make games.

AWARD	WINNER (DEVELOPER)
Lifetime Achievement	Peter Molyneux (below left)
Pioneer Award	Yu Suzuki
Ambassador Award	Tim Brengle and Ian MacKenzie
Game of the Year	*Red Dead Redemption* (Rockstar, below)
Best Writing	*Mass Effect 2* (BioWare)
Best Game Design	*Red Dead Redemption* (Rockstar)
Best Visual Arts	*Limbo* (Playdead)
Best Debut Game	*Minecraft* (Mojang)
Best Handheld Game	*Cut the Rope* (ZeptoLab)
Best Downloadable Game	*Minecraft* (Mojang)

Source: Game Developers Choice, presented in March 2011

INDEPENDENT GAMES FESTIVAL 2011

Focusing on innovation away from mainstream gaming, the Independent Games Festival Awards rarely overlap with the recipients of any other major awards of the year, but the winners often become hugely influential.

AWARD	WINNER (DEVELOPER)
Seumas McNally Grand Prize	*Minecraft* (Mojang)
Nuovo Award for short games	*Nidhogg* (Messhof)
Excellence in Visual Art	*BIT.TRIP RUNNER* (Gaijin Games)
Excellence in Audio	*Amnesia: The Dark Descent* (Frictional Games)
Excellence in Design	*Desktop Dungeons* (QCF Design)
Best Student Game	*FRACT* (University of Montreal)
Technical Excellence Award	*Amnesia: The Dark Descent* (Frictional Games)
Best Mobile Game	*Helsing's Fire* (Ratloop)
Audience Award	*Minecraft* (Mojang)
Direct2Drive Vision Award for Innovation	*Amnesia: The Dark Descent* (Frictional Games)

Source: Independent Games Festival, presented in March 2011

THE GAMER'S AWARDS

THE *DIRT* SERIES WAS ORIGINALLY ENDORSED BY RALLY DRIVER

NEW FOR 2012, GUINNESS WORLD RECORDS HAS DECIDED TO GET IN ON THE AWARDS ACTION BY GIVING OUR EDITORIAL CREW A CHANCE TO RECOGNIZE VIDEOGAMING EXCELLENCE ACROSS DECIDEDLY DIFFERENT CATEGORIES. HERE WE SINGLE OUT SOME OF THE MORE UNUSUAL ACHIEVEMENTS THAT HAVE TAKEN PLACE SINCE THE LAST *GAMER'S*.

THE "SHOCK AND AWE" AWARD FOR MOST MASS DESTRUCTION

Call of Duty: Modern Warfare 3 (Infinity Ward/ Sledgehammer Games, 2011)

The campaign portion of *Modern Warfare 3* further builds on the reputation *Call of Duty*'s *Modern Warfare* sub-series has established for blockbuster action and mind-blowing set pieces full of exploding things.

The new game sees the Russian war on the USA going global, expanding the battlefield across northern Europe, Africa and the Middle East, obligingly enabling players to employ a rich variety of NATO and Russian equipment as they try to top Captain John Price's nuclear strike on the USA from *Modern Warfare 2* for destructive exuberance.

RUNNER-UP: *Battlefield 3* (DICE, 2011). The scope for explosive tactics and jaw-dropping mayhem in *Battlefield 3* is not quite as global.

THE "HOT STUFF" AWARD FOR BEST DRAGONS

Skyrim from *The Elder Scrolls V: Skyrim* (Bethesda Softworks, 2011)

With its widespread population of dragons (left), the province of Skyrim on the continent of Tamriel easily takes this title. The latest chapter in *The Elder Scrolls* series moves the action up north, and with so many black dragons around and the prophesized return of Alduin, the dragon-god of destruction, it is a good time to be a dragon-slayer. Thankfully that is exactly the role the player-character is allotted. Lucky!

RUNNER-UP: *Dragon Age II* (BioWare, 2011). Simply too few dragons to compete.

COLIN McCRAE UNDER THE TITLE *COLIN McCRAE: DiRT*

THE "HOW DO YOU DO *THAT*?" AWARD FOR THE MOST DIFFICULT GAME

The Legend of Zelda: Ocarina of Time 3D (Grezzo, 2011)
While the original *Ocarina of Time* certainly had its difficult moments, particularly at the Water Temple, the Master Quest mode included on the 3DS version takes the game's commitment to toughness to a whole new level. The challenging combat and a reversed game world mode will leave some gamers questioning their sanity. Definitely one for the hardest of hardcore *Zelda* completionists.

RUNNER-UP: Dark Souls (From Software, 2011). It might boast more difficult combat sequences, but it doesn't make you play in reverse.

THE "SMASH IT UP" AWARD FOR MOST DETAILED CRASHES

DiRT 3 (Codemasters, 2011)
A racing game can distinguish itself in several ways – better handling, varied courses and more realistic cars are all welcome options – but the one that keeps us coming back for more is *DiRT 3*. Its spectacular car smashes are particularly effective in its obstacle course "Gymkhana" mode. Crashing is so much fun that some gamers smash their rides on purpose!

RUNNER-UP: MotorStorm: Apocalypse (Evolution Studios, 2011). Lots of crashes in this game, but you are often too busy dodging Crazies to enjoy them!

THE "BWAHAHAHAHA" AWARD FOR THE MOST UTTERLY EVIL SUPERVILLAINS

Batman: Arkham City (Rocksteady Studios, 2011)
Packed with villains from Gotham City's infamous detention facility for the criminally insane, *Arkham City* features dozens of bad guys and countless nefarious henchmen that Batman has to defeat to make the city safe again. The odds might be against him, but it is always foolish to bet against the Batman.

RUNNER-UP: Marvel vs. Capcom 3: Fate of Two Worlds (Capcom/Eighting, 2011). More heroes, but fewer villains.

THE GAMER'S AWARDS

DEUS EX (ION STORM INC., 2000) FEATURED EXCERPTS FROM MANY LITERARY

THE "DO YOU REMEMBER?" AWARD FOR BEST COMEBACK

Deus Ex: Human Revolution (Eidos, 2011)
Seven years since the release of *Deus Ex: Invisible War*, expectations were high for the latest sequel in the *Deus Ex* franchise. Thankfully, like its protagonist Adam Jensen, *Human Revolution* has been substantially augmented for its latest incarnation. The game focuses on "four pillars of gameplay" – combat, stealth, hacking and exploration – giving players the freedom to enjoy the game the way they want, with the possible exception of its boss fight sequences.

RUNNER-UP: Back to the Future: The Game (Telltale Games, 2010). Marty and the Doc really have come back to the future, benefiting from the gaming innovations of the 19 years since their last title was released.

THE "WHAT'S GOING ON?" AWARD FOR MOST CLUELESS DETECTIVE

Cole Phelps from L.A. Noire (Team Bondi, 2011)
For a sandbox game, *L.A. Noire* gives gamers surprisingly little control over how the story unfolds. As players soon learn, the main character, Police Detective Cole Phelps, spends much of his time picking up discarded beer bottles and sundry foodstuffs in a desperate search for clues. A somewhat misguided Phelps is also forced to arrest innocent suspects for various murders while the ultimate culprit remains infuriatingly untouchable for much of the game.

RUNNER-UP: Ghost Trick: Phantom Detective (Capcom, 2010). The game's main character, Sissel, needs no clues – he can travel back in time before each murder occurs, so as to prevent it. A neat trick if you can pull it off.

1.54 million The votes received for the Golden Joysticks 2010, the **most votes cast for a videogames awards event**.

THE "EWWWW, GROSS" AWARD FOR MOST GRUESOME GAMEPLAY

"X-Ray Moves" from *Mortal Kombat* (NetherRealm Studios, 2011)

While the *Mortal Kombat* series has never shied away from gratuitous acts of senseless brutality, the "X-Ray Moves" from the latest entry in the series are proof, if any were needed, that there are always more ways to depict the effects of violence. Connecting with one of these attacks gives players a brief, and somewhat disturbing, anatomy lesson as to exactly which bones are being broken.

RUNNER-UP: ***NeverDead* (Rebellion, 2011)**. Lead character Bryce Boltzmann can detach his limbs and then re-attach them!

THE "LAUGH-OUT-LOUD" AWARD FOR BEST NON-PLAYER CHARACTER

The "Space" personality core from *Portal 2* (Valve, 2011)

Once in a while a videogame character appears in a brief cameo that touches players in ways no one expected. This year's breakthrough performance comes from the "Space" personality core from *Portal 2*, voiced by Nolan North (see page 101). All the little guy wants to do is see the universe, or at least make it out of Aperture Science's underground laboratories...

RUNNER-UP: The Penguin from ***Batman: Arkham City* (Rocksteady Studios, 2011)**. Like the "Space" core, the Penguin is given his voice by Nolan North.

THE "BROWN TROUSERS" AWARD FOR BEST SCARES

***Dead Space 2* (Visceral, 2011)**

The subtle art of scaring gamers is dutifully advanced by *Dead Space 2*, which combines a creepy made-up religion, atmospheric audio, dim lighting and good ol' fashioned "monsters in closets" to keep us guessing where the next necromorph is coming from. An increased number of undead babies crawling around also ups the fear factor.

RUNNER-UP: ***Amnesia: The Dark Descent* (Frictional Games, 2010)**. With no weapons with which to fight the multitude of monsters, is it a surprise that main character Daniel's sanity, and underwear, are so taxed?

GAMING ROUND-UP

WE HAVEN'T WASTED A MINUTE SINCE WE FINISHED THE LAST *GUINNESS WORLD RECORDS GAMER'S EDITION*... AND NEITHER HAS THE REST OF THE GAMING WORLD. HERE ARE JUST A FEW OF THE SIGNIFICANT EVENTS FROM THE LAST YEAR IN VIDEOGAMES.

TOP FOR THE OPS: The NPD group reported in January 2011 that *Black Ops* (Treyarch, 2010), the latest instalment in the *Call of Duty* franchise, claimed the top spot as the most purchased videogame in the run-up to Christmas 2010, with *Just Dance 2* (Ubisoft, 2010) its nearest rival. See p.42 for more *Call of Duty* records.

POPULAR PAD

Following on from its phenomenally successful iPad, Apple launched the iPad 2. Going on sale in March 2011, the company's latest tablet boasted a new slimmer-form factor, front and rear cameras, and Apple's new, more powerful, Apple A5 Central processor.

KINECT CRACKER

Microsoft unleashed its Kinect motion-control device, designed to work exclusively with its Xbox 360 console, in November 2010. Within days of its release, a hardware expert named Hector Martin (above) became the first person to create open-source drivers for the gadget, opening up its sophisticated sensor array for development and uses far more varied than simply playing videogames. Microsoft eventually responded by releasing its own software development kit for the Kinect on 16 June 2011.

DELIVERING SALES:

As a gaming platform, the DS might have been at the end of its life cycle by January 2011, but it still had enough life in it to claim the record for being the **best-selling videogame console**, with 147 million units sold around the world since its launch in 2004. These figures saw the handheld finally surpass the previous title-holder, the PS2, which had lifetime sales of 143 million units.

AN *ANGRY BIRDS* FOR ALL SEASONS

Electronic Arts continued to expand into casual gaming in 2011, adding the developer PopCap and the publisher Chillingo, the original publisher of *Angry Birds*. However, what they didn't manage to buy was *Angry Birds* itself, and Rovio, the game's developers, have expanded the *Angry Birds* franchise with movie tie-in *Angry Birds Rio* and *Angry Birds Seasons*.

CAUGHT OUT: One of BioWare's employees got caught giving the company's game *Dragon Age II* an ultra-favourable review on the reviews site Metacritic. A spokesman defended the practice, claiming Barack Obama probably voted for himself too.

FOR SCIENCE!

In April 2011, gamers finally got their hands on *Portal 2*, the hotly anticipated sequel to Valve's iconic 2007 puzzle title. This time around the key innovation was an online multiplayer co-op mode, with multiple puzzles that required teamwork to complete successfully. Unfortunately for PS3 users, the game's release came the day before Sony was forced to close down the PlayStation Network, the service that governs multiplayer gaming on the console (see "Hacked Off").

HACKED OFF: Sony caused a storm of controversy when it became apparent that the accounts of 77 million users of their PlayStation Network had been compromised between 17 and 19 April 2011. Sony responded by shutting the service on 20 April, restoring it on 13 May after a major security update. The company also faced criticism for not informing users about the risk to their data as soon as the security breach became apparent.

TO INFINITY, AND BEYOND

Originally conceived as a Kinect game for Xbox 360, *Infinity Blade* (Chair Entertainment/ Epic Games) was eventually released for iOS at the end of 2010. The game, which used the Unreal Engine 3 – an engine more usually reserved for console and PC games – made its debut on the iPhone/ iPad and soon garnered the kind of coverage and rave reviews usually reserved for Triple-A titles (and *Angry Birds*). As of July 2011, the game had amassed a score of 87% on Metacritic, with one reviewer describing it as "*the* game to play on iOS".

APOCALYPSE: One unexpected consequence of Japan's Tohoku earthquake was Sony's decision to cancel the release of its disaster-themed racing game *MotorStorm Apocalypse* in Japan.

PREMIUM GRAPHICS

All good things come to those who wait, and racing game fans certainly waited some time for Polyphony Digital's *Gran Turismo 5* to be released. Coming out six years after *GT4*'s initial release in Japan, *GT5* was praised for the graphics on its premium cars, although some fans were disappointed that the new "damage" feature that enabled players to batter cars only had a limited effect on the cars' performance and was not easily accessible in the game's "campaign" and "arcade" modes.

GAMING ROUND-UP

DESPITE ITS IMPORTANCE TO GAMES DEVELOPERS AND PUBLISHERS, E3 HAS

EFFECTING THE MASSES

The hotly anticipated conclusion to the popular *Mass Effect* series generated a lot of interest at E3 2011. *Mass Effect 3* (BioWare) is set to give fans of the series their first chance to visit the homeworlds of a number of key alien races, such as the Salarians and Turians, as well as the epic invasion of Earth by the huge, robotic Reapers.

The E3 demo of the game showed off its revised combat systems, including visceral mêlée attacks, which will surely please more action-orientated gamers. Based on the reaction to this demo alone, *Mass Effect 3* is likely to be a key game of 2012.

THE BIGGEST SHOW IN TOWN: The Electronic Entertainment Expo (E3) is one of the world's most influential videogames trade shows. The annual event sees almost every major publisher and developer of videogames showing off the wares that they'll be releasing in time for Christmas and beyond. As ever, the *Gamer's* crew were there on the scene to report all the top news in person...

SIGNIFICANT MILESTONES: The biggest news at E3 2011 came from Nintendo's press conference, which opened with a symphony orchestra and choir performing music from *The Legend of Zelda* to celebrate the series' 25th anniversary. Statements about 3DS titles including *Zelda* and *Star Fox 64* (above left) were overshadowed by the announcement of the new Wii U console, complete with touch-screen controllers. Touted by Nintendo as being the first of a new generation of consoles, the Wii U should be available to buy in 2012. Will it outsell the old Wii?

SECRETS OF THE INFINITE

Footage of *BioShock Infinite* (Irrational Games) – a game with some serious buzz – was shown to a select few behind closed doors at E3 2011. Acting as a spiritual cousin to the first two *BioShock* games, *Infinite* takes place in the floating city of Columbia in 1912. Far from revisiting the Old West, Columbia provides a steampunk setting for former Pinkerton agent Booker DeWitt's quest to rescue a young woman with remarkable abilities from some mysterious forces.

The game's vertical exploration and combat impressed most E3 attendees. However, it will be Irrational Games' traditionally strong character development that will bring it to life and determine whether the game is as well-received as the first *Bioshock* game was in 2007.

275,000 The number of people attending the Cologne Gamescom 2011, making the event, held in August 2011, the **largest videogames convention**.

VOTE OF CONFIDENCE: In a poll conducted by IGN, a total of 258,367 gamers voted for their favourite game in exhibition at Cologne Gamescom. The winner, *Dota 2* from Valve Software, collected 68,041 votes, and its tally handed IGN Europe the record for the **most gamers voting for a single videogame award**, which IGNers Dan Kilby, Ian Chambers and Will Guyatt gratefully accepted from GWR's Gaz Deaves.

NO LONGER DOOMED

In September 2011, German authorities announced they would no longer restrict the sales of the shooters *Doom* and *Doom II* (both id Software, 1993 and 1994) to adults-only shops. Apparently, the decisions of Germany's Federal Department for Media Harmful to Young Persons can be appealed after 10 years. *Doom*'s current publisher, Bethesda Softworks, convinced German officials that the games no longer posed a risk to children, paving the way for their re-release in the country.

HAIL TO THE KING, BABY

After a wait of 14 years and 41 days, *Duke Nukem Forever* (3D Realms, 2011) was finally released on 10 June 2010. In the process, the title lost the record for the **longest development period for any videogame**, which it held in every *Gamer's Edition* until this one. Turn to page 168 to see which game now holds the record...

LIFE SAGA: August 2011 saw two dedicated fans of *Half-Life* stage a mini-demonstration outside the Kirkland, USA, HQ of developers Valve. Bearing hand-made placards, the pair were looking for news on a new game in the much-anticipated *Half-Life* saga. While the protest didn't result in any new info, it did net them a takeaway lunch from Valve's MD, Gabe Newell.

ACCEPT THE CHALLENGE

GO ON, IMPRESS US AND PROVE YOUR GAMING METTLE AT

CHALLENGERS

JUDGING YOU

Adam Moore (left) and Dan Barrett (right) are your hosts at Guinness World Records Challengers, the online community for superlative fans.

Adam is responsible for the video content across the GWR websites – he travels the globe to film folk performing fantastic feats and now he wants to see what YOU can do.

Dan is the community manager at GWR and looks after the company's online presence. You've got to work very hard to impress him.

"SHOW US WHAT YOU'RE MADE OF," SAY ADAM AND DAN, DA BOYZ FROM GUINNESS WORLD RECORDS CHALLENGERS. "IT'S SIMPLE: LOG ON, AND GET YOUR RECORD ON."

Brand new for the *Gamer's Edition* this year is our arrival on **guinnessworldrecords.com/challengers**. This is the online community for fans of record-breaking, where you can **PICK YOUR CHALLENGE** to attempt, or **SUGGEST A CHALLENGE** that could become a genuine Guinness World Record...

PICK YOUR CHALLENGE

1. Pick a challenge from the available choices on the site.
2. Train, train, train to beat the best score on your chosen challenge.
3. Perform your attempt and video it.
4. Upload the video to Challengers. Your feat may earn you a new world record!

"I've met some of the world's best... How do you stack up?!"
ADAM MOORE, VIDEO CONTENT MANAGER, GUINNESS WORLD RECORDS

KISH CHASE

So you've got yourself a world record, but how long do you think you can keep it? How many can you hold on to at once? As of September 2011, the Challenger to beat was Stephen Kish (UK, left), who earned himself a whopping six records, including one for the **highest score on *Angry Birds for Chrome*** (Rovio, 2011) with an epic score of 37,510 points racked up at his home in East Sussex, UK, on 23 August 2011. The chase is on – it's time to get gaming and put yourself in the running!

1st

/// "IN A WORLD RAVAGED BY WAR, DESTINY DEMANDS A HERO. WILL YOU ANSWER THE CALL?" ///

1,250 The average number of record claims Guinness World Records receives every week.

WWW.GUINNESSWORLDRECORDS.COM/CHALLENGERS ▶

GETTING SUGGESTIVE

One person who took up the challenge through our website was Cameron Jones (USA, right), who suggested the task of the **fastest completion of The Arena in *Kirby Superstar*** (Nintendo, 1996). His time of 6 minutes 10.33 seconds eventually took the record. Cameron also used the Challengers site to set an amazing five other records.

06'10''33

SUGGEST A CHALLENGE

If you don't see what you want to attempt, you can always suggest your record on the website – it could be chosen as a future challenge. And here's the best bit: all successful record attempts on Challengers are considered **official Guinness World Records**, so you're just a click away from being immortalized with one of our certificates!

Scan the QR Code here to go directly to the Guinness World Records Challengers website and start uploading your footage today!

"A good new gaming record suggestion is something that can be easily attempted at home by anyone and is fun!"

DAN BARRETT, COMMUNITY MANAGER, GUINNESS WORLD RECORDS

If your achievement in any given challenge is the fastest, you will be awarded a first-place award. Every Monday our adjudicators check the video footage and, if satisfied, award any new first-place holders with Guinness World Records!

IT'S IN THE GAME

By uploading video footage on to Guinness World Records Challengers, gamers have a direct route to making in-game achievements, such as high scores and speed runs, into official Guinness World Records feats.

That's exactly what Mason Pye (UK, right) did. His footage earned him the record for the **fastest time to type the alphabet on an iPad** for his 4.59-second run, recorded at his home in Northampton, UK, on 6 August 2011. Not satisfied with that, Mason went on to score two other non-gaming records, for the **fastest time to make a cup of tea** (11.2 seconds) and the **fastest time to unravel a toilet roll with one hand** (37.56 seconds). Well done Mason, you are a three-time world record holder!

CAMPANULA CLOSE

I Hold 3 'Guinness World Records'

HARDWARE

LARGEST GAME CONTROLLER

Holder: NES Controller (Netherlands)

Officially verified in August 2011 as the world's largest console gamepad, this fully functional NES pad measures an enormous 366 cm x 159 cm x 51 cm (12 ft x 5 ft 3 in x 1 ft 8 in). Its main creator is engineering student Ben Allen (right), who was helped by Stephen van't Hof and Michel Verhulst, all of whom study at the Delft University of Technology in the Netherlands. The fantastic facsimile is 30 times the size of a standard NES controller, and requires gamers to navigate its enormous buttons. If you wanted to use this like a standard handheld pad, you would need to be 51 m (167 ft) tall – the same height as London landmark Nelson's Column!

OVERVIEW

The relentless forward march of gaming systems continued apace in 2011, with new, faster handhelds from both Nintendo and Sony, as well as the official announcement of the first eighth-generation console in the form of the Wii U, due for release in 2012. Mobile games continued to quietly dominate from the sidelines with impressive offerings from both the Android and Apple app stores. This section of the book is where we cover the great and small of games platforms: if you can plug it in and play games on it, we've covered it here in all its boxy, flashy glory.

BIOGRAPHY

Gaz Deaves has been researching and ratifying the records that go into the *Gamer's Edition* for the past four years, but he still doesn't hold any records himself. He claims that the key to happiness as a gamer is staying healthy with a varied diet including the five major food groups: shooter, racer, strategy, RPG and puzzle.

NEStalgia

CONTENTS

BEST OF XBOX	24
BEST OF PLAYSTATION	26
BEST OF Wii	28
BEST OF PC	30
BEST OF 3DS AND DS	32
BEST OF MOBILE	34

BEST OF XBOX

WHEN MICROSOFT BEGAN WORK ON THEIR FIRST GAMING CONSOLE IN 1998,

SYSTEM UPDATE

At six years of age, the Xbox 360 is almost ancient in games console years, but there's no sign of the system slowing down just yet. 360 owners were not disappointed by this year's release schedule, with a broad selection of exclusive games, strong performance in multiplatform shooters and a plentiful supply of downloadable gems to entertain the adventurous. The arrival of the "second generation" of Kinect games – titles marked by the developers' increased familiarity with the system – welcomed in the arrival of some solid games and set the scene for even better, bolder things to come.

MARKING THE FIRST FULL YEAR OF THE KINECT SENSOR ON SALE, 2011 SAW THE XBOX 360 ARRIVE ON THE CASUAL GAMING SCENE WITH ALL THE BOMBAST THAT GAMERS HAVE COME TO EXPECT FROM MICROSOFT. AS INNOVATIVE AS EVER, THE 360 WON VALUABLE GROUND FROM RIVAL CONSOLE MANUFACTURERS.

TOPICAL

Tropico 4, the second Xbox release in the cult series, was released in 2011. These nation-building construction sims are the brainchild of Bulgaria's largest videogame development company, Haemimont Games. *Tropico 4* follows the lead of the third title, with players assuming the role of a dictator who has taken control of a stunning tropical island. As "El Presidente", gamers can affect social policies, religion, building construction and international politics.

GAMERS' DOZEN

There have been 12 different versions of the standard Xbox 360 console so far, with variations including "form factor", on-board storage and HDMI support. *Gears of War* received its very own limited edition Xbox 360 Slim console (pictured below).

GEARS OF WAR 3

The definitive shooter, *Gears of War 3* (Epic Games, 2011) returns with bigger explosions, mech-based combat, new enemies and awesome new boss fights. While the plot of the single-player campaign was spoiled for many web users after this third part of the trilogy was leaked online, the arcade-style horde mode once again stole the show from the blockbuster twists of the story missions. Horde mode in the third *Gears of War* adds a range of new features to boost defences, including optional fortifications and ammo bought with points earned during each round. The game's April 2011 release was put back to September 2011 due to a "business decision". For more information, check out our Critical Hit! on page 52.

XBOX 360
GEARS OF WAR

"Consumers will enjoy news, sports and their favourite local channels, all just a voice command away, on Xbox 360."

MICROSOFT PRESS RELEASE ON THE USA'S FORTHCOMING XBOX LIVE TV CHANNEL

BASTION

The beautiful, broken world of Caelondia is the setting for *Bastion* (Supergiant, 2011), a compelling action RPG available through the Xbox Live marketplace. The game's hero, known as the Kid, awakens after a terrible calamity has befallen the land, and embarks on a quest to return the world to order. Spectacular watercolour visuals make up a world that builds itself around the Kid as he walks through it. The adventure is narrated by the southern drawl of Rucks, who reports on every move the Kid makes. The narration changes according to decisions the player makes – for example, Rucks will comment on an upcoming enemy. A variety of weapons, locations and impressive set pieces serve to elevate *Bastion* well above the accepted standard for downloadable games.

CHILD OF EDEN

The designer of *Child of Eden* (Q Entertainment, 2011), Tetsuya Mizuguchi (Japan), has carved out an impressive niche in "synaesthetic" games, in which sound and visuals combine to take the player deep into his colourful creations. One of the first shooters for Kinect, *Child of Eden* proved to be a fitting successor to Mizuguchi's classic Dreamcast shooter *Rez*, to which it owes a great deal. It expands on the rhythm-rail shooter formula with the introduction of controller-free inputs. While the game is rather short on plot, it does make reference to Mizuguchi's other projects, including the PSP and PS2 title *Lumines*. As well as stunning, dazzling visuals, there is an innovative sound-control facility: by shooting at objects, players can generate various audio effects.

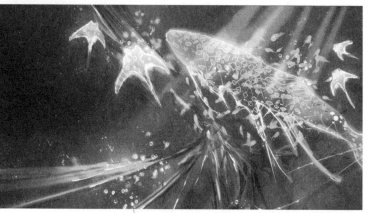

FORZA MOTORSPORT 4

Now undeniably a competitor to the once unassailable *Gran Turismo*, the *Forza* series has assured the status of the Xbox 360 as a great console for petrolheads. New features in *Forza Motorsport 4* (Turn 10 Studios, 2011) include Kinect-based head-tracking and "Autovista", a virtual car showroom mode that allows fans to get up-close and ogle a digitized representation of some of the cars featured in the game. Season Play from *Forza 3* is replaced by World Tour Mode, and players can now choose which car they win at the end of each race. There are also more types of races available this time around, including Drift, multi-heat and Autocross, as well as the classic bumper-to-bumper contests. To find out more, turn to our *Forza Motorsport* Critical Hit! feature on page 70.

BEST OF PLAYSTATION

IT WAS ANOTHER GREAT YEAR FOR PLAYSTATION GAMERS, WITH A NEW HANDHELD AND PLENTY OF PLATFORM-EXCLUSIVE TITLES TO ENJOY.

PLAYSTATION VITA

Sony's highly anticipated new portable stays true to the idea behind the original PSP – giving gamers a device with a widescreen display and the serious processing power to provide the highest-quality graphics available on a handheld. In addition to its touch-screen, the big talking point of the new system is the touchpad located on the rear of the device. This enables players to take control of action on the screen without the disadvantage of their fingers blocking (or smearing) the screen.

By owning so many developers, Sony is also in a strong position to ensure the Vita receives good software support. It has pledged to bring the *Uncharted* and *Disgaea* series, among others, to the platform for its global launch in 2012.

UNCHARTED: GOLDEN ABYSS

Bringing action archaeologist Nathan Drake to Sony's new handheld, *Uncharted: Golden Abyss* was developed by Sony's Bend Studios (formerly Eidetic) in collaboration with the main series' developer, Naughty Dog.

Set before the events chronicled in *Uncharted: Drake's Fortune* (Naughty Dog, 2007), *Golden Abyss* is set to allow players to choose how they control the game, with touch- and motion-based controls for navigation and aiming in addition to the dual analogue controls more akin to those of the PS3 games. This could be the benchmark by which the Vita's launch titles are judged.

SYSTEM UPDATE

The big news for Sony consoles in 2012 is the release of the Vita. Although its global launch was delayed, missing the 2011 holiday season in the West, the console included features that many had wanted since the PSP launched in 2005: touch-screen controls, 3G connectivity and dual analogue sticks to make shooters more fun to play.

MOTORSTORM: APOCALYPSE

Moving away from the natural environments that provided the setting for the previous titles in the series, *MotorStorm: Apocalypse* (Evolution Studios, 2011) brought the driving action to a post-apocalyptic urban setting. In addition to mastering the tracks, drivers also had to contend with race-sabotaging city residents and attempt to avoid their riotous actions.

The game's path to market also faced an unexpected roadblock, too, in the form of the Tōhoku earthquake and tsunami in March 2011. The game's Japanese release was cancelled and the UK and North American launches were both delayed.

143.96 million The number of units the PlayStation 2 has sold worldwide as of August 2011, making it Sony's most successful home console.

THE LATIN WORD *"SONUS"*, MEANING "SOUND"

inFAMOUS 2

Super-powered protagonist Cole MacGrath made a triumphant return in *inFAMOUS 2* (Sucker Punch Productions, 2011), once again challenging gamers to take him down the path of good or evil, to defeat, or perhaps become, the "beast" predicted at the conclusion of the first game.

Gamers were impressed with the results and they weren't alone – Sony liked what they saw so much that they bought the studio in August 2011. However, this move is unlikely to have much of an impact on the developer's output as Sucker Punch has produced nothing but PlayStation titles for over 10 years.

LITTLEBIGPLANET 2

Literally "building" on the success of its predecessor, *LittleBigPlanet 2* (Media Molecule, 2011) brought the multiple-award-winning platform game back with a whole raft of new level-creation features.

Within six months of the game's official launch in January 2011, players had access to over 10 million pieces of downloadable content created by its active fan community, with new levels ranging in genre from the traditional 2D platformers to puzzle games, motorbike races and even shooters!

To help celebrate the launch of *LittleBigPlanet 2*, Media Molecule's David Dino, Lauren Guiliano and Sean Crowley (all USA) took part in an epic Guinness World Records feat – the **longest marathon playing a platform game**. The trio managed to play their own game for an amazing 50 hr 1 min in New York, USA, from 17 to 19 January 2011.

> "There's the regular gameplay, where you get your combat rifle and off you go... and then you get the *jetpack*..."
> **STEVEN TER HEIDE, *KILLZONE 3*'S SENIOR DESIGNER, ON ITS TACTICAL POSSIBILITIES**

KILLZONE 3

The PS3's big-gun console exclusive shooter returned to much critical acclaim in early 2011. The latest title in the series was praised for its wide selection of new environments, detailed character animation and spectacular set-piece battles. Its new co-op and multiplayer "operations" mode also helped to make the battles with, or against, other players just as exciting as battles against the Helghast baddies in the single-player mode. The addition of PlayStation Move controls and stereoscopic 3D made for an innovative package that wowed PS3 users around the world.

BEST OF Wii

"NINTENDO", A TRANSLITERATION OF THREE JAPANESE KANJI CHARACTERS,

SYSTEM UPDATE

Unveiled to a mass of gamers at the Nokia Theatre in Los Angeles, USA, during the 2011 E3 Expo, the Wii U is Nintendo's first HD-capable console. Its most striking feature, however, is its distinctive controller, which features a 15-cm (6-in) touch-screen, dual analogue nubs and plenty of motion-sensing equipment. When it launches, the Wii U will easily take the record for the largest standard videogame controller. Much of the interest at its first public demonstration, however, came from the controller's ability to display full console games, freeing up the standard TV-viewing screen for other things. The system's processing power reportedly puts it on a par with the Xbox 360 and PS3, and it will feature both full backwards-compatibility with existing Wii games and cross-compatibility with Wii controllers. Are we seeing the dawn of a new age of consoles? Nintendo is certainly hoping so...

THE 25TH ANNIVERSARY OF THE MUCH-LOVED *ZELDA* SERIES CAUSED GREAT EXCITEMENT FOR NINTENDO FANS IN 2011. ADD TO THAT THE ANNOUNCEMENT OF A NEW HOME CONSOLE IN THE WORKS AND IT WAS ANOTHER FANTASTIC YEAR FOR NINTENDO-LOVERS.

Wii U DEMOS

Nintendo had a range of playable demos available at E3 2011, set up specifically to show off some of the Wii U's key features. One of the most exciting was dubbed *Battle Mii* (pictured above and below).

An arena combat game that uses gamers' Mii avatars, *Battle Mii* pits two players using the standard Wii Remote/nunchuk combo against a single opponent using the new Wii U controller. The Wii Remote users' characters run around on foot and their actions are viewed split-screen on a TV display while the player using the Wii U pad controls a character flying a UFO. The guys on foot might have a more basic set-up and fewer advantages, but they have superior manpower in this frantic third-person shooter.

Battle Mii is a prototype only, so may never see the light of day as a full retail release. But Nintendo will be keen to exploit the innovative gameplay potential of its new Wii U console as it attempts to woo away from their Xbox 360s and PlayStation 3s the hardcore gamers the company lost with the Wii.

MEANS "ENTRUSTED TO HEAVEN" – OR TO CHANCE ▶

Shield bash

C

Z Lock on

THE LEGEND OF ZELDA: SKYWARD SWORD

Link's latest adventure really brought players into the game, using Wii MotionPlus-enhanced Remotes to simulate swordplay. Players delighted in wielding their controls like a big blade, helping Link cut his enemies down to size.

The game's airborne sequences were dazzling and visually it struck a balance between the cel-shaded graphics in *The Wind Waker* (2002), disliked by some fans of the series for being too cartoon-like, and the dark fantasy of *Twilight Princess* (2006). It also filled in a significant gap in the history of Link's native Hyrule by detailing the creation of his recurring weapon, the Master Sword.

KIRBY'S EPIC YARN

Finally getting a European release in early 2011, Kirby's latest adventure, *Kirby's Epic Yarn*, stayed true to the character's bizarre roots. This time the cuddly, cute, pink blob was transformed into a piece of wool after eating a cursed tomato!

The highly stylized graphics made the most of the title's woolly theme and gave rise to Kirby's new ability to change shape. Players could transform the character into a variety of things, including a train, a dolphin and a car, as he ploughed through the platforms. They could even give him a giant robotic tank (above) to drive.

CHASE Mii!

Another demonstration game for the Wii U, *Chase Mii* also made use of Mii avatars in a two-on-one contest. This time the two Wii Remote players had to catch the other player. However, the gamer using the Wii U Remote had access to a map of the playing area to help them avoid their pursuers.

> "We really want to change the structure of home entertainment... we thought, 'What if we were able to be independent from the TV?'"
>
> **SATORU IWATA, PRESIDENT AND CEO OF NINTENDO, ON PLAYING THE WII U WITHOUT A TV**

CAVE STORY

Making its console debut after six long years as a freeware title for PC, *Cave Story* (Studio Pixel, 2004) received a warm welcome on Nintendo's WiiWare store. The game was praised for being an enormous 2D adventure in the style of *Metroid* (Nintendo, 1986) and *Castlevania* (Nintendo, 1986). With its compelling storyline about an amnesiac robot and spectacular boss fights, it's hard to believe that the game's PC original was developed by a lone programmer, the Japanese Daisuke "Pixel" Amaya. Let's hope his future games make it on to the Wii U.

BEST OF PC

SYSTEM UPDATE

History has shown that the popularity of PC titles can be linked to the lifecycle of consoles. With the current generation (PS3, Xbox 360 and Wii) getting a little long in the tooth, the graphics and performance of PC titles now compare very favourably to their console cousins. A wide selection of exclusive releases in many different genres meant that PC gamers were spoilt for choice in 2011, with excellent strategy games, RPGs, puzzlers and shooters to get stuck into. MMORPGs remain hugely popular, and the genre is still dominated by the desktop and laptop, rather than the console. It's all a very long way from *Reversi*, the **first Windows game on version 1.0**, back in 1985.

WHILE CONSOLES SPENT MUCH OF 2011 FOCUSING ON THEIR MOTION-CONTROLLED OFFERINGS, PC OWNERS FOUND PLENTY OF MORE SERIOUS TITLES TO SATISFY THEIR APPETITE FOR DEEP AND VARIED GAMEPLAY EXPERIENCES...

BARACK MAC

It is common practice for national leaders and dignitaries to present one another with gifts during trips, meetings and summits. On a state visit to Poland in May 2011, President Barack Obama was the lucky recipient of a copy of *The Witcher 2: Assassins of Kings* from the Polish Prime Minister, Donald Tusk. Unfortunately, President Obama is likely to struggle to play the game, since he is well-known for being a Mac user. Just as well, then, that Prime Minister Tusk also gave his American counterpart an iPad.

THE WITCHER 2: ASSASSINS OF KINGS

Geralt of Rivia returns in *The Witcher 2: Assassins of Kings* (CD Projekt RED, 2011), the follow-up to Poland's most successful gaming export. Based on the series of fantasy novels by Andrzej Sapkowski, this third-person RPG follows the monster hunter Geralt as he finds himself accused of regicide. He embarks on a quest to track down the true culprit. While the first game was known for its "mature themes", the sequel has refined the formula but maintained the distinctive flavour that has made the series so popular. A well-realized world and a plot that offers huge amounts of control over the storyline have made this the must-play RPG of the year.

SMALLEST GAMING LAPTOP

Holder: Alienware M11x
This powerful laptop features a dinky 11.6-in (29.4-cm) screen, but its highest-spec versions pack in enough processing muscle to run any current PC game on impressive settings. The latest models feature optional Intel Core i7 and up to 16GB of RAM.

Shown with iPhones for scale

EUROPE IN 2011, COMPARED WITH THE SAME PERIOD IN 2010

AMNESIA: THE DARK DESCENT

Hovering somewhere between survival horror and graphic adventure, *Amnesia: The Dark Descent* (Frictional Games, 2010) draws on the well-established principle that the imagined is much more terrifying than the obvious. You control a character who awakens in a medieval castle with no clues as to their past except for a hastily scrawled note in their own handwriting. You quickly find yourself frantically lighting tinderboxes to keep out of the oppressive darkness, jumping at even the slightest hint of the game's excellent, atmospheric audio. The use of madness is the game's real achievement, however: looking at the monsters or remaining in darkness for too long starts to bring on panicky episodes, reflected in the game as horrible hallucinations and slower controls, making it even harder to continue.

> "Consoles are limited because they don't have enough memory... a lot of scenes hit an upper limit. Now we're looking at PCs that have ten times the horse-power of home consoles."

id SOFTWARE'S TECHNICAL DIRECTOR, JOHN CARMACK

TOTAL WAR: SHOGUN 2

Acting as a sequel to the very first *Total War* game, *Total War: Shogun 2* (The Creative Assembly, 2011) returns gamers to the Sengoku period of feudal Japan. The player's ambitious task is to unify the country under one ruler, while subduing rival clans with military might, economic pressure or duplicitous, scheming ninjas. The art style used throughout the game's interface and maps evokes the period wonderfully, and combines with exceptional detail on battlefield units to produce a visually stunning strategy title. The *Total War* series has always been known for the apparently limitless depth of its gameplay, and while *Shogun 2* has streamlined some of its systems in comparison with its forebears, there is still a great deal of variety to be explored in this samurai saga.

RIFT

Proving that there's still ample room to innovate in fantasy MMORPGs, *Rift* (Trion Worlds, 2011) manages to make real advances and dispense with some of the clutter that had been caught up with the core tenets of the genre. A clever change to the traditional class system allows players to switch roles more effectively and fill gaps within a party without running around the world trying to recruit a healer before a raid. The eponymous "Rifts" are portals filled with enemies that open up randomly within the game's world, offering huge challenges and great rewards for players who are able to repel them. The solid "player vs player" offering, built on a foundation in objective-based teamwork rather than simple slaughter, shows there is plenty to differentiate *Rift* from the status quo of established MMOs. With an average Metacritic rating of 84%, *Rift*'s desire to be different clearly met with critical approval.

NINTENDO WAS ORIGINALLY A MANUFACTURER OF PLAYING CARDS BEFORE

SYSTEM UPDATE

Nintendo gave gamers a whole new two-screen console in 2011. On the bottom was the standard touch-screen interface while the top used a parallax barrier, a special layer of material containing a series of holes. The holes are positioned so that each eye sees a slightly different image through them, giving gamers the impression of 3D action. Some were dissatisfied with the limited range of games made specifically for the 3DS when it was launched, but even the sternest of critics melted at the chance to play the classic N64 title *The Legend of Zelda: Ocarina of Time* reconfigured for the device. An online store featuring other titles from Nintendo's past optimized for 3D display greatly extended the range of games available to download and play, too.

THE ARRIVAL OF THE 3DS IN FEBRUARY 2011 BROUGHT WITH IT ALL THE USUAL EXCITEMENT OF A MAJOR HANDHELD CONSOLE LAUNCH. THOUSANDS OF GAMERS WAITED OVERNIGHT TO BE THE FIRST TO GET THEIR HANDS ON THE DEVICE.

CATS 'N' DOGS

After the success of the portable pet sim on the original DS, it came as no surprise to see Nintendo had let the dogs out again (this time with some feline friends) for the 3DS title *nintendogs + cats* (Nintendo, 2010). Players could pose for photos while "holding" their pets, with the use of the 3DS's augmented reality facility (right). Find out more on page 171!

"The expansion of the game audience has been a Nintendo theme for a number of years now. We can bring new and interesting experiences."

HIDEKI KONNO, DEVELOPMENT HEAD AT NINTENDO ON HIS HOPES THAT THE 3DS WILL EXPAND NINTENDO'S AUDIENCE

SUPER STREET FIGHTER IV: 3D EDITION

The 3DS version of *Super Street Fighter IV* (Capcom, 2011) allowed players to take their tussles literally into the streets as the series exploited the portable potential and the stereoscopic graphics of Nintendo's latest handheld. Prominent innovations included new camera angles that showed off the game's 3D features, plus the capacity for players to access characters' "special", "super" and "ultra" moves via a touch-screen, making these moves much more accessible for beginners.

The game also allows users to stage two-player battles between 3DS handhelds via wireless connections. The "Download Play" feature offers a special downloadable demo so that owners can play against other 3DS users who don't have the game.

POKÉMON BLACK/WHITE

Arriving in the West shortly before the launch of the 3DS, *Black/White* (Game Freak, 2010) was the last major *Pokémon* title for the DS. The game met with universal acclaim, including a perfect review score from Japanese games magazine *Famitsu*, and brought a huge selection of new features to eager pokémaniacs.

The game not only introduced 156 brand new "Generation V" monsters, but it also added new moves, abilities, environmental hazards and even in-game seasons, changing the way gamers catch and trade their pocket monsters. But although popular with fans, the title has a way to go to beat the 31 million units *Pokémon Red/Green/Blue* (Game Freak, 1996) shifted to make it the **best-selling Japanese RPG title**.

3DS MINI-GAMES

To demonstrate the new capabilities of the 3DS straight out of the box, Nintendo pre-loaded some simple games into the system's hard drive.

StreetPass Quest (Nintendo, 2011) was a gentle, Japanese-style RPG in which players collected the Mii avatars of other 3DS users they passed in the street via the wireless signals each device transmits. Gamers could then use the Miis they had collected to fight monsters in the game.

But the most eye-catching offering was *AR Games* (Nintendo, 2011), a software package that used augmented reality technology and a set of question-mark and character cards (pictured below) that came supplied with the 3DS. The cards served as an anchor on which simple virtual games and characters appeared when viewed through the 3DS's camera.

FACE ME

Face Raiders (HAL Laboratory, 2011) was another free title for the 3DS. The game was a shooter that had a key innovation – players could use the console's cameras to capture 3D images of their friends' faces. These faces then became the enemies in the game that had to be shot down! Perfect for when the face isn't listening.

BEST OF MOBILE

SYSTEM UPDATE

With the continued growth of games in the iOS App Store and great leaps forward made in titles for both Android and Windows Mobile, smartphone gaming has become a very real threat to handheld gaming devices. Handsets and tablets now boast dual-core processors, and high-resolution displays are increasingly common, which allows games developers to offer graphics to compete with the 3DS and PSP.

AS HANDSETS BECOME EVER MORE POWERFUL AND CAPABLE, ONE OF THE MAIN AREAS MANUFACTURERS ARE COMPETING IN IS THE QUALITY OF GAMES AVAILABLE FOR THEIR PLATFORMS: IT'S A GREAT TIME TO BE A MOBILE GAMER!

Y21 M3 W3	$141,135.2K
93	

Bunny Killer
17,406,412 units — Rank #6

Save — Menu

GAME DEV STORY

A cross-platform game about making videogames, *Game Dev Story* (Kairosoft, 2010) tasked players with transforming a small games maker into a major developer by hiring staff, deciding what to make and who to sell to. The simple gameplay, an unusual premise and gaming in-jokes made it popular with gamers.

THE BIGGER APPLE

On 27 July 2011, the US government released figures revealing that it had an operating cash balance of $73.7 billion (£45.3 billion). Apple's tax filing revealed that it could boast $76.4 billion (£46.5 billion) in cash reserves as of 25 June 2011, giving the technology company more spending power than the US government!

iPAD 2

Lighter and faster than the original iPad, and a third slimmer, Apple's latest tablet has dominated the market since it hit the shelves in March 2011. In the three months after its launch, Apple sold 9.25 million iPad 2s.

INFINITY BLADE

For many gamers, the action RPG title *Infinity Blade* (Chair Entertainment, 2010, shown left) was the game that proved that the iPad could support a large, graphically complex gaming experience. The title, which sees the player ascending a castle to confront the "God King", was originally planned for Xbox Kinect, but was transferred to iOS later in its development.

2 million The number of copies of *Tiny Wings* (Andreas Illiger, 2011) downloaded to iOS devices, according to Apple's Game Center.

PHONEY?

Apple and Samsung are not just locked in battle for dominance of the smartphone market – the two tech giants are also locked in a legal dispute over the look of the user interface of their phones. Apple think the Galaxy series is too similar to their iPhones. The conflict looks like it will continue for some time.

GALAXY S II

Hailed by many as the great alternative to the iPhone, the Galaxy S II from the South Korean tech giant Samsung is thinner and has a larger screen than the iPhone 4, and supports the latest version of Bluetooth, Wi-Fi and even 4G connectivity. Will gamers embrace it as readily as they have the iPhone? Only time will tell.

TEGRA ZONE

Compared to Apple's tightly controlled iTunes Store, the Android Market for apps on Android phones has a reputation for being less well organized. In 2011, Nvidia provided an alternative for folk using phones containing their battery-life-friendly do-everything "Nvidia Tegra chips". Focusing on apps designed to get the most out of Nvidia's hardware, the Tegra Zone store provided improved reliability and performance from the apps it offered.

iPHONE 4S

October 2011 marked the arrival of the turbo-charged iPhone 4S, featuring the dual-core A5 chip previously only found in the iPad 2. This latest version of the market-leading smartphone offers faster graphics and better gameplay experiences.

TINY WINGS

Walking a fine line between the platform, rhythm action and racing genres, *Tiny Wings* (Andreas Illiger, 2011) saw players controlling a little bird who dreams of soaring but whose wings are too small for sustained flight. The single-touch controls dictate whether the bird flaps its wings for lift or folds them for speed, allowing the player to use the game's hills as ramps for longer jumps and higher scores.

PLAYING FOR TIME

According to the data analyst firm Medio, the mobile game *Angry Birds* (Rovio, 2009) racks up roughly 1.4 billion minutes of play per week.

XPERIA PLAY

Resembling Sony's PSPgo, Ericsson's gaming smartphone employed the Android operating system to give gamers access to both Android games and a selection of downloadable PlayStation and PSP titles, as well as the standard smartphone features.

N.O.V.A. 2

Available on both iPhone and Android, *N.O.V.A. 2: The Hero Rises Again* (Gameloft, 2010) did an excellent job of transporting the standard control sticks and triggers required for comfortable play to a one touch-screen. The biggest gripe some gamers had with it was the game's resemblance to the genre-defining shooter series *Halo*.

XBOX 360 vs PS3

NINTENDO'S CURRENT HOME CONSOLE DOESN'T PROVIDE HD GAMING, BUT

CLASH OF THE CONSOLES, BATTLE OF THE BOXES

THE TWO HEAVYWEIGHTS OF THE HD GAMES MARKET HAVE BEEN DUKING IT OUT FOR YEARS – BUT HOW DO THEY STACK UP?

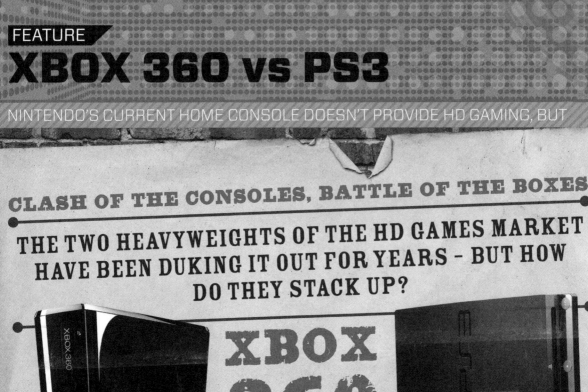

THE MICROSOFT MIRACLE...

Microsoft's Xbox 360 launched in late 2005.

❋ ❋ ❋

Its main processor – the brains of the unit – is a tri-core CPU made by IBM. Think of it as three super-brains on one chip.

❋ ❋ ❋

Ships with a choice of three integrated hard drives, offering 4 GB, 250 GB or 320 GB of memory.

XBOX 360 S	PS3 SLIM
CPU	**CPU**
POWER PC TRI-CORE XENON	CELL BROADBAND ENGINE
MEMORY	**MEMORY**
512 MB OF GDDR3 RAM	256 MB XDR
NETWORKING	**NETWORKING**
ETHERNET WI-FI INFRARED	ETHERNET WI-FI BLUETOOTH 2.0

THE SONY SUPERSTAR...

Sony's PlayStation 3 launched in late 2006.

❋ ❋ ❋

One main processor backed up by seven smaller SPUs (Synergistic Processing Units) that add to the main chip's computational strength.

❋ ❋ ❋

Ships with a choice of two upgradable hard drives, offering 150 or 320 GB of memory.

/// "CHOOSE YOUR POSSE, YOUR WEAPONS, YOUR STRATEGY – THE ADVENTURE IS YOURS" ///

WHO SAYS?

Richard Leadbetter is the director of Digital Foundry Ltd, technical specialists who create custom-made equipment for the capture and analysis of HD gameplay. He also writes for many gaming magazines.

GAME DESIGN

PlayStation 3: Many games are designed for a specific gaming system and then ported over to others. Sadly for PS3 users, the *Call of Duty* games are ported to the platform and not designed for it. Some ports are good, some are not, and many gamers using the Sony system reported bugs in the multiplayer mode on *Black Ops*.

Xbox 360: *Black Ops* was built for the centralized graphics-processing architecture of the Xbox 360, giving it smoother gameplay and more responsive controls on that console. And as a result of an agreement Microsoft made with the publisher Activision, Xbox 360 owners also get all downloadable content earlier than their PS3-playing pals.

OPTICAL DRIVES

PlayStation 3: Sony's proprietary Blu-Ray disks hold more data than the standard DVDs used by the Xbox 360, so big games, such as *Final Fantasy XIII*, fit on one disk for the PlayStation 3. *Final Fantasy XIII* was also designed especially for the PS3, so the game ran more efficiently on that console.

Xbox 360: *Final Fantasy XIII* was ported for the Xbox 360 late in the game's development, so Square Enix was forced to cram 40 GB of game on to three Xbox 360 DVDs. The quality of the graphics and cutscenes on the Xbox 360 version suffered in comparison to those on the PlayStation 3 version, too, mainly due to rushed conversion issues.

GAMES AND CONSOLE EXCLUSIVES

PlayStation 3: Sony's internal studios are much larger than Microsoft's, pumping out more console-exclusive hit franchises, such as *Uncharted, Killzone, Gran Turismo, God of War* and *LittleBigPlanet* (right), each designed to show off the PS3's technical strengths.

Xbox 360: Microsoft typically has fewer high-profile exclusives. Its franchises, such as *Halo, Forza Motorsport, Gears of War* and *Fable,* are still incredibly popular, even if they are not quite as technically advanced as the Sony titles.

CONTROLLERS

PlayStation 3: Both the PS3 and the Xbox 360 ship with a joypad/analogue stick controller but the PS3 has recently added support for its Move motion-control system. The Move uses a camera to track the controller's movement.

Xbox 360: Microsoft's Kinect uses its stereoscopic camera to identify players, judge depth, track their movements and recognize their voices, enabling gamers to effectively become the controller. The Kinect also has more exclusive titles and its controller-free gameplay has been a massive hit with casual gamers.

THE RESULT...

It used to be the case that most games released across both consoles would typically perform better on the Xbox 360, but this changed over the course of 2011: there is now a closer parity between the two systems. In terms of exclusive games, Sony retains an edge because of its enormous network of in-house studios that concentrate on getting the most out of the PS3. The success of Microsoft's Kinect has brought an entirely new audience to the Xbox 360, however – something the PlayStation Move has not done. The battle of these two HD console behemoths looks set to continue, and this is one fight where *you* decide – by choosing which platform you prefer to play your games on.

SHOOTING GAMES

FASTEST-SELLING VIDEOGAME

Holder: *Call of Duty: Black Ops* **(Treyarch, 2010)**

Released by publisher Activision on 9 November 2010, *Call of Duty: Black Ops* sold 5.6 million copies on its launch day, and the game made $1 billion (£618 million) by 22 December 2010. This massive sales record is, however, expected to be beaten by *Call of Duty: Modern Warfare 3* (Infinity Ward, 2011) when the game's launch figures are officially released.

OVERVIEW

Whether you're staring down the sights of a gun, over the shoulder of your protagonist or running left to right along a scrolling landscape, shooters have you taking aim and firing upon your in-game enemies in endless battles for dominance, defence or exploration.

Today's popular shooter franchises, such as *Call of Duty* and *Gears of War*, are as well known for their online multiplayer modes – which allow gamers to trade bullets across a battlefield that can span the globe – as they are for their campaigns, but shooters have been around since the 1960s and have always rewarded a sharp eye and quick trigger finger.

BIOGRAPHY

Kirsten Kearney has been a journalist for 15 years and has written about games for eight, contributing to magazines and websites such as *GamesMaster* and *PocketGamer*. She once held the record for the **longest marathon playing a first-person shooter** for a 24-hour 4-minute stint on *Tom Clancy's Rainbow Six: Vegas 2* (Ubisoft, 2008), and is currently the editor of Ready-Up.net and the community editor for Play-Gamer.com.

CONTENTS

CRITICAL HIT!: *BATTLEFIELD* 40
FIRST-PERSON SHOOTERS 42
THIRD-PERSON SHOOTERS 44
2D SHOOTERS 46
ONLINE SHOOTERS 48
RAIL SHOOTERS 50
CRITICAL HIT!: *GEARS OF WAR* 52

BATTLEFIELD

EX-SAS SOLDIER AND AUTHOR ANDY McNAB WORKED ON

MOST PROLIFIC FPS SERIES

Holder: *Battlefield*
(EA Digital Illusions CE, 2002–11)
With 19 entries in the series, including expansions and spin-offs, the *Battlefield* franchise is the most prolific in the first-person shooter genre (pictured is *Battlefield 3*). Snapping at the game's heels are *Medal of Honor*, with 17 entries, and *Call of Duty*, with 15. The count for *Battlefield* could have been even higher but for a technicality: the number does not include the game regarded by many fans as the spiritual prequel to the series, *Codename Eagle* (Refraction Games, 1999).

FIRST GAME IN THE CORE *BATTLEFIELD* SERIES TO FEATURE A SINGLE-PLAYER CAMPAIGN

Holder: *Battlefield 3*
(EA Digital Illusions CE, 2011)
A direct sequel to *Battlefield 2* (EA Digital Illusions CE, 2005), *Battlefield 3* is the first game in the main series to have a single-player story. Every previous *Battlefield* game has been solely a multiplayer experience. (The *Battlefield: Bad Company* spin-off series was separate, with its focus on story-driven solo campaigns.) The narrative in *Battlefield 3* is set in 2014, and players adopt the role of Staff Sergeant Henry "Black" Blackburn, with most of the action taking place in the Middle East. Blackburn is in charge of a US army squad on a mission to find a soldier missing in action, while dodging the bullets of a determined insurgency.

18,414,811,520 Total body count logged online in *Battlefield: Bad Company 2* (EA Digital Illusions CE, 2010) across PC, PlayStation 3 and Xbox 360 versions, as of 5 September 2011.

BATTLEFIELD 3 (2011) TO HELP MAKE IT AS AUTHENTIC AS POSSIBLE ▶

MOST DESTRUCTIBLE ENVIRONMENTS IN A MILITARY FIRST-PERSON SHOOTER

Holder: *Battlefield: Bad Company 2* **(EA Digital Illusions CE, 2010)**

Using its Frostbite 1.5 engine, *Battlefield: Bad Company 2* was the first game to introduce fully destructible environments to the *Battlefield* series. Players have the ability to flatten buildings, destroy walls and cut through chain-link fences. Around 90% of the environment is deformable or destructible – even the ground can be deformed. *Battlefield 3*, with its Frostbite 2.0 engine, is expected to offer players even more destruction, including the option of annihilating a seven-storey building.

> "Even our most far-reaching ideas are becoming a reality. This is the game we've always wanted to create."
>
> PATRICK BACH, EXECUTIVE PRODUCER OF *BATTLEFIELD 3*

FASTEST-SELLING DOWNLOAD-ONLY GAME ON XBOX LIVE

Holder: *Battlefield 1943* **(EA Digital Illusions CE, 2009)**

Battlefield 1943 became the fastest-selling day-one and week-one download-only game worldwide on the Xbox LIVE Marketplace. The title's success on the Xbox 360 in 2009 was quickly followed by a repeat of both these sales feats on North America's PlayStation Network. In its first two weeks, *Battlefield 1943* sold more than 600,000 copies on the download services.

MOST KILLS IN *BATTLEFIELD: BAD COMPANY 2* ON XBOX 360

Holder: WinslowLee420 **(USA)**

With a horrific total of 278,039 kills on the *Bad Company* sequel on the Xbox 360, WinslowLee420 stands 61,128 kills ahead of his closest rival, CNT CrazyLoveX, as of 26 July 2011. WinslowLee420's weapon of choice is the 870 Combat shotgun and his favourite vehicle is the AH-64 Apache.

MOST DOG TAGS OBTAINED IN *BATTLEFIELD: BAD COMPANY 2*

Holder: PlayStation 3 gamers

The dog tag system awards players with an opponent's tag when they are defeated by a knife attack. Across PC, PS3 and Xbox 360 platforms a total of 451,208,242 tags have been collected. But PS3 gamers have collected more dog tags than their counterparts on any other platform – they are almost 8 million tags ahead of their closest rivals on the Xbox 360. It seems gamers are as quick with a blade as they are with a gun!

LARGEST CASH PRIZE WON IN A *BATTLEFIELD* TOURNAMENT

Holder: Team Legends **(USA)**

The record sum of $250,000 (£144,000) was paid out to the aptly named gamers Team Legends after they beat more than 200 rivals to claim victory at the *Best of the Battlefield* tournament on 17 February 2006 in Redwood City, California. Playing *Battlefield 2: Modern Combat* on the Xbox, each member of the 10-man group earned $25,000 (£14,400). Runners-up Team Professional Skills (USA) were consoled with a sum of $50,000 (£29,000).

TOP 10 VEHICLES USED IN *BATTLEFIELD: BAD COMPANY 2* ON PC (BY DISTANCE TRAVELLED)

DISTANCE	VEHICLE
35,421,000 km	AH-64
33,333,352 km	M1A2
27,847,990 km	T-90
26,330,691 km	MI-28
20,879,900 km	Quad
19,977,760 km	UH-60
17,491,951 km	UAV
10,586,352 km	M3A3
9,887,829 km	Mi-24
6,389,027 km	HMMW

Source: BattlefieldBadCompany2.com

FIRST-PERSON SHOOTERS

DURING THE LAUNCH OF *KILLZONE 3* (GUERRILLA GAMES, 2011), 7-ELEVEN STORES

BEST-SELLING AVATAR ITEM IN THE XBOX LIVE MARKETPLACE

Holder: *Night Vision Goggles – Call of Duty: Modern Warfare 2* **(Infinity Ward, 2009)**
Since November 2008, gamers have been able to have their own avatar to represent them on Xbox Live. The little characters can be used as players in a number of games, and users can buy apparel and props to customize their avatar and update its appearance. According to xbox.com, the all-time most popular item is the Night Vision Goggles from *Call of Duty: Modern Warfare 2* for both male and female avatars, which costs 240 MS points – that's £2 ($3) in real money.

HALO, DARLING

Hidden messages from developers, planted in obscure locations within games, are often deliberately very difficult to spot. One of the best-hidden Easter eggs of all time appears in *Halo: Combat Evolved* (Bungie, 2001). This was the first in the massively successful *Halo* series, and appeared on the Xbox prior to its release for PC and Mac. Level designer Jamie Griesemer hid a special dedication to his girlfriend, Meg, in the form of her first initial spelled out in bullet holes in the roof of a hidden room in the Pillar of Autumn level. It's hard to find, and you can't survive once you've located it. It was only discovered after Griesemer left a series of clues on online message boards.

/// "MONEY, POWER, RESPECT, THAT'S WHAT OUR CODE IS ALL ABOUT" ///

100,000 The number of entries in the "Name in the Game" competition for *Bioshock Infinite* (Irrational Games, 2012). The winner will have their name appear on in-world advertising.

IN THE USA SOLD A *KILLZONE*-THEMED SLURPEE CALLED "BATTLE FUEL" ▶

TOP 10 PLAYERS ON *BULLETSTORM* MULTIPLAYER

RANK	GAMER	TOTAL KILLS
1	Xenophobia UK	268,002
2	Wayne 1949 02	227,473
3	choccolatte	199,171
4	BurialRaindrop2	193,982
5	mkaj	144,883
6	MATIASCASTRO	93,626
7	ZED DIRTY ANGEL Z	79,487
8	RA1DER 75	77,000
9	jedikyle2	75,901
10	N3RGAL	70,959

Source: in-game leaderboard   *Accurate at 23 August 2011*

MOST GUNS IN A VIDEOGAME

Holder: *Borderlands* **(Gearbox, 2009)**
Borderlands has a tagline that jokingly boasts of "87 bazillion" guns in the game. In reality, the figure is 17,750,000 – still by far the most guns in any videogame. Weapons are generated randomly, with a number of different modifying factors including components, elemental effects, ammo type, damage multipliers and manufacturers. There are also eight rarity levels, with the rarest – and most powerful – being pearlescent.

MOST CHARACTER CUSTOMIZATION OPTIONS IN A SHOOTING GAME

Holder: *Brink* **(Splash Damage, 2011)**
Although first-person shooters haven't usually focused on the player character, who cannot be seen during play, it has become more common to allow gamers to customize the look of their in-game avatar. *Brink* allows over 102 quadrillion, or, to be more exact, 102,247,681,536,000,000 unique character combinations, including clothing, tattoo and scar options. But you can still only play as a male!

MOST CRITICALLY ACCLAIMED SHOOTER ON THE PLAYSTATION 3
Holder: *Call of Duty: Modern Warfare 2* **(Infinity Ward, 2009)**
Despite *Call of Duty: Black Ops* (Treyarch, 2010) selling faster than *Call of Duty: Modern Warfare 2* (see page 38), the latter garnered much higher praise from games critics, according to reviews site Metacritic. *Modern Warfare 2*

remains the highest-scoring shooter on the PS3, with a metascore of 94%, while *Black Ops* lags behind with a "mere" 88%.

LONGEST FPS MARATHON
Holders: Christopher Gloyd and Timothy Bell (Canada)
This is a record that is often challenged. Christopher Gloyd and Timothy Bell played *Halo: Reach* (Bungie, 2010) for a thumb-numbing 45 hours in a row. The duo accomplished this feat in Selkirk, Canada,

from 13 to 15 March 2011. The previous holders, Irish gaming team Gunna Scréach, had taken the record just one month previously, also playing *Halo: Reach*, but for 42 hours. Gloyd and Bell aren't the only Canadians with a marathon record: Canucks René Rinfret, Jerome Louie, Anesu Mutangadura and Jamie Tang hold the record for the **longest marathon playing a soccer videogame**, for a 31-hour session in February 2011 on *FIFA 11* (EA, 2010).

/// "A JOURNEY WHERE YOU NEVER KNOW WHO YOU'LL RUN INTO NEXT" ///

VANQUISH FEATURES AN "O'NEILL CYLINDER", A SPACE STATION DESIGNED BY

FIRST GAME TO FEATURE "ROCKET SLIDING"

Holder: *Vanquish* **(Platinum, 2010)**
Fast-paced shooter *Vanquish* added a fun gameplay innovation to the third-person shooter genre in the form of "rocket sliding", a special move in which players slide their characters from one piece of cover to another at great speeds while still being able to aim and shoot. The move was named Gamespot.com's "Best Original Game Mechanic" of 2010 and its influence can be seen on other more recent shooters, such as *Bulletstorm* (People Can Fly, 2011) and *Crysis 2* (Crytek, 2011).

8.6 million The number of copies the first six titles in the *Twisted Metal* series sold across all formats, a figure set to rise with the release of the new game.

THE ———— AMERICAN SCIENTIST AND WRITER GERARD O'NEILL ▶

MOST CRITICALLY ACCLAIMED PSP SHOOTER

Holder: *Syphon Filter: Dark Mirror* **(Sony, 2006)**
Although Agent Gabe Logan (left) may not be as famous today as he was during the *Syphon Filter* series' heyday around the year 2000, his profile is still high among the fans of shooters on the PSP. *Syphon Filter: Dark Mirror* and *Syphon Filter: Logan's Shadow* (Sony, 2007) claim the top two spots for such games on Sony's handheld console list on reviews website Metacritic, scoring 87% and 85% respectively.

MOST MARS BARS EATEN IN ONE MINUTE

Holders: Pat Bertoletti and **Joey Chestnut (both USA)**
To help promote the release of *Red Faction: Armageddon* at the San Diego Comic-Con on 22 July 2010, professional speed-eaters Pat Bertoletti and Joey Chestnut each chomped through three Mars bars in one minute. The choice of Mars bars for the attempt was to mark the fact that the game they were promoting is set on the planet of the same name.

HIGHEST SCORE ON "RUIN MODE" ON *RED FACTION: ARMAGEDDON*

Holder: Papa-Wheelie
"Ruin mode" in *Red Faction: Armageddon* (Volition, Inc, 2011) is all about blowing things up – every building in the game must be destroyed! The PS3 player known as Papa-Wheelie scored an impressive 22,627,306 points by smashing up the "Junction map". The same gamer has the top scores for the mode on every other map, too.

TOP 10 PLAYERS ON *SOCOM: SPECIAL FORCES*

RANK	GAMER	KILLS
1	TaZmAnIaN_619	42,657
2	Noxage	41,060
3	Robert562-	36,315
4	oG_riT	34,924
5	SOCOMmando	33,613
6	SpiritRose	32,992
7	XxIVIP-SoulJaxX	32,805
8	vERECTION	31,880
9	x-SupeRioR	31,199
10	Sleeping-Reaper	30,858

Source: in-game leaderboard

FIRST COVER-BASED SHOOTER

Holder: *Kill Switch* **(Namco, 2003)**
Although the likes of *Time Crisis* (Namco, 1995) and *The Getaway* (Sony, 2003) experimented with cover systems, *Kill Switch* was the first game to make cover-based shooting its core gameplay mechanic. *Kill Switch* introduced innovations such as blind firing from behind cover, and its legacy can be seen not only in games such as *Gears of War* (Epic, 2006) but also beyond the shooting genre in titles such as *Red Dead Redemption* (Rockstar, 2010) and *Deus Ex: Human Revolution* (Eidos, 2011).

> "In any war there's always a winning side and a losing side, there are winners and losers, but one of the themes in the story is, what makes a true victor in any conflict?"
>
> SHINJI MIKAMI, DIRECTOR OF *VANQUISH*

LONGEST-RUNNING PLAYSTATION FRANCHISE

Holder: *Twisted Metal* **(SingleTrac, 1995–2011)**
When developer Eat Sleep Play brought the vehicular combat series *Twisted Metal* to the PS3 in October 2011, it claimed the mantle of being the longest-running PlayStation game series from *Gran Turismo* (Polyphony Digital, 1997–2010). Sharing its name with the first game in the series, the new *Twisted Metal* features the return of classic characters such as the killer clown Sweet Tooth (right).

2D SHOOTERS

ⱯⱯ ×02

CHAIN STATUS

VULCAN LV06

HOMING LV05

SPREAD LV05

LONGEST WAIT FOR THE HD REMIX OF A SHOOTER

Holder: *Radiant Silvergun* **(Treasure, 1998)**
Previously only available in Japan, Western fans of classic shooter *Radiant Silvergun* have waited over 13 years for a chance to play the game without having to import it (and buy a console to play it on). Fortunately, the high-definition version was slated for an international release via the Xbox Live Arcade in late 2011. The widely acclaimed game was released on the Sega Saturn in 1998, and second-hand copies regularly sell for more than $200 (£123).

TOP 10 SCORES ON *SUPER STARDUST HD*, "ARCADE" MODE

RANK	GAMER	SCORE
1	TLO-MEK	2,016,958,340
2	BRIDY	1,839,104,255
3	DYNAMIC_NEET	1,715,941,840
4	ER777	1,593,405,745
5	BATTLEQURS	1,319,123,340
6	ROIN10	1,228,885,255
7	FEENA78	1,113,248,530
8	ZRRQ2	1,109,021,580
9	O-MONI-	1,056,638,970
10	LAGMONSTER	1,041,120,530

Source: in-game leaderboard

FIRST SIDE-SCROLLING SHOOTER

Holder: *Defender* **(Williams Electronics, 1980)**
Inspired by *Space Invaders* (Taito, 1978) and *Asteroids* (Atari, 1979), American developer Eugene Jarvis is famed in the world of gaming for pioneering horizontal scrolling in the shooter genre with *Defender*. The title's key innovation was a gameplay area that was wider than the width of a screen. Off-screen areas were represented in the form of a dynamic "mini-map", indicating to players where they needed to fly their ship to defend humanity from evil aliens.

FIRST ARCADE GAME TO BE ADVERTISED ON TELEVISION

Holder: *Zaxxon* **(Sega, 1982)**
Today, game publishers have huge advertising budgets to sell their wares, and sophisticated game trailers in prime-time TV slots are the norm, but such coverage for videogames was once unheard of. Sega was first to take the big step of advertising an arcade game on TV, when it promoted space shooter *Zaxxon* in 1982. The game itself was notable for being the **first to feature an isometric viewpoint display** and to give its characters shadows.

MOST CRITICALLY ACCLAIMED DOWNLOADABLE 2D SHOOTER

Holder: *Geometry Wars: Retro Evolved 2* **(Bizarre Creations, 2008)**
The top-down multi-directional shooter series *Geometry Wars* started out as a mini-game, playable in an in-game garage in *Project Gotham Racing 2* (Bizarre Creations, 2003). The sequel, *Geometry Wars: Retro Evolved 2*, is a download-only game on Xbox Live Arcade. It has proved particularly popular among shooter fans and has an aggregate score of 90% on reviews site Metacritic.

GENRE IN WHICH GAMERS MUST NAVIGATE A WALL OF INCOMING FIRE! ▶

WEAPON

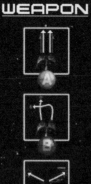

HIGHEST SCORE ON *GALAGA LEGIONS DX*

Holder: UnspokenSix8 (Japan)

To help celebrate the 30th anniversary of the classic arcade space shooter *Galaga* (Namco, 1981) in 2011, Namco Bandai released *Galaga Legions DX* on Xbox Live Arcade. Similar to the *PAC-Man Championship Edition DX* (Namco Bandai, 2007) and created by the same team of designers, the game boasts all-new HD graphics as well as a host of new modes and regular online tournaments. A *Galaga* fan known as UnspokenSix8 has the top score on nine of the game's regular modes, with an impressive cumulative score of 66,887,500 points, and also ranks second on its special "Championship" mode.

> **"I was so captivated by it, I just became obsessed with this one game."**
>
> ANDREW LAIDLAW ON HIS RELATIONSHIP WITH *GALAGA*

HIGHEST SCORE ON *GALAGA*

Holder: Andrew Laidlaw (USA)

Announced by Twin Galaxies on 31 December 2010, Andrew Laidlaw achieved an incredible score of 4,525,150 points on *Galaga* (Namco, 1981) on Twin Galaxies' Tournament Settings, which uses the game's hardest "difficulty" setting and allows players just five lives. Andrew's feat beat the previous record set by fellow American Phil Day by 1,249,430 points. According to local newspaper reports, it was the pair's rivalry that led to them becoming friends, with Phil sending Andrew footage of his gameplay to help his challenger prepare for the record.

HIGHEST SCORE ON *DEATHSMILES* (IOS)

Holder: sigRSW

Developer Cave employed cute, occult-loving goth girls Windia (right) and Casper (far right) instead of the spaceships often seen in the genre as the controllable characters in *Deathsmiles* (Cave, 2007), their side-scrolling *danmaku* shooter for the Xbox 360. In 2011, the game was adapted for the iPhone. On this portable version of *Deathsmiles* it is the gamer known only as sigRSW who holds the highest score, with an impressive 410,354,034 points accrued as of July 2011, using new character Tiara.

ONLINE SHOOTERS

AMERICAN COMPOSER MIKE MORASKY HAS WRITTEN THE MUSIC FOR HUGE

MOST POPULAR GAME ON STEAM

Holder: *Team Fortress 2* **(Valve Software, 2007)**

Team Fortress 2 overtook *Counter-Strike* (Valve, 2000) as the most played game on digital download service Steam in June 2011, with figures reaching as high as 97,000 players per day, compared to *Counter-Strike*'s 61,000. In the years since Steam launched in 2003, *Counter-Strike* had been almost immovable at the top, so this represents a major popularity shift. *Team Fortress 2* shot to No.1 after it became free to play.

FIRST CROSS-PLATFORM SHOOTER

Holder: *Quake III Arena* **(id Software, 1999)**

Now that digital distribution service Steam includes its Steamworks features in PS3 games, cross-platform online gaming could well become huge. But allowing PC gamers to play against and alongside console gamers began back in 2000. A year after its PC release, *Quake III Arena* launched on the Sega Dreamcast to great critical acclaim (its Metacritic score was 93% as of August 2011). The game allowed four-player online play between the two platforms. There are still gamers who play this version of the game over a decade later, for its excellent frame rate and online play, despite there being more recent Steam and Xbox Live versions available.

MOST POPULAR FPS ON FACEBOOK

Holder: *UberStrike* **(Cmune, 2010)**

With 1 million user installs, *UberStrike* is the most popular first-person shooter on Facebook, and one of the few "social shooters" around. Originally released in 2008 as *Paradise Paintball* – the **first multiplayer 3D game on Facebook** – the game was relaunched in 2010 with a more adult theme, a new name and more weapons. Although some fans were critical, *UberStrike* enjoyed an increase in users.

MOST CRITICALLY ACCLAIMED ONLINE SHOOTER

Holder: *Unreal Tournament* **(Epic, 1999)**

With a Gamerankings.com rating of 93.57%, *Unreal Tournament* is still, more than a decade after its release, the most critically acclaimed online shooter. It is also one of the first to focus almost entirely on multiplayer gameplay. Its main online FPS competitor, *Quake III Arena*, was released 10 days later and sold more copies in its first year, but *Unreal Tournament* has remained the critics' choice.

89
The average percentage rating for Valve Software's online co-op shooter *Left 4 Dead 2*, according to reviews aggregate website Metacritic.

ONLINE SHOOTERS *TEAM FORTRESS 2, LEFT 4 DEAD* AND *LEFT 4 DEAD 2* ▶

FIRST ONLINE FPS FOR iPHONE

Holder: *iFPS Online* (GarageGames, 2009)

The first FPS playable online using both the iPhone and iPod Touch is deathmatch title *iFPS Online*. The game has a multiplayer option for up to 10 gamers, using Wi-Fi and 3G. Other recent, popular online shooters for the iPhone include *N.O.V.A. 2* (Gameloft, 2010) and *Archetype* (Munkyfun, 2010).

BIGGEST LAN PARTY

Holder: DreamHack (Sweden)

A local area network, or LAN, connects various computers to each other. Swedish LAN party DreamHack has beaten its own record for the world's largest LAN party. The record now stands at 12,754 computers and 13,608 visitors at their Winter 2010 event. The record-breaking party hosted *Counter-Strike* and *Quake Live* tournaments.

DreamHack previously held the record with 10,544 computers and 11,060 attendees at their Winter 2007 event.

HEARTWARMING

In *Left 4 Dead 2* (Valve Corporation/Turtle Rock Studios, 2009), players become survivors in a society full of zombie-like beings, and the aim of the game is to survive the infected hordes and go from safe house to safe house. On the Xbox 360, *Left 4 Dead 2* contains 65 "Achievements" (compared to 73 on the PC version), which players must complete in order to add to their "gamerscore". A mere 2% have managed to master the Heartwarmer "Achievement", and little wonder – dodging infected zombies, players must find and carry a defibrillator to the next safe house, then exit the safe house to find, then revive, a dead team-mate. The easiest Achievement, which 79.1% of players have completed, is called "Acid Reflex".

> **"Just make sure you have a good internet connection and fast reflexes to avoid being blown up."**
> VALVE SOFTWARE DEVELOPER ROBIN WALKER ON *TEAM FORTRESS 2*

FIRST CROSS-PLATFORM TITLE ON GAMES FOR WINDOWS LIVE

Holder: *Shadowrun* (FASA Interactive, 2007)

Integrating PC titles into Microsoft's Live service (most popularly used for the Xbox 360) has been a difficult process. Only a few titles have allowed cross-platform gaming so that players can hook up and trade bullets on the PC and Xbox 360. The first game to achieve this was *Shadowrun*, which lets online gamers play as a human, elf, troll or dwarf and use magic spells alongside weapons such as shotguns.

TOP 10 SCORES ON *QUAKE ARENA ARCADE* IN "FREE-FOR-ALL" MODE

RANK	GAMER	FRAGS*
1	Sleath	8,373
2	BeanBrains14	6,893
3	getdanKK	5,533
4	THExBIBLE	4,939
5	miss mouFy	4,359
6	Ambient Nujabes	4,297
7	APOCALYPSE 514	4,285
8	Shotgun 10111	3,088
9	Shimair	3,070
10	Tdart189	2,519

Source: in-game leaderboard   * Accurate at 1 August 2011

RAIL SHOOTERS

A RAIL SHOOTER MILESTONE, THE ORIGINAL *STARFOX* (NINTENDO, 1993) FOR THE

ON TRACK?

Just as a train cannot move off its tracks, so rail shooters restrict player movement to a single route. But unlike most rail journeys, there are usually plenty of lurking baddies who need to be disposed of with a few shots.

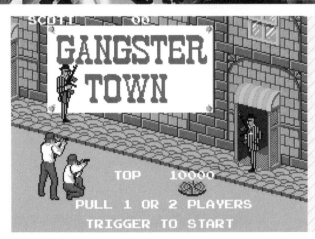

FIRST LIGHT-GUN RAIL SHOOTER

Holder: *Gangster Town* (Sega, 1987)
The history of the light gun goes back to the Seeburg *Ray-O-Light* in 1936, a simulated shooting gallery that was the **first light-gun game**. It wasn't until 1987, and the Sega title *Gangster Town*, that developers shifted away from such formats to moving the player "on rails" through a set path filled with enemies. *Gangster Town* had players use their Sega Light Phaser to fire at gangsters, with a scrolling car chase in which they shot at enemies as they loomed into range.

FIRST LASERDISC GAME
Holder: *Astron Belt*
(Sega, 1983)
Much of the early excitement about LaserDisc games at the Amusement and Music Operators Association show, held in the USA in 1982, was due to one title – *Astron Belt*. A classic rail shooter, the game itself caused less of a stir than the LaserDisc's large storage capacity, which enabled it to feature full-motion video clips, something with which rival game systems of the time could not compete.

34,000 The number of copies the psychedelic Xbox 360 shooter *Child of Eden* sold in July 2011, its first full month on global release.

MOST CRITICALLY ACCLAIMED KINECT GAME

Holder: *Child of Eden*
(Q Entertainment, 2011)

With a score of 83% on the reviews site Metacritic, *Child of Eden* is the highest-rated game for Microsoft's hands-free Kinect controller. The brainchild of Japanese game developer Tetsuya Mizuguchi, the man behind the visually dazzling *Rez* (Q Entertainment, 2001), *Child of Eden* has players control a missile gun with one hand and direct a stream of fire with the other.

> "You'll be able to trace the DNA of these elements all the way back to my earliest games."

TETSUYA MIZUGUCHI ON HIS GAME, *CHILD OF EDEN*

FIRST FULL-MOTION VIDEO CONSOLE GAME

Holder: *Sewer Shark*
(Digital Pictures, 1992)

Playing out like an interactive movie, rail shooter *Sewer Shark* was a CD-Rom game for Sega's short-lived Sega CD add-on to the Genesis/Mega Drive. A major improvement on *Astron Belt* (Sega, 1983), *Sewer Shark* employed full-motion video, which was directed by the Oscar-winning American visual effects supervisor John Dykstra. With a larger storage capacity than the console's regular games cartridge, the CD-Rom could play video smoothly at a rate of 60 frames per second. The actual game was perhaps rather less inspiring, tasking players with fighting off giant scorpions, mechanical moles and mutant alligators while keeping the sewers of Solar City clean.

HIGHEST SCORE ON *GYRUSS*

Holder: **Michael Bangs (USA)**

On 5 July 1987, gamer Michael Bangs racked up an impressive 47,024,400 points on the "marathon" mode of the epic arcade rail shooter *Gyruss* (Konami, 1983). The **highest score** on *Gyruss* under **"Tournament" settings** (in which players have only five lives) is the 1,306,100 points scored by Richard Marsh (USA) on 2 June 2004.

BEST-SELLING RAIL SHOOTER

Holder: *Star Fox 64* **(Nintendo, 1997)**

Although, *Star Fox 64* sold 4.03 million copies, more than any other rail shooter, it was the last time the game's protagonist, the much-loved Nintendo character Fox McCloud, would star in a pure rail shooter for almost 15 years. After some free-roaming adventures, the 3DS *Star Fox 64 3D* (Nintendo, 2011) brings the character firmly back on the rails.

TOP 10 SCORES ON "SCORE ATTACK" IN *REZ HD*

RANK	GAMER	SCORE
1	CASTINGD	301,270
2	MisoraHebari	300,270
3	TrueBlu Bomber	299,500
4	Sheequet	297,950
5	Pierre Mikawa	296,240
6	SMASHING DRIVE	294,150
7	sandsfel	285,400
8	duralist	285,270
9	Perplexity777	273,090
10	HurricaneJesus	268,970

Source: in-game leaderboard

KING OF LIMBS

A prequel to the survival-horror game *Dead Space* (EA, 2008), *Dead Space Extraction* (Visceral Games, 2009) brings some of the series' unique features to the rail-shooter genre for Wii and PS3.

As with the main games, players kill the attacking mutated monsters, or necromorphs, by severing their limbs, performing "strategic dismemberments" using the Wii Remote (Wiimote) controller or PlayStation Move to indicate where their character's plasma cutter should do its gory work.

Each weapon also possesses a secondary-fire option that can be activated by turning the controller, either a Wiimote or PlayStation Move, on its side. By using a "kinesis" module, players can also lift or throw heavy objects at foes.

MOST VALUABLE XBOX SOLD AT AUCTION

Holder: *Panzer Dragoon Orta* Special Edition Xbox **(2002)**

Limited-edition consoles are some of the most sought-after gaming collectables. Excluding one-off competition prizes, and other consoles that were never available at retail, the rarest is the white *Panzer Dragoon*-themed original Xbox. Released to help promote *Panzer Dragoon Orta* (Sega, 2002), only 999 such Xbox consoles were ever produced. On 10 June 2011, one of these units sold on eBay for $1,250 (£760).

GEARS OF WAR

GEARS OF WAR 3 FEATURES THE VOCAL TALENTS OF

UN-BETA-BLE BONUS
Beta testers of *Gears of War 3* could unlock a number of exclusive weapons, including the Golden Retro Lancer, for use in the full game by completing 90 matches in any game type and earning 100 kills while testing.

MOST COUNTRIES PARTICIPATING IN A MULTIPLAYER BETA
Holder: *Gears of War 3* **(Epic Games, 2011)**
Beta-testing is the stage of game development in which an early version of a game is examined for playability problems. Sometimes developers recruit actual gamers to take part. For *Gears 3*'s multiplayer beta, Epic Games recruited 1.29 million gamers from 145 countries. Participating players received an in-game medal that marked their testing "service" in the game's final retail release.

HIGHEST SCORE IN "HORDE MODE" IN *GEARS OF WAR 2*
Holders: **SVT Merc and SwaggaLykUs (both USA)**
In *Gears of War 2*'s "horde mode", players face 50 waves of attacking enemies. These foes increase in strength and energy every 10 waves. The aim is to survive while scoring highly. As of 4 July 2011, Xbox Live players SVT Merc and SwaggaLykUs share the honours in this task with 994,400,000 points apiece.

6.1 million The number of copies the first *Gears of War* game has sold worldwide, just ahead of the 5.95 million units shifted by *Gears 2*.

FASTEST PRE-ORDERED XBOX 360 TITLE

Holder: *Gears of War 3* **(Epic Games, 2011)**

Even before it was released, *Gears of War 3* was breaking sales records. Over a million fans of the series had placed pre-orders for the game by May 2011, more than four months before its scheduled release date.

> **"*Gears of War 3*'s campaign is very important to us, and we're going to have the longest damn campaign of the series in *Gears 3*."**
>
> CLIFF BLESZINSKI, DESIGN DIRECTOR, EPIC GAMES

FIRST XBOX 360 GAME TO ENTER THE JAPANESE TOP 10

Holder: *Gears of War* **(Epic Games, 2006)**

Microsoft's consoles have never really cracked the Japanese market, so it is particularly remarkable that the platform-exclusive *Gears of War* managed to blast its way to number seven in the Japanese sales chart. The game moved 33,212 copies in Japan in its first week on sale in January 2007.

TEN *GEARS OF WAR 2* QUOTES

QUOTE (CHARACTER)

"I always wanted a horsey" (Augustus Cole)

"Anya, it's a giant worm! They're sinking cities with a giant worm!" (Marcus Fenix)

"Suck pavement!" (Marcus Fenix)

"No, no, it was bigger than that! It looked like a weird monkey-dog thing!" (Benjamin Carmine)

"Mom, Dad? Are we there yet?" (Damon Baird)

"Everyone wants to see The Cole Train play!" (Augustus Cole)

"We're not here to sell cookies" (Marcus Fenix)

"I'm coughing up blood that ain't even mine!" (Damon Baird)

"Where the lights go? Can't have no game without no lights" (Augustus Cole)

"You're the first humans to ever desecrate this palace with your presence..." (Myrrah)

Source: Gears of War 2

MOST CRITICALLY ACCLAIMED THIRD-PERSON SHOOTER

Holder: *Gears of War* (Epic Games, 2006)

According to reviews site Metacritic, *Gears of War* seriously outguns all other third-person shooters with a review score of 90%, a full 4% ahead of its closest rival, *Syphon Filter* (Eidetic, 1999) on the PSP. The key question is: can *Gears 3* (below) beat this score?

SPORTS GAMES

HIGHEST SUM PAID FOR A PS3 GAME

Holder: *NBA Elite 11*
(EA Canada, 2011)

Rarely does a cancelled title get so close to release that retail discs are printed and posted, but that's exactly what happened to *NBA Elite 11*. After "concerns about game polish" prompted EA to pull the plug, the game instantly became a highly sought-after rarity. Israeli collector Damian Fraimorice was lucky enough to secure two factory-sealed copies, one of which he sold to a buyer in the USA for an incredible $1,500 (£915) in August 2011. Only 10 unopened copies are known to exist.

BIOGRAPHY

Joseph Ewens writes about videogames and films for a variety of publications, including *Kotaku*, *Den of Geek* and *Film International*. He also writes about dwarves for *Fantasy Flight Games*, and is a regular poker columnist. He has scored more goals in *FIFA* than you've had hot dinners and will one day definitely finish that *NHL* franchise he started in 2007.

OVERVIEW

Whether played on court, field or street, sport is a universal language across the globe. Its gaming equivalents are no exception, uniting millions of players around the world in shared entertainment. The history of sports gaming is one of the richest in the videogames medium. Defining titles such as *Pong* (Atari, 1972) and *John Madden Football* (EA, 1988) proved both massively popular and highly influential. Sports games are constantly evolving and innovating; today's heavy-hitters could be inspired by underground skate parks or established federations, such as FIFA or the NHL. All they need to showcase is a love for competition and a desire to be the best.

CONTENTS

CRITICAL HIT!: *SSX*	056
SOCCER	058
AMERICAN SPORTS	060
EUROPEAN SPORTS	062
EXTREME SPORTS	064

SSX

WHEN THE LATEST GAME IN THE SERIES, *SSX* (2012), WAS ANNOUNCED IN 2010,

BOARDER CROSSING

It's no coincidence that the racing element of every *SSX* title bears a strong resemblance to boardercross – in which four snowboarders race each other down snow-covered slopes. The inventor of the sport, Steve Rechtschaffner (USA), was an Executive Producer on the original *SSX* from 2000. The first boardercross contest was staged in 2001 and it has been an Olympic event since 2006.

MOST REAL-LIFE MOUNTAIN RANGES IN A VIDEOGAME
Holder: *SSX* (EA Canada, 2012)
Using data provided by NASA, EA Canada accurately mapped 300 mountains from around the world with ASTER Global Digital Elevation Model satellite imagery. Using this information, it has reproduced as many as 70 mountains across up to 13 different ranges for the sixth game in the series, also called *SSX*, including the Andes, Himalayas and Rockies. Players are even able to explore peaks in snow-capped wastelands such as Antarctica and Greenland, with bespoke terrain deformation adding ramps and half pipes to the natural terrain. EA use a tool called "Mountain Man" to apply ramps, jumps and rails to the realistic slopes. The game's main menu presents a Google Earth-type 3D model of the Earth, which players can zoom in on to choose a range.

TOP SCORE

The *SSX* series has long been famed for its multiple-artist soundtracks, but this all changed with *SSX Blur* (EA Montreal, 2007). The entire score was composed by Dutch musician Junkie XL (aka Tom Holkenborg), who took his remix of Elvis Presley's "A Little Less Conversation" to No.1 in the UK chart in 2002.

/// "NOTHING IS TRUE.
EVERYTHING IS PERMITTED" ///

93 The average Metacritic score for *SSX 3* (EA Canada, 2003) on the PlayStation 2, equalling the average for *SSX* (EA Canada, 2000).

ITS ORIGINAL TITLE WAS *SSX: DEADLY DESCENTS* ▶

MOST CRITICALLY ACCLAIMED SNOWBOARDING GAME

Holders: *SSX* (EA Canada, 2000) and *SSX 3* (EA Canada, 2003)

The very first *SSX* offered gamers a new spin on the snowboarding genre, delivering a complete package of racing, tricks and attitude. By the time *SSX 3* appeared, the team at EA had refined their game into an open-world mountainscape with an abundance of new boarding opportunities. So it's no surprise that the two games each earned a rating average as high as 93% from the review aggregator Metacritic.

MOST DECORATED SPORTS FRANCHISE

Holder: *SSX* (EA Canada, 2000–present)

The Academy of Interactive Arts & Sciences hands out its Interactive Achievement Awards every year. No sports series has received more accolades than *SSX*. Debut title *SSX* amassed five awards, *SSX 3* (EA Canada, 2003) picked up two trophies, and fourth title in the series *SSX on Tour* (EA Canada, 2005) gained a single nod for Outstanding Achievement in Soundtrack.

"**When we found out we had the chance to bring back *SSX*, we knew we wanted to do something really big...**"
TODD BATTY, CREATIVE DIRECTOR OF *SSX*

SNOW-BUSINESS

It's quite common to hear Hollywood talent in epic RPG games or gritty shooters, but less so in a snowboarding game. Way back in 2001, *SSX Tricky* (EA Canada) hired *Charlie's Angels* star Lucy Liu to provide the voice for cover character Elise Riggs. The game also features vocal work from actors David Arquette and Billy Zane, as well as turns from musicians Macy Gray and Bif Naked.

BEST-SELLING PS2 SNOWBOARDING GAME
Holder: *SSX 3* (EA Canada, 2003)

Aficionados may prefer *SSX Tricky* (EA Canada, 2001), but there's no doubting which fan-favourite topped the sales chart. *SSX 3* for the PlayStation 2 had sold 1,379,862 copies as of 29 July 2011, easily making it the most successful snowboarding title on Sony's console. The **best-selling snowboarding game ever** is *1080° Snowboarding* (Nintendo, 1998), which sold 2.03 million copies.

MOST PROLIFIC FICTIONAL VIDEOGAME DJ
Holder: DJ Atomika

Fans of *SSX 3* (EA Canada, 2003), *SSX Blur* (EA Montreal, 2007) and *Burnout Paradise* (Criterion Games, 2008) will be familiar with the tunes of DJ Atomika. Voiced by Mark Hildreth (Canada), the character has personally introduced 35 tracks during his tenure. By contrast, real-life DJ and *GTA* veteran Lazlow Jones can boast only 17 songs played under his aegis, although he has multiple stints as a talk radio host.

FIRST USE OF CUSTOM AUDIO FOR A DYNAMIC SOUNDTRACK
Holder: *SSX* (EA Canada, 2012)

Dynamic soundtracks, which alter as you play a game, have been common since LucasArts debuted the iMUSE system in *Monkey Island 2* (1991). The *SSX* series is famed for its own use of dynamic music. Instruments and vocals are partially excluded when a song starts, feeding back in as players complete increasingly impressive tricks. *SSX* is the first game to apply this to a player's own imported tracks, so that their music changes according to how they play.

TOP 10 *SSX 3* HIGH SCORES

RANK	PLAYER	SCORE*
1	REVirus	27,105,628
2	Alex "Ikki2504" B	20,044,160
3	Lt-UnReaL "ChaosRacer2"	19,236,712
4	JTS	18,128,867
5	Rastapo	18,112,298
6	Rastapo	17,512,665
7	bakalhau	16,023,714
8	fatzo14	14,976,780
9	Onizuka	14,858,241
10	Onizuka	14,084,567

Source: Cyberscore.me.uk   * Accurate at July 2011

THE FIRST *MARIO* TITLE TO FEATURE SOCCER WAS FIVE-A-SIDE GAME *SUPER*

LARGEST VIDEOGAME TOURNAMENT

Holder: **2011 FIFA Interactive World Cup**

Since its origins in 2004, the FIFA Interactive World Cup has ballooned to record-breaking proportions, with 869,543 players competing for a ticket to the 2011 Grand Final in Los Angeles, USA. Only 24 players won their way to LA, with 16-year-old Portuguese Francisco Cruz romping home to the $20,000 (£12,500) title. Cruz (front row, fifth player from left) powered his way to victory without losing a single match along the way.

MOST PLAYER CELEBRATIONS IN A SPORTS VIDEOGAME

Holder: *FIFA 12* **(EA Canada, 2011)**

Firing in a screamer is your cue to unleash that patented victory dance, and in *FIFA 12* your players can join in the fun. With 143 different celebrations to execute, *FIFA 12* holds the record for the most goal-scoring jigs in a sports game. EA Sports modified the victory routines in *FIFA 11* (EA Canada, 2010), introducing signature celebrations for particular players. *FIFA 12* picks up where *11* left off, from the straightforward to the elaborate. Among the more interesting options are the Prancing Bird, the Samba Dance and the Uncontrolled Backflip.

MOST VIEWED SOCCER VIDEO FAQ

Holder: **Marius Hjerpseth (Norway)**

FIFA 10 (EA Canada, 2009) master Marius Hjerpseth is best known for his stylish goal compilations on YouTube. A desire to emulate his silky skills and master the game has led to 5,052,558 views of his *FIFA 10* "New Skills" Tutorial, as of 20 July 2011. In total, Hjerpseth's videos have been viewed an incredible 24 million times.

5.82 million The total sales, across all platforms, of *Pro Evolution Soccer (PES) 2010* (Konami, 2009). This is 1.7 million more than successor *PES 2011*.

MARIO STRIKERS (NEXT LEVEL, 2005) ON THE NINTENDO GAME CUBE ▶

TOP 10 BEST-SELLING SOCCER TITLES

RANK	TITLE	PLATFORM	SALES
1	*FIFA 11*	PlayStation 3	4.41 million
2	*PES 6*	PlayStation 2	4.13 million
3	*FIFA 06*	PlayStation 2	3.93 million
4	*PES 5*	PlayStation 2	3.82 million
5	*FIFA 07*	PlayStation 2	3.78 million
6	*FIFA 10*	PlayStation 3	3.64 million
7	*PES 4*	PlayStation 2	3.57 million
8	*FIFA 05*	PlayStation 2	3.51 million
9	*PES 2008*	PlayStation 2	3.44 million
10	*FIFA 11*	Xbox 360	3.33 million

Source: VGChartz.com

DIRTY DOZEN

FIFA 12 (EA Canada, 2011) proved popular with critics at the 2011 Electronic Entertainment Expo (E3), where it picked up the Best Sports Game award from IGN and two gongs from 1UP – Best Sports Game and Best Mobile Game. Looking more physically realistic, and with more damaging injuries, *FIFA 12* is set to become the pinnacle of the series so far – and the most painful!

FIRST SOCCER MANAGEMENT GAME

Holder: *Football Manager* **(Addictive Games, 1982)**
Developed by Addictive Games for the ZX Spectrum, *Football Manager* has no connection to the famous Sports Interactive franchise. Gamers of 1982 could delve into the transfer market and even watch match highlights. The game offered at least 60 clubs to choose from, although savvy managers quickly noticed that every team started with exactly the same squad.

OWN GOAL

He's one of the most famous soccer players in the world, but few know that David Beckham had his very own Game Boy Advance title. This is probably for the best, considering that *David Beckham Soccer* (Rage Software, 2002) was universally derided. In the words of IGN's Peer Schneider, "the only way to enjoy *David Beckham Soccer* is to not play it".

HIGHEST-RATED *FIFA 11* PLAYER

Holder: Lionel Messi (Argentina)
It should come as no surprise to discover that diminutive South American dynamo Lionel Messi – currently the FIFA World Player of the Year – has the highest overall rating on *FIFA 11* at 90. Just as Real Madrid finished behind Barcelona in the 2010–11 La Liga season, a pair of Real players ranked marginally behind Barcelona ace Messi in the *FIFA 11* rankings: Cristiano Ronaldo (Portugal) and club captain Iker Casillas (Spain) are both rated at 89.

"You only have a chance of being the best if you take on the best players in the world on a regular basis."

2011 FIFA INTERACTIVE WORLD CUP CHAMPION FRANCISCO CRUZ

BALLS, BASICALLY

The first soccer games appeared as basic arcade titles in 1973. *Space Invaders* creator Tomohiro Nishikado unveiled *Soccer* (Ramtek) in Japan, while Florida-based Allied Leisure Industries debuted *Super Soccer*. Both were highly derivative of runaway hit *Pong* (Atari, 1972), and bore the barest resemblance to the beautiful game. Players manoeuvred multiple paddles to block and deflect the ball.

FASTEST-SELLING SPORTS GAME

Holder: *FIFA 11* **(EA Canada, 2010)**
In its opening weekend, *FIFA 11* sold an amazing 2.6 million copies, easily outstripping previous record holder *FIFA 10*, which managed a "mere" 1.7 million.

To date, *FIFA 11* has sold 10 million copies across all platforms. Closest rival *PES 2011* has managed just 4.13 million since its release. The first EA Sports football game was 1993's *FIFA International Soccer*.

AMERICAN SPORTS

MOST ONLINE WINS IN *NCAA FOOTBALL 11*

Holder: YUNG 24 GO HARD (USA)

Virtual American Football isn't all about the *Madden* series (EA Tiburon). The developers at EA Sports have an appreciation for the burgeoning college football scene, adding a new release to their *NCAA Football* franchise every year. Online expert YUNG 24 GO HARD has mastered the series, amassing a world-beating 1,172 wins on *NCAA Football 11* (EA Tiburon, 2010).

FIRST WOMAN TO WIN THE MADDEN BOWL

Holder: Maria Menounos (USA)
The first Madden Bowl took place in 1995. Held every year during the Super Bowl weekend, it features some of the NFL's top athletes battling it out on the virtual playing field. In February 2011, for Madden Bowl XVII, the competitors used Online Team Play to form groups of three. Among the winning trio was TV presenter Maria Menounos, who triumphed alongside San Francisco 49er Patrick Willis and then Cincinnati Bengal Chad Ochocinco. After over 15 years of the competition, Maria became the first woman to lift the trophy.

MOST POPULAR AMERICAN SPORTS GAME ON GAMETRAILERS.COM

Holder: *Madden NFL 08* (EA Tiburon, 2007)
Despite more recent releases in the franchise, *Madden NFL 08* remains the top American sports game on video site Gametrailers.com, with 3,307,817 views across 84 uploads as of 12 August 2011. It is the third most popular sports game overall, behind EA's *Skate* and *FIFA 08*.

FIRST COLLEGE BASKETBALL VIDEOGAME

Holder: *NCAA Basketball* (Sculptured Software/ HAL Laboratory, 1992)
Japan's HAL Laboratory, creators of the *Kirby* series, collaborated with the USA's Sculptured Software to create *NCAA Basketball* for the SNES in October 1992. As well as being the first game to feature real American college teams, it was the first time 3D graphics had been seen on a console basketball release.

A HOST OF HIDDEN CHARACTERS, UNLOCKED BY SECRET CODES ▶

LONGEST PERIOD COVERED IN A BASEBALL SIMULATION

Holder: *Old Time Baseball* **(Stormfront Studios, 1995)**

Baseball fans are known for their love of the game's history. With *Old Time Baseball*, they can get a taste of what it was *really* like to play ball in previous eras. This MS-DOS title allows players to select any year between 1871 and 1995, depending on their preference for "Early Baseball" (when pitchers served underarm), the Babe Ruth era or the "Golden Age" of the 1940s and 1950s.

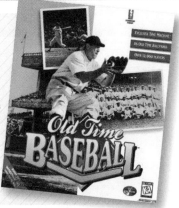

MOST CRITICALLY PANNED SPORTS GAME

Holder: *Elf Bowling 1 & 2* **(Black Lantern Studios, 2005)**

There's some stiff competition for the flat-out worst sports game ever, but *Elf Bowling 1 & 2* (released as one title) is the unwelcome winner. According to reviews site Metacritic, it scores a paltry 12%. A flash title that went viral before being ported to the Nintendo DS in 2005, the game was described by one IGN critic as being "god-awful... one joke that's just gone on for far too long".

TOP 10 *NCAA 2011* PLAYERS

GAMER	POINTS*
YUNG 24 GO HARD	5,002
BAMA_ASSASIN428	4,900
garattee	4,850
GALLOPING GHOST	4,801
GODzTHUMBz22	4,720
Clint41	4,594
Kool_Jetfly_SWAG	4,506
chiefloudordie	4,459
RUNEXT305	4,387
JwOiHnAdNsNor	4,301

Source: www.EaSports.com   * Accurate at 8 August 2011

"Goalie fights is probably the most requested feature we got after last year's game."

SEAN RAMJAGSINGH, PRODUCER OF *NHL 12* (EA CANADA, 2011), THE 21ST GAME IN THE *NHL* SERIES

COVERED

Running back Peyton Hillis is the first ever Cleveland Brown to become a *Madden* cover star, having been voted on to the *Madden NFL 12* (EA Tiburon, 2011) box by fans of the series. He is the second player to be chosen by gamers, following quarterback and *Madden NFL 11* (EA Tiburon, 2010) headliner Drew Brees.

FIRST PERSON TO PITCH A PERFECT GAME IN *MLB 2K11*

Holder: Brian Kingrey **(USA)**

A "perfect game" in baseball occurs when a single pitcher throws for a whole match without an opposing batter hitting a single ball. Publishers 2K offered a $1,000,000 prize to the first player able to complete a perfect game on *MLB 2K11* (Visual Concepts, 2011). The victor, on 1 April 2011, was American Brian Kingrey (near left), who spent days calculating the best combination of pitcher and opposition.

EUROPEAN SPORTS

FIRST TENNIS GAME IN STEREOSCOPIC 3D

Holder: *Top Spin 4* **(2K Czech, 2011)**
Once upon a time, the advent of 3D polygons was gaming's new frontier. Now those pixels are protruding from the screen in the latest visual revolution – stereoscopic 3D. The first game to embrace this technology is *Top Spin 4*. It pipped rival *Virtua Tennis 4* (SEGA-AM3/Sumo Digital, 2011) to the record by a single month.

FIRST OFFICIALLY LICENCED OLYMPIC VIDEOGAME

Holder: *Olympic Gold* **(U.S. Gold, 1992)**
Games involving feats of Herculean athleticism go back a long way, but *Olympic Gold* for the Sega Mega Drive was the first to do so with the blessing of the International Olympic Committee. *Olympic Gold* was the official videogame of the 1992 Barcelona Olympics and featured three difficulty levels for seven sports – the 100 metres, diving, swimming, hammer throw, hurdles, pole vault and archery. The gameplay owes a debt to classics such as *Track & Field* (Konami, 1983), with button-mashing mastery required to conquer many of the events.

BEST-SELLING GOLF GAME

Holder: *Golf*
(Nintendo, 1984)
The *Tiger Woods* series might have ruled the roost in recent years, but it was never able to dethrone one of the first golfing games – the functionally titled *Golf*. This early NES release has sold 4,009,599 units, compared to 2,841,563 of *Tiger Woods PGA Tour 08* (EA Tiburon, 2007), the highest-selling game from EA's franchise.

/// "FAKE GUITARS ARE OVER –
IT'S TIME TO ROCK IT REAL!" ///

4 The number of games that feature both Mario and Sonic, three of which are part of the *Mario & Sonic at the Olympic Games* (SEGA Sports R&D) series.

WHICH, IN ITS VARIOUS VERSIONS, HAS BEEN AVAILABLE SINCE 1997 ▶

RAREST SPORTS GAME

Holder: *Stadium Events* **(Bandai, 1987)**
When Nintendo purchased the rights to produce their own version of the Bandai Power Pad in 1988, they had all unsold copies of launch title *Stadium Events* recalled and destroyed. It is estimated that there are fewer than 20 complete versions of the North American edition of *Stadium Events* in existence and one collector paid as much as $22,800 (£14,171) for a factory-sealed copy. *Stadium Events* comprises a series of traditional track and field sports.

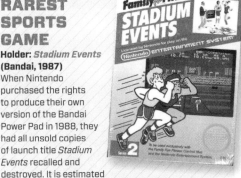

TOP 10 SCORES ON THE ARCADE VERSION OF *TRACK & FIELD*

RANK	PLAYER	SCORE
1	Hector T Rodriguez	95,350
2	Kelly Kobashigawa	95,040
3	Jason Wilson	93,240
4	Gary West	93,100
5	Phil Britt	92,190
6	Tommi J Tiihonen	91,520
7	Mark Sellers	89,970
8	Peter J Skerritt, Jr	89,020
9	Donald Hayes	88,960
10	David Nelson	88,860

Source: TwinGalaxies.com

BIGGEST SALES DROP FOR A Wii SEQUEL

Holder: *Wii Sports Resort* **(Nintendo, 2009)**
When the Wii launched in late 2006, *Wii Sports* (Nintendo, 2006) was the console's flagship title. Bundled with the console in most territories, it had sold an enormous 77,176,000 copies at the time of going to press. Its sequel, *Wii Sports Resort*, was released in tandem with the updated Wii Motion Plus controller. Although it outperformed almost every other game on the platform, the sequel showed a drop of 49,136,000 units below the sales of the first game in the series.

> **"**If the insinuation is it's a reflection of EA Sports backing away from its relationship with Tiger, that's not the case whatsoever.**"**
>
> PETER MOORE, PRESIDENT OF EA SPORTS

MOST BALLS RETURNED IN Wii TENNIS TRAINING

Holder: ondra123
Tennis is one of the most played motion-controlled challenges on the immensely popular *Wii Sports* mini-game compilation. Nintendo created a training mode that allows players to practise their skills by returning balls indefinitely. A gamer known as ondra123 holds the record for this exercise, having made 319 consecutive returns on 1 December 2007.

TIGER TAMED?

Following poor sales of *Tiger Woods PGA Tour 11* (EA Tiburon, 2010) – and despite the addition of US Open champion Rory McIlroy on the cover – EA took the decision to drop Tiger Woods' recognizable face from the front of the follow-up title *Tiger Woods PGA Tour 12: The Masters* (EA Tiburon, 2011).

MOST DOWNLOADABLE CONTENT FOR A VIDEOGAME LAUNCH

Holder: *Tiger Woods PGA Tour 12* (EA Tiburon, 2011)
While it's certainly not unusual for a videogame to be supported by downloadable content on its launch date, the most recent entry in EA's long-running *Tiger Woods PGA Tour* series took this approach to new heights with an unprecedented 53 in-game items available in the game's first week. The digital goodies on offer include additional golf courses, snazzy outfits and a selection of new clubs sponsored by the official manufacturers. Committed Tiger fans would have to shell out £153.47 ($245.55) to own the complete set – that's around five times the price of the game itself!

/// "BEYOND SURVIVAL... THERE'S A WHOLE NEW BREED" /// WWW.GUINNESSWORLDRECORDS.COM/GAMERS **063**

EXTREME SPORTS

THE FIRST EVER EXTREME SPORTS GAME WAS ATARI'S 1986

MOST SUCCESSFUL CREATIVE TEAM IN *SKATE 3*

Holder: SUPER-HEROS

Like-minded players in skateboarding simulator *Skate 3* (EA Black Box, 2010) can group together to form teams. Top squad SUPER-HEROS have sold 1,103,851,600 custom-designed boards as of 15 September 2011. Team founder THE CHRONTROLLA holds the individual record for **most board sales in *Skate 3***, with 179,100,411 units. He leads a roster of other hardcore skaters (some of whom are represented below).

/// "HE HAD ONLY AN INSTANT, IMPRESSED ON A PEDAL, TO COLLECT THE LOST PIES, AND SHOW TIME HIS FULL METTLE" ///

751,847,639,459 The number of custom skateboards sold by players in *Skate 3* (EA Black Box, 2010). Players can also create custom skateparks.

TOP 10 BEST-SELLING SKATEBOARDING GAMES

RANK	GAME	TOTAL SALES	YEAR
1	*Tony Hawk's Pro Skater*	7.9 million	1999
2	*Tony Hawk's Pro Skater 3*	6.2 million	2001
3	*Tony Hawk's Pro Skater 2*	5.3 million	2000
4	*Tony Hawk's Underground*	4.7 million	2003
5	*Tony Hawk's Pro Skater 4*	4.0 million	2002
6	*Tony Hawk's Underground 2*	3.0 million	2004
7	*Tony Hawk's American Wasteland*	2.5 million	2005
8	*Tony Hawk's Project 8*	2.4 million	2006
9=	*Tony Hawk: Ride*	1.9 million	2009
9=	*Tony Hawk's Proving Ground*	1.9 million	2007

Source: VGChartz.com

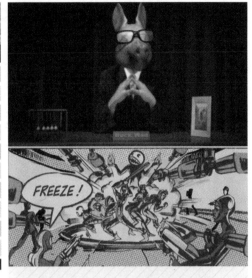

> "Originally, it was just the skaters who played it, but then it really broke into the gaming community. Now it's everyone."

TONY HAWK ON THE UNIVERSAL SUCCESS OF HIS VIDEOGAME SERIES

MOST CUTSCENES IN AN EXTREME SPORTS GAME

Holder: *Amped 3* **(Indie Built, 2005)**
Extreme Sports games aren't known for hilarious video shorts, but then *Amped 3* isn't exactly conventional. While the gameplay is standard snowboarding fare, the real gems are found between the levels. Cutscenes here involve stop-motion action figures, fake American anime and a decapitated pig head with a New York accent. There are 54 mini-movies in total.

FIRST CEL-SHADED SPORTS GAME

Holder: *Jet Set Radio* **(Smilebit, SEGA, 2000)**
This innovative inline skating game brought cel-shading technology to the forefront of videogame design. Players could tag levels with their own custom graffiti, pull off extravagant tricks and evade tyrannical cops. Cel-shaded graphics created a comic-book world that wowed critics and consumers sufficiently to spawn a sequel, *Jet Set Radio Future* (Smilebit), which was released for the Xbox in 2002.

HIGHEST SCORE ON *VS. EXCITEBIKE*
Holder: **Hector T Rodriguez (USA)**
NES classic *Excitebike* (Nintendo, 1984) was reduxed and re-released for arcades in 1984 as *Vs. Excitebike* (Nintendo), with updated graphics and cabinet controls. The side-scrolling motocross racer has remained a popular source of record-breaking attempts. Prolific high-score expert Hector T Rodriguez topped all-comers on 17 February 2011 with a new record of 3,644,445 points.

FIRST SKATEBOARDING WORLD CYBER GAMES CHAMPION
Holder: **Dustin "DuVaL_AK47" Valcalda (USA)**
Regarded as the Olympics of videogaming, the World Cyber Games (WCG) is held every year in a different city. From 3 to 7 October 2007, the seventh WCG took place in Seattle, USA. Appearing on the roster for the first time was a skating game, *Tony Hawk's Project 8* (Neversoft, 2006). After a hard-fought knockout contest, the gold medal went to 21-year-old American Dustin Valcalda, who managed to beat Brit David "Zaccubus" Treacy in the final.

WORST-RATED TONY HAWK GAME

Holder: *Tony Hawk: Shred* **(Robomodo, 2010)**
The giant skateboard peripheral debuted to much derision in *Tony Hawk: Ride* (Robomodo, 2009), with a 46% score on review aggregation website Metacritic. The motion board was put to not-so-good use in a 2010 sequel – *Shred* sold only 3,000 copies in its opening week, the lowest figures of any Tony Hawk game.

PRO-GAMING REVIEW

PRO-GAMING IS A TRULY INTERNATIONAL AFFAIR – GERMAN TEAM SK GAMING'S

AFTER A DIFFICULT FEW YEARS FOR THE eSPORTS SCENE, 2011 WILL BE REMEMBERED AS THE YEAR THAT COMPETITIVE GAMING RETURNED WITH A BIG BANG. CORPORATE SPONSORS EMERGED TO SUPPORT THE MAJOR TOURNAMENTS AND THE SIZE OF AUDIENCES – BOTH ONLINE AND LIVE – SAW MASSIVE GROWTH. POPULAR TITLES IN THE 2011 ROSTER INCLUDED *LEAGUE OF LEGENDS*, *STREET FIGHTER* AND *STARCRAFT II*, AND THE IMPENDING ARRIVAL OF VALVE'S *DOTA 2* SUGGESTS AN EXCITING AND ENTERTAINING YEAR AHEAD…

> "Our audience is growing every week. It's not remaining stagnant, and that's exciting."
>
> **MARCUS "DjWHEAT" GRAHAM,
> ONLINE eSPORTS COMMENTATOR**

WHO SAYS?

Robert "Moyes" Haxton competed around the world for eight years across a wide array of games. Having won his final championship in 2008 with *World in Conflict*, he decided to focus his energy on supporting eSports by reporting upon its ongoing development into a professional activity recognized the world over.

WHAT *IS* PRO-GAMING?

Put simply, a pro-gamer earns money for playing videogames. It may sound like a dream job, but despite the creation in 2002 of Major League Gaming – which claims to be the largest professional videogame league – there is still a long way to go before gaming can call itself a popular sport in the standard sense. The more recent success of online titles *League of Legends* and *StarCraft II* has certainly reinvigorated interest in pro-gaming, while the individuals, teams and organizers involved in competitive gaming are seeing an influx of interest from some unlikely places. The growing number of corporate sponsors willing to back events (see image, above top right) suggests eSports is attracting more money and moving into the mainstream. Organizers hope that sponsors' cash can, in turn, fuel more media coverage and public interest.

The surge in popularity and availability of internet broadcasts is another significant development. Few prestigious online or offline tournaments now operate without broadcasting a selection of their competitive action over the internet. The success of South Korea's gomtv.net demonstrates the commercial potential of high-quality, online pro-gaming coverage.

But eSports still struggles to attract the attention of the Western media. Since the demise of the Championship Gaming Series in 2008, there has not been a renewed attempt to screen competitive gaming to a mainstream television audience. As pro-gamers become ever more skilful at their craft, public interest remains a step behind – for now.

PROFILE: djWHEAT

One of the most important elements in pro-gaming is its people – individuals who turn the business of competitive gaming into entertainment that engages the public and boosts interest. American Marcus "djWHEAT" Graham has been at the forefront of eSports for years. He was a successful player (famous for *Quake 3*), and then a coach, and now he's a "shoutcaster" (an online gaming commentator), prolific Tweeter and media producer/broadcaster.

PRESTIGIOUS eSPORTS COMPETITIONS

COMPETITION	WEBSITE
Intel Extreme Masters	www.esl-world.net/masters
Major League Gaming	www.majorleaguegaming.com
World Cyber Games	www.wcg.com
Electronic Sports World Cup	www.eswc.com
Global *StarCraft II* League	www.gomtv.net

HIGHEST EARNING eSPORTS TEAM

Holder: Fnatic (UK)

London-based Fnatic eSports team, which specializes in *Counter-Strike*, is led by 26-year-old Swedish gamer Patrik Sättermon (left). It has earned a total of $470,655 (£286,442) in tournaments worldwide as of July 2011, making Fnatic the most financially successful team in videogaming. It is managed by CEO Sam Matthews (UK), who employs 33 pro-gamers.

MAJOR LEAGUE GAMING (MLG)

Founded some 10 years ago, Major League Gaming has become a leading cross-platform, online videogame competition. The league operates the annual MLG Pro Circuit, which consists of six live events across the USA, where the world's best videogame players compete for big cash prizes. Through www.majorleaguegaming.com, MLG reaches roughly 5 million people each month, attracts more than 4,000 new members daily, holds more than 700,000 online matches each month and delivers millions of live stream views of its Pro Circuit competition. Men's fragrance Old Spice is a sponsor!

RACING GAMES

FASTEST COMPLETION OF MARIO CIRCUIT 1

Holder: Sami Çetin (UK)

Speedy Sami has been a fixture of the competitive *Mario Kart* scene for over 10 years, but 2010 was his golden season. He took the chequered flag for the fastest completion of the iconic Circuit 1 on the very first game in the series, *Super Mario Kart* (Nintendo, 1992). He holds the record on both the PAL and NTSC versions of the game, with times of 58.34 seconds and 56.45 seconds respectively as of August 2011.

OVERVIEW

Racing games are all about speed – whether you are going from A to B while avoiding the police in an open world such as *Grand Theft Auto*, conquering real-life circuits around the globe in *Forza* or whipping through the countryside in *DiRT*.

Things have come a long way since the first racing game, Atari's *Gran Trak 10*, was released in 1974. Improvements to physics engines offer ever-increasing levels of reality in track simulations and the vehicles gamers drive around them. Be it two wheels, four or more, it's about getting there first and sometimes taking out opponents along the way...

BIOGRAPHY

John Brown describes himself as a technology adventurer, but a couch potato he is not. He races motorbikes, snowboards and travels extensively. Racing and driving games are, however, where he spends a lot of his "down-time". John writes for popular community gaming website *Ready Up*, and also produces podcasts in spare moments.

CONTENTS

CRITICAL HIT!:
FORZA MOTORSPORT   70
SIMULATION RACING   72
ARCADE RACING   74
STREET RACING   76
KART RACING   78

FORZA MOTORSPORT

CRITICAL HIT!

FORZA MOTORSPORT 3 AND FORZA MOTORSPORT 2 OCCUPY THE TOP TWO SPOTS

MOST POLYGONS PER CAR IN A RACING GAME

Holder: *Forza Motorsport 4* **(Turn 10, 2011)**

The race for ever-increasing reality in videogame car graphics is driving the developers to increase the number of polygons, the discrete 2D shapes used to build the cars. The previous polygon record holder was PS3 title *Gran Turismo 5* (Polyphony Digital, 2010), with 400,000 polygons per vehicle. *Forza Motorsport 4* has now comfortably eclipsed this figure by doubling it with an astonishing 800,000 polygons per car.

FASTEST LAP OF NÜRBURGRING NORDSCHLEIFE IN *FORZA MOTORSPORT 3*

Holder: BeFreak (Austria)

On 3 July 2011, Xbox 360 user BeFreak set a blisteringly fast lap time of 5 min 32.509 sec around the Nordschleife circuit, using the Aston Martin Lola car number 007 in the X Class. BeFreak's closest rival is four milliseconds behind him. In terms of the real-life equivalent, the fastest recorded lap around the modern Nordschleife circuit for a non-production car is 6 min 47 sec, set in a Pagani Zonda in June 2010.

The overall fastest lap ever timed on the actual circuit dates back to 1983, when the late Stefan Bellof of Germany completed a 6-min 11-sec qualifying lap in a Porsche 956, followed by a race lap time of 6 min 25 sec. The in-game experience, although increasingly realistic, still appears to be considerably faster than reality!

MOST CRITICALLY ACCLAIMED XBOX 360 RACING GAME

Holder: *Forza Motorsport 3* **(Turn 10, 2009)**

With an impressive score of 92%, *Forza Motorsport 3* rates as the most acclaimed racing game on the Xbox 360, according to the Metacritic website. Critics particularly admired the new car design features, which allow players to create original artwork, and the new in-game camera, which can take photos at any point during a single-player race. Based on the buzz it has caused in the industry, *Forza Motorsport 4* (left) looks all set to be just as popular.

9.96 million The combined sales of *Forza Motorsport* (Turn 10, 2005), *Forza Motorsport 2* (2007) and *Forza Motorsport 3* (2009).

IN THE WORLDWIDE SALES CHART FOR RACING GAMES ON THE XBOX 360 ▶

FOURTH GEAR

Forza Motorsport 4 comes with a new and special feature – the BBC's *Top Gear* test track, based in Surrey, England, is part of the game. In addition, *Top Gear* presenter Jeremy Clarkson provides the commentary. If you want to drive on the real track, you'll need to be a "star in a reasonably priced car" or work for McLaren, who also use the facility.

MOST SUCCESSFUL "DRIFTING" TEAM IN *FORZA MOTORSPORT 3*

Holder: Team Shift n Drift (UK)
"Drifting" is the tricky technique of deliberately over-steering a car so that it slides across a track sideways, without ever crashing. The most skilled drifters use this technique while preventing the car from spinning wildly out of control. In *Forza Motorsport 3* (Turn 10, 2009), Team Shift n Drift has excelled at drifting with a combined score of 78,381,162.

> "One of the best racing games released on any console to date and a must-have for any Xbox owners."
>
> GAMINGEXCELLENCE.COM'S DANIEL ACABA, RATING *FORZA MOTORSPORT 3* AS 9.8/10

TOP 10 F-CLASS LAP TIMES FOR SILVERSTONE GRAND PRIX CIRCUIT IN *FORZA MOTORSPORT 3*

RANK	GAMER TAG	TIME*
1	GSR Sup3R ZAGO	02:07.563
2	V12 Matti Dude	02:07.571
3	GSR Veleno	02:07.794
4	V12 STEFANO	02:07.982
5	V12 STEVO	02:08.048
6	AGM Monkey88	02:08.088
7	V12 Painjunky	02:08.298
8	V12 BackONE AbS	02:08.360
9=	GSR Hakkinen	02:08.467
9=	AGM THE WOLF	02:08.467

*Source: ForzaMotorsport.net * Times in minutes and seconds*

FIRST RACING SIMULATOR RESPONSIVE TO DRIVERS' HEAD MOVEMENTS

Holder: *Forza Motorsport 4* **(Turn 10, 2011)**
Using Microsoft Kinect technology to its fullest, the fourth *Forza Motorsport* title is the first racing simulator to track the movements of a player's head and reflect them in the game. If a player moves his or her head to the left or right, the Kinect peripheral translates those movements directly into the game. This enables what players see on their TV screens to be controlled by their head movements. It also means that there are fewer blind spots, and better visibility when using the bonnet cam view.

FIRST TEAM GARAGES IN A RACING VIDEOGAME

Holder: *Forza Motorsport 4* **(Turn 10, 2011)**
Until now, racing gamers formed alliances by adding prefixes to their gamertags but there was no other way a grouping could be shown in gameplay. The latest *Forza Motorsport* title has created an in-game garage environment so that team-mates can drive both individually and as teams through team challenges. Players share a garage with other members of their "Forza Club", allowing them to paint cars in team colours and drive any other car in their particular garage. This ability to club together is similar to the "friends" function on social network sites. In a "Forza Club", players can constantly enlarge their circle of racing allies.

SIMULATION RACING

GRAN TURISMO 5 PROLOGUE (POLYPHONY DIGITAL, 2007) WAS THE FIRST

BEST-SELLING FORMULA 1 GAME

Holder: *F1 2010* **(Codemasters, 2010)**

With 2.3 million copies sold across the Xbox 360, PlayStation 3 and PC, Codemasters' first outing with the Formula 1 licence became the best-selling title since the sport began to be portrayed in videogames in the early 1980s. *F1 2010*'s weather system was a major advance on previous F1 games, with the effects on handling from rain given an unprecedented level of realism.

TOP 10 LAP TIMES AT SILVERSTONE IN *F1GP* FOR THE PC

RANK	NAME	LAP TIME / GAP-1ST*	SPEED
1	Rene Smit	1:15.552 / 0:00.000	152.57 mph
2	Steven Mestdagh	1:15.683 / 0:00.131	152.31 mph
3	Mark Guest	1:15.686 / 0:00.134	152.30 mph
4	Ivanhoe Vasiljevich	1:15.884 / 0:00.332	151.91 mph
5	Michael Wollenschein	1:15.967 / 0:00.415	151.74 mph
6	Pascal Dukers	1:16.225 / 0:00.673	151.23 mph
7	Chris Foden	1:16.275 / 0:00.723	151.13 mph
8	Ralf Ernst	1:16.307 / 0:00.755	151.06 mph
9	Toni Kuusela	1:16.314 / 0:00.762	151.05 mph
10	Mike Wallace	1:16.395 / 0:00.843	150.89 mph

Source: SimRacingWorld.com   * Accurate at 1 August 2011

BEST-SELLING RACING GAME ON AN HD CONSOLE

Holder: *Gran Turismo 5* **(Polyphony Digital, 2010)**

The latest in the popular *Gran Turismo* series, *Gran Turismo 5*, had sold an impressive 6,379,856 units worldwide as of 29 July 2011. This is all the more remarkable given that the game is exclusive to the PlayStation 3. It is not, however, the best-selling title in the series. That accolade belongs to *Gran Turismo 3: A-Spec* (Polyphony Digital, 2001) for the PlayStation 2, which has shifted at least 14 million copies worldwide.

FIRST RACING COMMUNITY TO BE RECOGNIZED BY AN OFFICIAL RACING GOVERNING BODY

Holder: The Online Racing Association

The Online Racing Association (TORA) is an internet community for users of *Forza Motorsport*, *Need for Speed: Shift 2* and *F1 2010* on the Xbox 360. In May 2010, the UK's Motor Sports Association (MSA) recognized TORA as a governing body for virtual motorsport, making them the first simulation racing organization to be officially acknowledged by a motorsport governing body.

292 years The total amount of time gamers spent driving in *DiRT 3* (Codemasters Southam, 2011) during the first 28 days after its launch.

MOST CRITICALLY ACCLAIMED MOTORCYCLE SIMULATION GAME
Holder: *MotoGP2* (Climax Group, 2003)
The MotoGP championship has produced some of the most exciting motorcycle races in recent years, and the *MotoGP* videogame series has sought to capture the sport's action within game environs. The reviewers of Metacritic have spoken, and rated *MotoGP2* as the best representation both of that class and of motorcycle sims in general, with a combined Xbox and PC average of 86%.

FASTEST LAP TIME AT JEREZ IN *MOTOGP 10/11*
Holder: | Ghostrider | (France)
Bikes are notoriously difficult to ride both fast and well, so the achievement of racing gamer | Ghostrider | is considerable. He took his 2010-spec Suzuki MotoGP bike on to the track at Jerez, Spain, in *MotoGP 10/11* (Monumental Games, 2011). The Frenchman rode a time trial and set an impressively speedy lap time of 1 min 47.07 sec, making this the fastest lap anyone has completed around the track.

HIGHEST-PLACED GAMER IN A REAL-LIFE DRIVING COMPETITION
Holder: Lucas Ordoñez (Spain)
As the winner of the *Gran Turismo* academy in 2008, Lucas Ordoñez beat 25,000 gamers and earned the once-in-a-lifetime opportunity to take part in the Dubai 24 Hour Race in 2009. Lucas showed such skill that sponsors Nissan signed him to a new team, and in 2011, he achieved a podium finish with his team, Signatech Nissan, who finished second in the LMP2 class and ninth overall at the legendary 24 Hours of Le Mans.

> **"Codemasters' EGO engine is the best racing engine out there, providing the best graphics and best crashes."**
> **JUSTIN TOWELL OF GAMESRADAR.COM, REVIEWING *DiRT3* ON THE XBOX 360**

FIRST RACING GAME TO INTEGRATE USER UPLOADS TO YOUTUBE
Holder: *DiRT 3* (Codemasters Southam, 2011)
Rally driving title *DiRT 3* is the first racing game to build in player uploads to the internet's most popular video site. Video playback has long featured, but the addition of a simple one-click upload function to a player's YouTube account means that sweet slides, awesome overtakes or spectacular wipeouts can be shared with viewers worldwide. With over 170,000 videos of racing action uploaded in the first four weeks of *DiRT 3*'s release, it seems that sharing is proving popular!

ARCADE RACING

IN THE *MX* vs *ATV* SERIES, "MX" STANDS FOR MOTOCROSS (TWO-WHEELED BIKES)

FIRST TRIPLE BACKFLIP ON *MX* vs *ATV: ALIVE*
Holder: TheChrisDood (Australia)
There is more to *MX* vs *ATV: Alive* (THQ, 2011) than the simple thrill of being first past the post. The game also gives players the chance to explore their free-riding and freestyle skills with a library of tricks to choose from. Backflips are the "must have" trick in any freestyle motocross routine, but Australian gamer TheChrisDood went several stages further when he pulled off the first triple backflip and posted footage of his incredible feat on YouTube.

MOST HITS SCORED ONLINE ON *BLUR*
Holder: Steven "Xx Seamonkey xX" Kovacs (USA)
Winning at any cost, through fair means or foul, is the name of the game in *blur* (Bizarre Creations, 2010), even if it requires crashing into your opponent's car until it is wrecked. Gamer Steven Kovacs is particularly skilled at this kind of skullduggery, scoring a total of 271,001 hits against other racers and causing a total of 27,237 wrecks as he sped through the game's tracks, which include courses inspired by the streets of Los Angeles and London.

TOP 10 TIMES FOR ATV 450s ON THE ONSENKI PARK TRACK ON *MX* vs *ATV: ALIVE*

RANK	GAMERTAG	LAP TIME	ASSIST OPTIONS USED
1	Blasterboy207	00:46.89	None
2	The Ginga Goon	00:47.01	None
3	Aaron 481	00:47.04	None
4	II LaChance II	00:47.46	"Jump" and "Corner"
5	MazookaRacing 7	00:47.55	"Jump" and "Corner"
6	brettbraaap	00:47.58	None
7	PHILLY CHEESE10	00:47.63	None
8	ltr450Jeremy	00:47.79	"Jump" and "Corner"
9	mystro85	00:47.94	None
10	ButterMX212	00:48.02	None

Source: in-game leaderboard

AND "ATV" STANDS FOR ALL-TERRAIN VEHICLES (MAINLY QUAD BIKES) ▶

MOST CRITICALLY ACCLAIMED DOWNLOADABLE MOTORCYCLE GAME

Holder: *Trials HD* **(Red Lynx, 2009)**
Xbox Live Arcade title *Trials HD* achieved an aggregated score of 86% on reviews site Metacritic. The aim of the game is to complete the motorcycle course in the shortest time and with the minimum number of crashes (known as "faults"). Players also try out skills challenges, such as achieving as many flips as possible within a set time limit.

HIGHEST SCORE ON *OUT RUN* (ARCADE)

Holder: Richard Jackson (USA)
On 21 February 1987, Richard Jackson scored 52,897,690 points on the classic arcade racer *Out Run* (Sega, 1986), setting a record that has not been beaten in 24 years!

The game had a sequel, *Turbo Out Run* (Sega, 1989), which was released as both a new cabinet and as an upgrade kit that could be installed on the original game's chip board. The **highest score on Turbo Out Run (arcade)** was set by Martin Bedard (Canada), with 52,087,460 points.

"The idea of *blur* was that everyone could see all of the content as they progressed through the game... people who were better at it would just get through it faster."
GARETH WILSON, *BLUR*'S LEAD DESIGNER

FIRST SNOWMOBILE RACING GAME

Holder: *Sled Storm* **(EA, 1999)**
Racing games are usually associated with smoking tyres, hot tarmac and car brands such as Ferrari, Porsche, Bugatti and Lamborghini. PlayStation title *Sled Storm* took the genre down a different track – one that was covered with snow! Players could choose between two campaign modes – straightforward "Open Mountain" racing and a more tricks-based mode known as "Super SnoCross".

HIGHEST "DRIVER SCORE" ON *BLUR*

Holder: Richard "AAA Dopeymonkey" Goodall (UK)
The "Driver Score" in *blur* (Bizarre Creations, 2010) is calculated from multiplayer game data, including the number of races participated in and the number of cars beaten (instead of simple race wins; a gamer who wins a 20-car race scores higher than one who wins a three-car race). Richard completed 32,555 races to give him an overall Driver Score of 290,000 points. When asked what car he used to achieve his record score, Richard replied: "I only ever use the first car in each class to prove it's not the car you drive, but the way you drive it."

STREET RACING

NEED FOR SPEED: THE RUN (EA, 2011) IS THE FIRST GAME IN THE SERIES TO USE

LONGEST WHEELIE ON *BURNOUT PARADISE*

Holder: Matthew "MTC" Cutler (UK)

Street-racing games are typically about fast cars, but *Burnout Paradise* introduced bikes into the mix and, with them, a whole new set of tricks. Matthew Cutler proved that one wheel is better than two, or four, when he pulled a wheelie over 5,513 m (18,087 ft) in the game!

MOST DRIVERS SPONSORED BY A VIDEOGAME PUBLISHER

Holder: Team Need for Speed

Proving their interest in real-life racing, games publisher Electronic Arts sponsors seven drivers across the Formula Drift, Time Attack and FIA GT3 motor-racing disciplines under the name of Team Need for Speed. In addition, the team also sponsors drivers in marquee single-event endurance races, such as the Le Mans 24-Hour Rally, in which Abdulaziz T Al Faisal (Saudi Arabia, far left) competed in 2011, and the Nürburgring 24-Hour Rally, in which fellow Team Need for Speedster, driver Edward Sandström (Sweden, left), came fourth in 2010.

DICE'S ADVANCED FROSTBITE 2 GRAPHICS ENGINE ▶

TOP 10 FASTEST CARS OVER A QUARTER OF A MILE IN *BURNOUT PARADISE*

RANK	VEHICLE	SECONDS
1	Carson GT Nighthawk	7.90
2	Carson Extreme Hot Rod	8.28
3	Carson Opus XS	8.60
4=	Carson Opus Hemi	8.63
4=	Krieger Unerschall 8	8.63
4=	Krieger Unerschall Clear-View	8.63
7	Krieger Carbon Unerschall 8	8.73
8=	Rossolini Tempesta GT	8.80
8=	Hunter Citizen	8.80
8=	Carson Thunder Custom	8.80

Source: in-game leaderboard

"It is easy to learn and hard to master."

ALAIN JARNIOU, GAME DIRECTOR OF *TEST DRIVE UNLIMITED 2* ON THE APPEAL OF HIS GAME

LIFE IN THE FASTLANE

Fastlane Street Racing (Atod AB, 2008) for iOS (the iPad/iPhone platform) was originally written to run on the ill-fated Gizmondo, a handheld gaming device launched in 2005 and discontinued a year later, but it only saw the light of day as an iOS game.

BEST-SELLING STREET-RACING SERIES
Holder: *Need for Speed* **(EA, 1994–present)**
As of August 2011, the *Need for Speed* series had shifted a total of 69.26 million units worldwide in its 16-year history, putting it way ahead of its two main rival series, *Burnout* (Criterion Games, 2001–present) and *Test Drive* (Distinctive Software, 1987–present), which have sales of 11 million and 5 million units, respectively.

HIGHEST-SCORING FLAT SPIN ON *BURNOUT PARADISE*
Holder: **SuperNemesis001 (USA)**
According to the folks at Burnoutaholics.com, a fan community for those who love street racing, the gamer SuperNemesis001 hit a score of 8,615 points for his flat spin – making his car spin around lengthways as it flies through the air – on *Burnout Paradise* (Criterion Games, 2008).

LONGEST-RUNNING RACING SERIES

Holder: *Test Drive* **(Distinctive Software, 1987)**
The *Test Drive* series is the grandaddy of the racing genre, spanning 10 main titles over the 26 years since the game made its debut in 1987. The latest release, *Test Drive Unlimited 2* (Eden Games, 2011, below), features the accurately modelled streets of Ibiza, Spain, and Oahu, Hawaii, USA, allowing gamers to drive a sports car through the streets of these beautiful islands – an experience usually reserved only for millionaire playboys!

KART RACING

FORMULA 1   DRIVERS LEWIS HAMILTON AND MICHAEL

FIRST FLYING KART GAME

Holder: *Mario Kart 7*
(Nintendo, 2011)
Famed for its innovation, the *Mario Kart* series has now pioneered the use of flying karts, which make their debut in *Mario Kart 7* on the 3DS. When a racer gets big air, wings sprout from their kart to help it glide over a track shortcut. *Mario Kart 7* is also the **first underwater kart-racing game**. Its karts feature propellers that pop out when they go underwater, helping racers cruise along the sea floor.

FIRST CROSSOVER CHARACTERS IN A KART GAME

Holder: *Mario Kart Arcade GP*
(Namco, 2005)
Crossover characters are becoming increasingly popular in various genres, but *Mario Kart Arcade GP* was the first kart game to put PAC-Man, Ms. PAC-Man and Blinky the red ghost into karts as playable characters. The second version of this arcade game also included Mametchi from *Tamagotchi*.

BEST-SELLING KART SERIES
Holder: *Mario Kart* (Nintendo)
The *Mario Kart* games continue to set new world records. The **best-selling handheld racing game** is still *Mario Kart DS*, with a total sales figure of over 22 million. The **best-selling racing game** is still *Mario Kart Wii*, with a total now running at over 27 million. It seems *Mario Kart*'s lead is unassailable, as total series sales have now reached 80.28 million.

/// "WELCOME BACK, COMRADE!" ///

533.64 The total review score for all six *Mario Kart* games listed at Gamerankings.com. The average score for each game is 88.94%, as of August 2011.

SCHUMACHER STARTED THEIR CAREERS IN KARTING ▶

TOP 10 BEST-SELLING KART-RACING GAMES

TITLE	PLATFORM	SALES IN MILLIONS
Mario Kart Wii	Wii	27.31
Mario Kart DS	DS	22.06
Mario Kart 64	N64	9.87
Super Mario Kart	SNES	8.76
Mario Kart: Double Dash!!	GameCube	6.96
Mario Kart: Super Circuit	Game Boy Advance	5.45
Crash Nitro Kart	PS2	1.88
NASCAR Kart Racing	Wii	0.41
Dreamworks Madagascar Kartz	Wii	0.38
Dreamworks Madagascar Kartz	DS	0.28

Source: VGChartz.com   Accurate at 2 August 2011

MOST UGC AVAILABLE FOR A GAME AT THE TIME OF PLATFORM LAUNCH

Holder: *ModNation Racers* **(SCEA San Diego Studios, 2011)**
The Sony Vita handheld console, scheduled for a 2012 release in Europe and North America, represents the first of the next generation in portable devices, with a touch-screen and touch-sensitive back plate. Vita-owning kart racers have double cause for excitement, as all of the *ModNation Racers* (United Front Games, 2010) user-generated content (UGC) created for the PS3 will be accessible on the new handheld device. At the time of going to press, Sony had confirmed that over 2 million tracks, vehicles and mods that have been created by the *ModNation* PS3 community will be available.

BEST-SELLING PLAYSTATION KART GAME

Holder: *Crash Team Racing* **(Naughty Dog, 1999)**
The most successful kart game on the PlayStation is *Crash Team Racing*, with a mammoth worldwide sales total of 4.79 million. The videogame also holds the honour of being the best-selling kart game *not* produced by Nintendo.

> **"If you can dream it, you really can make it in *ModNation Racers*."**

REVIEW SITE IGN, GIVING THE GAME 9/10

HIGHEST-RANKED CREATOR IN *MODNATION RACERS*

Holder: **Peto-Mad** (France)
ModNation Racers (United Front Games, 2010) is the **most customizable kart-racing game**. Players are rewarded with what is known as "Create XP" whenever their custom creation is downloaded or used by another racer. Peto-Mad has earned the highest amount of Create XP in the game with a total of 56,414,631.

FIRST KART-RACING VIDEOGAME

Holder: *Super Mario Kart* **(Nintendo, 1992)**
The heroic plumber made his first karting appearance in *Super Mario Kart* on the SNES. The game changed everything, spawning many imitations and sequels on consoles including the N64 and Wii. *Super Mario Kart* sold a total of 8.76 million copies, making it the third best-selling SNES title, after *Super Mario World* and *Donkey Kong Country*.

GO, KART, GO!

The designers of *Mario Kart Wii* tested roughly 30 different prototypes with different shapes, colours and weights (based on real-life go-karts) before deciding on the final Wii Wheel design. It became the first gaming wheel without a drive shaft, enabling it to be held in mid-air. It was designed to be as light as possible so that gamers would not become easily tired. To accompany the release of *F1 2009*, Nintendo released a special-edition version shaped like a Formula 1 wheel.

PARTY GAMES

OVERVIEW

Gaming isn't just about sitting on the sofa and twiddling your thumbs any more. Some of today's best-selling titles involve belting out a tune, shaking your stuff on the dance floor or even working out to improve your physical fitness. The best party games are easy to pick up and play regardless of the player's age or experience – think *SingStar* and *Dance Central*. When it comes to the music genre, *Guitar Hero* and *Rock Band* are still topping the charts. In the field of self-improvement, *EA Sports Active* and *Wii Fit* are great for burning off calories, while *Brain Training* is ideal for keeping the mind sharp.

BIOGRAPHY

Ellie Gibson is the deputy editor of Eurogamer.net. Although she's a big fan of puzzlers, platformers and action-adventure titles, she also loves the kind of games that get you jumping around the living room. Her favourite party title is currently *Just Dance*, but she never says no to a *SingStar* session!

CONTENTS

CRITICAL HIT!: *KINECT* 082
LIFESTYLE & FITNESS 084
AUGMENTED REALITY 086
RHYTHM – INSTRUMENTS 088
RHYTHM – DANCING 090

LARGEST SIMULTANEOUS ONLINE 100 M SPRINT

Holder: Xbox Live users (worldwide)
The record for the largest simultaneous online 100 m sprint was set during the Xbox Nations Free Live Weekend on 23 April 2011. A total of 10,539 Xbox Live users booted up *Kinect Sports* (Rare, 2010) to take part in the record event, racing around living rooms across the globe. Each participant was rewarded with an exclusive avatar T-shirt. Shown here is Microsoft's own "virtual presentation" of the Guinness World Records certificate.

KINECT

CRITICAL HIT!

YOOSTAR 2 LETS YOU RE-ENACT THE ██████████ KISS BETWEEN PRINCE

BEST-SELLING KINECT GAME

Holder: *Kinect Sports* **(Rare, 2010)**
Developed by UK studio Rare and released on 4 November 2010, Kinect Sports had sold more than 3 million copies by May 2011. The game (which is not bundled with the Kinect) features six events to choose from – bowling, boxing, track and field, table tennis, football and beach volleyball.

MOST VALUABLE KINECT SENSOR

Holder: Swarovski Kinect
At a whopping $1,242 (£773), the Swarovski crystal-encrusted Kinect designed by PlayBling is the most expensive of its kind in the world. The 6,000-crystal sensor was inspired by pop princess Kylie Minogue's 2011 European tour, and is available exclusively as a prize to the winner of a competition organized to promote the Kinect title *Dance Central*.

FIRST SIMULTANEOUS TWO-PLAYER KINECT DANCING GAME

Holder: *Dance Central 2* **(Microsoft, TBA)**
The first Kinect dancing game to allow two players to perform simultaneously is *Dance Central 2*. It was announced at Microsoft's E3 press conference in 2011, where two players took to the stage and danced side-by-side.

The original game features a multiplayer mode but players have to take it in turn to try to score the most points.

FIRST KINECT GAME TO WIN A BAFTA

Holder: *Kinect Sports* **(Rare, 2010)**
The British Academy of Film and Television Arts (BAFTA) has recognized videogame achievements since 2003, and the first Kinect game to win a BAFTA was *Kinect Sports*. A total of six Kinect titles were nominated for awards – including *Kinect Adventures*, *Kinectimals* and *Dance Central* – but *Kinect Sports* was the only game to win, walking away with the trophy for Best Family Game.

10.9 million The number of standalone Kinect games sold up until the end of May 2011, according to Microsoft.

WILLIAM AND KATE MIDDLETON ON THE BALCONY AT BUCKINGHAM PALACE! ▶

BORN IN BRAZIL

Kinect was first unveiled at Microsoft's E3 press conference on 1 June 2009. Back then it was code-named Project Natal. The name was chosen by Alex Kipman, one of the brains behind the technology. Microsoft likes to use cities as code-names and Natal is the name of a city in Brazil, Kipman's home country. He liked the way it means "to be born" in Latin, which seemed fitting for a device designed to attract new types of people to the world of gaming.

TOP 10 MOST DOWNLOADED YOOSTAR 2 CLIPS

RANKING	CLIP NAME	MOVIE
1	"Life is like a box of chocolates"	*Forrest Gump*
2	"I ask you for justice"	*The Godfather*
3	"Everyone and their mums"	*Hot Fuzz*
4	"Dorothy meets the Cowardly Lion"	*The Wizard of Oz*
5	"Please don't hurt me!"	*Tropic Thunder*
6	"This is Sparta"	*300*
7	"She looks too pure to be pink"	*Grease*
8	"What's the last thing we remember?"	*The Hangover*
9	"My dad is…"	*Kindergarten Cop*
10	"Make it out of here"	*Platoon*

Source: Xbox.com *Accurate at 31 May 2011*

MOST DOWNLOADED *YOOSTAR 2* CLIP
Holder: *Forrest Gump*
Topping the download chart of *Yoostar 2* movie clips is the "chocolate box" scene from *Forrest Gump* (USA, 1994), in which players take the place of leading man Tom Hanks (*see table above*).

LARGEST SIMULTANEOUS DANCE-MAT ROUTINE
Holder: Pupils of Westmount Secondary School, ON, Canada
A total of 832 participants danced to *Just Dance* on the Xbox Kinect at Westmount Secondary School in Hamilton, Ontario, Canada, on 4 May 2011. The image of the game was projected on to the wall of the school gymnasium, and the choice of song was the 1980 hit "Funkytown" by Lipps Inc.

FIRST XBOX 360 MOVIE KARAOKE GAME

Holder: *Yoostar 2* **(Blitz Games Studios, 2011)**
The first movie karaoke game for Xbox 360 was *Yoostar 2*. Released on 11 March 2011, the game allows players to record themselves performing famous scenes from film and TV shows using the point-tracking capacity of the Kinect camera. The performances are then inserted alongside the real film clips, with the players replacing the original actors. Players can rate, share and edit their performances via Facebook application Yoostar Playground.

FASTEST-SELLING VIDEOGAMES PERIPHERAL

Holder: Kinect
The Kinect sensor launched on 4 November 2010 and, by 3 January 2011, had sold 8 million units – an average of 133,333 a day. The device briefly held the record for the world's fastest-selling consumer electronics product, and it remains the fastest-selling peripheral. Pictured is *Kinect Adventures*, which was bundled with the device.

> **"**I really love Kinect… It's a treasure trove of new interactivity.**"**
> MICROSOFT GAME STUDIOS BOSS AND BAFTA FELLOWSHIP RECIPIENT PETER MOLYNEUX

LIFESTYLE & FITNESS

AMONG THE CELEBRITIES LINED UP TO PROMOTE

BEST-SELLING FITNESS GAME SERIES

Holder: *Wii Fit* **(Nintendo, 2007)**
As of September 2011, the *Wii Fit* series has sold 41.84 million copies. The original *Wii Fit* accounts for 22.71 million units of this figure, while sequel *Wii Fit Plus* (Nintendo, 2009) has shifted 19.13 million. The games are played using the Wii Balance Board, a device that acts like a set of scales and measures both a player's centre of gravity and their weight.

MOST POINTS TRACKED BY A FITNESS GAME

Holder:
Your Shape: Fitness Evolved **(Ubisoft, 2010)**
Most games using Microsoft's motion-sensing Kinect peripheral do so by tracking the movement of just 16 points on the body, but Ubisoft's Player Protection System used in *Your Shape: Fitness Evolved* tracks more than 1 million points. This degree of data capture makes for a much more accurate representation of the body and ensures a far smoother animation of the player's on-screen avatar.

WORKOUT TURNOUT

In 2010, the University of Wisconsin's Dr John Porcari conducted a study into *EA Sports Active* (EA, 2009). He found that the game met the fitness guidelines for an effective workout, as put forth by the American College of Sports Medicine. According to Porcari, if played on a regular basis *EA Sports Active* can increase aerobic capacity and improve body composition in users who are generally healthy and lead an active lifestyle. As if to prove the point, 605 EA staff demonstrated the game's virtues in a mass workout at EA's Burnaby Campus Sports Field in Burnaby, British Columbia, Canada, on 22 May 2009.

337,309,509 The number of calories burned so far by gamers around the world playing *EA Sports Active*, as of 26 May 2011.

EA SPORTS ACTIVE 2 IS ENGLAND SOCCER STAR DAVID BECKHAM

TOP 10 *EA SPORTS ACTIVE* CHALLENGE TEAM MEMBERS

RANK	PLAYER	MINS PLAYED
1	Aries19ca	71,568
2	Amyloulopez	64,132
3	Deanac20	43,919
4	Rainessa	38,329
5	Cassiecat	33,523
6	Dectrop	29,622
7	Eugenerugosa	28,733
8	Tami1101	26,468
9	Nadonna	25,046
10	Chansen_20001	24,581

Source: SparkAmerica.com

BEST *WII FIT* GAMES FOR BURNING CALORIES
Holder: *Free Run* and *Island Run*

According to a study carried out by the American Council on Exercise, running challenges *Free Run* and *Island Run* are the *Wii Fit* mini games that burn the most calories. Played for 30 minutes, the pair both caused users to burn an average of 165 calories. *Rhythm Boxing* was in second place with 114 calories, and *Super Hula Hoop* came third with 111 calories. It would take nearly 48 minutes to burn off a Mars bar by playing *Free Run* or *Island Run*.

MOST PEOPLE EXERCISING TO A VIDEOGAME

In an event held to promote a healthier lifestyle to school children and celebrate the release of *Get Fit with Mel B* (Lightning Fish Games, 2010), a record-breaking total of 783 pupils from five schools in the Clarke Associated Schools Group converged on The Pines Senior Public School in Newcastle, Ontario, Canada, on 5 May 2011, to perform a five-minute exercise routine with the game.

BEST-SELLING PERSONAL SCALE
Holder: Wii Balance Board (Nintendo)

The Wii Balance Board sold 32,114,428 units between its launch in 2007 and November 2010. Its primary function is as a balance-board controller, but it has outsold any model of bathroom weighing scales.

HIGHEST FEE PAID FOR A VIDEOGAME ADVERT APPEARANCE
Holder: Helen Mirren (UK)

Hollywood film actress Dame Helen Mirren was paid a reported £500,000 (then $800,000) to appear in a series of UK television adverts as part of a major campaign for *Wii Fit* (Nintendo, 2007) during 2010. Nintendo were keen to work with the actress to help them emphasize that their games were not just for kids. Other celebrities to have featured in Wii-related adverts are the British pop act JLS, promoting *Wii Party* (Nintendo, 2010), and Irish broadcaster Sir Terry Wogan.

HIGHEST *Wii FIT* "HULA HOOPING" SCORE
Holders: Andy Fulwood and Stephen Kish (both UK)

On 16 April 2009, gamer Andy Fulwood scored 325 points on the "Hula Hooping" challenge on *Wii Fit* (Nintendo, 2007) at the ASDA Supermarket in Derby, UK. His score was later matched by Stephen Kish on 6 June 2011, who uploaded evidence of his achievement to us via our website at www.guinnessworldrecords.com/Challengers.

FIRST FITNESS GAME
Holder: *Jack LaLanne's Physical Conditioning* (Mattel, 1979)

A full 25 years before Nintendo popularized fitness gaming, Mattel's Intellivision blazed a trail for health-conscious software with *Jack LaLanne's Physical Conditioning*. The game featured the recorded voice of the veteran American fitness fanatic Jack LaLanne (then already 65 years old), encouraging gamers to try various exercises while simple animations showed the movements on screen.

AUGMENTED REALITY

NINTENDO 3DS ARCADE SHOOTER *FACE RAIDERS* ALLOWS GAMERS TO TAKE A

FIRST PHONE-CONTROLLED FLYING MACHINE

Holder: AR.Drone (2010)

The AR.Drone is a hovering, rotor-powered device which can be used to play augmented reality games. A quadricopter, it can be controlled using an iPad, iPod or iPhone. An on-board camera allows the player to see the landscape from the device's point of view, making it easier to target virtual enemies. The AR.Drone creates its own Wi-Fi link to allow iPhone control, and can fly as high as 50 m (164 ft), although the limit for maintaining stable flight is 6 m (20 ft). The device can fly for 12 minutes on a single 90-minute charge.

FIRST PORTABLE AR GAME

Holder: *ARQuake* (University of South Australia, 2000)

The first augmented reality game to break free from the constraints of desktop computers and mainframes was the experimental shooter *ARQuake*, developed by the Wearable Computer Lab at the University of South Australia. The game used a semi-transparent display to overlay virtual items and enemies from the massively successful *Quake* (id Software, 1996) on to the player's current position in the real world. With the necessary hardware alone costing over $10,000 (£5,100), *ARQuake* has never been made available to consumers.

LARGEST NINTENDO Mii CHARACTER

Holder: Tetsujin 28-go

The world's largest Mii character was created by a group of Japanese 3DS fans in March 2011. First, they designed a huge augmented reality marker by taping together 256 sheets of A3 paper. They placed the marker next to the Tetsujin 28-go giant robot statue in Wakamatsu Park, Kobe, Japan. Then, using the 3DS, they were able to generate a Mii character as big as the real-life statue, which weighs 50 metric tonnes and stands a whopping 18 m (60 ft) tall.

/// "THEY DON'T EXPECT YOU TO SURVIVE. THEY CALL IT A SUICIDE MISSION. PROVE THEM WRONG" ///

500,000 The number of player accounts held for augmented reality iPhone MMO *Parallel Kingdom*, as of June 2011. The game was launched in 2008.

SELF-PORTRAIT WITH THE 3DS CAMERA AND BECOME AN IN-GAME BOSS ▶

WHAT *IS* AUGMENTED REALITY?

Augmented reality (AR) is a modified representation of real things. The modifying device is a computer, with AR games and apps increasingly appearing on smartphones or handheld consoles. An AR marker is a 2D symbol, printed on a surface such as a piece of card or a wall, which generates imagery and data once "scanned" by a suitable computer or camera. The PS3's PlayStation Eye Camera was launched in 2007, and the first game to use it was *The Eye of Judgment*, in which gamers place specially marked trading cards (*see below right*) on a mat which is read by the Eye Camera. The Eye-scanned cards form the basis of the battle which players embark on.

ON YOUR MARKERS

In March 2010, Nintendo announced plans to give away extra large augmented reality markers as a special bonus to members of Club Nintendo. These would allow 3DS owners to generate scaled-up Mii characters using their handhelds. To demonstrate this, Nintendo president Satoru Iwata took a photo of himself holding hands with his very own life-sized Mii. Just like the Wii, the 3DS can store up to 100 individual Mii avatars (such as the one pictured here).

TOP 10 HIGHEST SCORERS ON PARALLEL KINGDOM

RANK	PLAYER	SCORE
1	*XB*	31,716,643
2	Elen	13,472,666
3	Linake	11,473,428
4	iPimpy	11,369,254
5	Jopie	8,446,285
6	Luhngjai	8,303,346
7	ALDOGGY	7,964,658
8	RavenStorm	7,549,708
9	squirrelthegreat	7,427,491
10	Schzap	7,086,566

Source: ParallelKingdom.com

HARDEST INVIZIMAL TO CATCH
Holder: Salma Pup

In AR game *Invizimals* (Novarama, 2009), players capture and battle virtual creatures within the real world. The two toughest creatures to catch are the Salma Pup and Tusker: both require the player to whistle a tune in response to the beast's calls but Salma Pup's whistle requires a much more complicated melody. Some enterprising gamers have solved the problem by using a recording device to play back the calls, while others have tried a rotating circular saw blade to trick the PSP's microphone into registering the right notes.

"The Battle Master is a horrifyingly destructive war engine of death! You may think I'm being melodramatic; I'm not."

BLACKCUBIC.COM REVIEWER "ICEPICK" ON THE MOST FEARSOME *EYE OF JUDGMENT* TRADING CARD

FIRST AR GAME FOR THE iPHONE
Holder: *Fairy Trails* (Freeverse, 2009)

Fairy Trails blazed a trail for augmented reality on the iPhone when it was released in the App Store on 26 September 2009. The game uses the iPhone's camera and compass to generate virtual fairies and butterflies within the real world. Players have to try to catch them in "jars" by tapping on the iPhone's touch-screen. The more fairies captured, the more power gained to detect other fairies.

FIRST AR MARKER TATTOO FOR 3DS
Holder: Cranberryzero

Blogger and Nintendo 3DS fan Cranberryzero, of IHeartChaos.com, decided to make his augmented reality marker for the 3DS more permanent than most. He had the famous question mark box image tattooed on the inside of his left forearm in May 2011. Anyone considering doing the same might want to think carefully before committing, especially since, according to Cranberryzero, "the tattoo doesn't always work in really bright light, like sunlight".

MOST EXPENSIVE *EYE OF JUDGMENT* CARD
Holder: Dioskuri (number 311)

According to the *Eye of Judgment* Collectors' Price Guide, the most expensive trading card on the market is number 311, Dioskuri. This ultra-rare card currently changes hands for $150 (£77) and above. Dioskuri's Magic Attack targets all enemy creatures and its force is determined by the combined energy – known as "mana" – of both players. It can be combined with the Pollux or Kastor cards for even greater effect.

RHYTHM - INSTRUMENTS

GUITAR HERO CREATOR CHARLES HUANG WAS TOLD TO EXPECT SALES

MOST DOWNLOADABLE CONTENT FOR A CONSOLE GAME

Holder: *Rock Band* (*Harmonix, 2007*)

As of May 2011, the console videogame offering players the biggest library of downloadable content was *Rock Band*. Since the game's original release, more than 2,700 additional tracks from around 900 musical artists have been made available to download. "We have everybody from Otis Redding to Metallica to Bon Jovi to Green Day to Duran Duran... And much more," Harmonix's Chris Rigopulos told *Game Informer* magazine.

BEST-SELLING *LIPS* TRACK

Holder: "Take On Me" by A-ha

The best-selling track in the online library for the Xbox 360 game *Lips* (Microsoft, 2008) is "Take On Me" by Norwegian band A-ha. (Pictured is lead vocalist Morten Harket.) It has a top user-rating of four-and-a-half stars.

▪ The **biggest-selling collection of tunes in the *Lips* store** is the Coldplay song pack.

▪ The **least downloaded song** is "Workin' for a Livin'" by Huey Lewis and The News.

▪ The **most expensive karaoke game peripheral** is a *Lips* microphone produced by CrystalRoc as part of a limited edition of 100 units at a cost of $640 (£430). It is encrusted with 1,040 Xilion Rose Flat Back crystals!

BEST-SELLING INSTRUMENT GAME ON A SINGLE PLATFORM

Holder: *Guitar Hero III: Legends of Rock* for PS2 (*Neversoft, 2007*)

More than 4.67 million copies of the PS2 version of *Guitar Hero III: Legends of Rock* have been sold. That makes it the best-selling single-platform instrument game ever – despite the subsequent releases of Xbox 360 and PS3 versions, along with various sequels.

/// "IN A WORLD OF CHAOS, SEIZE CONTROL" ///

OF JUST 150,000 UNITS. THE SERIES HAS NOW SHIFTED OVER 50 MILLION COPES! ▶

TOP 10 BEST-SELLING *ROCK BAND* TRACKS ON XBOX LIVE

RANKING	TRACK	BAND
1	"All the Small Things"	Blink-182
2	"Move Along"	The All-American Rejects
3	"Dirty Little Secret"	The All-American Rejects
4	"The Kill (Bury Me)"	30 Seconds to Mars
5	"Buddy Holly"	Weezer
6	"B.Y.O.B."	System of a Down
7	"Don't Stop Believin'"	Journey
8	"Toxicity"	System of a Down
9	"Juke Box Hero"	Foreigner
10	"Crushcrushcrush"	Paramore

Source: Xbox.com   Accurate as of 21 May 2011; does not include free tracks

ARE GUITAR GAMES DEAD?

Is it all over for guitar-based videogames? In 2011, Activision cancelled plans to release another *Guitar Hero* title, despite the fact that work on the game had already begun. Harmonix also said it would not be releasing another *Rock Band* title that year, admitting that the latest instalment in the series was being outsold by the floor-filling Kinect game *Dance Central*.

But while gamers might not be buying as many guitar-based titles, they still seem to be playing them. According to Harmonix's Chris Rigopulos, more than a million unique users are still logging on to download *Rock Band* tracks every month. Nearly 5 million unique account holders have purchased a song since the *Rock Band* store launched in 2007.

MOST BUTTONS ON A VIDEOGAME CONTROLLER

Holder: *Rock Band 3* wireless Fender Mustang PRO-Guitar controller **(Mad Catz, 2010)**
With 113 different buttons representing every possible finger position on a 17-fret guitar, the wireless Fender Mustang PRO-Guitar controller for *Rock Band 3* has more individual inputs than any peripheral in console history – even more than a standard PC keyboard, in fact!

> "Anyone can now rock out – even if they have never shredded before in their life."

MUSICIAN KID ROCK ON WHY HE SIGNED UP TO PROVIDE TRACKS FOR *POWER GIG*

FIRST VIDEOGAME TO WORK WITH A REAL GUITAR

Holder: *Power Gig: Rise of the SixString* **(Seven45 Studios, 2010)**
The first videogame to work with a real guitar instead of a plastic peripheral is *Power Gig: Rise of the SixString*. It was released in North America on 19 October 2010 for Xbox 360 and PS3. The game is played using a controller that is both a genuine six-string guitar – which can be plugged into a standard amplifier and played as a real instrument – and an input device for note-matching games.

LEAST POPULAR *GUITAR HERO* TRACK

Holder: "We've Got a Situation Here" by **The Damned Things**
At the time of going to press, the download track "We've Got a Situation Here" by the New York heavy-metal supergroup The Damned Things has a popularity rating of just +3 on the *Guitar Hero* website – meaning that only three people have elected to click the "like" symbol! "Memories of the Grove" by Maylene and The Sons of Disaster is in second place with a score of +4.

The **most popular** *Guitar Hero* track is Amon Amarth's "Twilight of the Thunder God", boasting an impressive rating of +862.

BEST-SELLING KARAOKE GAME SERIES

Holder: *SingStar* **(Sony)**
The best-selling karaoke game series of all time is Sony's *SingStar* (2004–10). More than 22 million discs have been sold and over 15 million tracks have been downloaded from the SingStore. To date, more than 1.5 million players have uploaded nearly 300,000 videos of their performances to the My SingStar Online service.

RHYTHM - DANCING

BEST-SELLING MUSIC GAME

Holder: *Just Dance 2* (Ubisoft, 2010)

As of May 2011, more than 7.32 million copies of Ubisoft's Wii game *Just Dance 2* had been sold around the globe. That makes it more successful than the single-platform versions of all other music games. The second best-selling title in the genre is the original *Just Dance* (Ubisoft, 2009) with sales of 5.78 million.

MOST EXPENSIVE DANCE MAT

Holder: iON Master Metal Arcade 4 in 1 dance pad
The most expensive dance pad designed for home use is the iON Master Metal Arcade 4 in 1. It carries a recommended price of nearly $1,300 (£800). The pad is made from heavy-duty stretched metal and weighs 42.6 kg (94 lb). It can support players weighing up to 400 kg (882 lb) – that's the average weight of a fully grown polar bear!

MOST CRITICALLY ACCLAIMED DANCING GAME

Holder: *Dance Dance Revolution* (Konami, 2001)
Reviews aggregator site Metacritic reports that the PlayStation version of *Dance Dance Revolution* (*DDR*) is the most critically successful dancing game ever, racking up an average review score of 90 out of 100. In fact, nine of the top ten best-scoring dancing games are *DDR* titles. The exception is *Dance Central* (Microsoft, 2010), which shimmies into fifth place with a score of 82.

FIRST RHYTHM GAME

Holder: *Family Trainer: Aerobics Studio* (Nintendo, 1987)
Launched in Japan on 26 February 1987, *Family Trainer: Aerobics Studio*, a pioneer of the dance-mat controller for the Nintendo Famicom, was the first rhythm videogame released.

Tom
4650

PERFECT

DISCO INFERNO?

The *Just Dance* series may be popular with gamers but it hasn't always been a hit with the critics. On the aggregate scoring site Metacritic, *Just Dance 2* has an average review score of only 74 out of 100, despite being the best-selling music game ever. The original game fares even worse, with an average score of just 49!

> "Kinect lets you and your mates dance in your own living room with no controllers... so you can dance your way to a hot body, just like mine."

PINEAPPLE DANCE STUDIO CHOREOGRAPHER
LOUIE SPENCE (UK) ON *DANCE CENTRAL*

MOST PROLIFIC DANCING GAME HIGH SCORER

Holder: Elizabeth Bolinger (Ottumwa, Iowa, USA)
Elizabeth "Kitty McScratch" Bolinger holds more Twin Galaxies high-score records for *Dance Central*, *Just Dance* and *Just Dance 2* than any other player. She is no.1 on the leaderboard for more than 85 different songs. Her highest score is for *Dance Central* track "C'mon Ride It (The Train)" by Quad City DJs, for which she scored 432,793 points on 5 December 2010.

TOP 10 BEST-SELLING *DANCE CENTRAL* TRACKS ON XBOX LIVE

#	TRACK	ACT
1	"I Gotta Feeling"	The Black Eyed Peas
2	"Disturbia"	Rihanna
3	"Temperature"	Sean Paul
4	"Because of You"	Ne-Yo
5	"Word Up"	Cameo
6	"Whoomp! (There It Is)"	Tag Team
7	"Girls & Boys"	Blur
8	"Control"	Janet Jackson
9	"I Got You Dancing"	Lady Sovereign
10	"We Run This"	Missy Elliott

Source: Xbox.com   - Accurate as of 22 May 2011

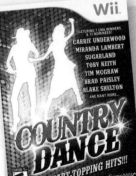

FIRST COUNTRY-MUSIC-THEMED DANCING GAME

Holder: *Country Dance* (High Voltage, 2011)
The first ever country-music-themed dancing game was released in the USA on 29 March 2011 by High Voltage Software. Titled *Country Dance*, it is exclusive to the Wii and features 27 tracks for wannabe cowgirls and cowboys to shake their spurs to, including "Achy Breaky Heart" by Billy Ray Cyrus, "Ring of Fire" by Johnny Cash and "Cowboy Casanova" by Carrie Underwood (who also shares a world record with Reba McEntire for the **most country no.1s by a female artist**, with 10 singles).

GAMING FAIL

SOME EARLY VIDEOGAMES HAVE SO-CALLED "KILL SCREENS" – LEVELS THAT

GAMES ARE MEANT TO BE FUN, BUT SOMETIMES THEY ARE MORE ABOUT THE FAIL. IF YOU MISSED THESE LESS-SUCCESSFUL GAMES THE FIRST TIME ROUND, HERE ARE SOME CLASSICS FROM THE HALL OF SHAME.

WHO SAYS?

Hello! I'm Stuart Ashen, but you may know me as Ashens. Instead of having a real job, I make YouTube videos poking fun at things I think are rubbish. I've been a gamer for over 25 years, and during that period I've wasted far too much money and time on some really appalling videogames.

E.T. THE EXTRA-TERRESTRIAL
(Atari, 1982 for Atari 2600)
A legend of gaming fail, *E.T. the Extra-Terrestrial* was based on the successful 1982 Steven Spielberg movie of the same name. Rush-developed and mass-produced for Christmas 1982, the resultant game was dull, had very basic graphics and tasked the player with searching for pieces of a phone to help E.T. call home. It reportedly sold 1.5 million units, but more than double that figure remained unsold and many were buried in a landfill site.
Grade: E+

INTERGALACTIC CAGE MATCH
(Mastertronic, 1987 for Commodore 64)
As it is impossible to hit your opponent, the fighting element of this game is almost irrelevant, and even more so when you realize that all you need to do to win is climb up the fighting cage's fence faster than your opponent and that climbing fighters cannot be hit.
Grade: D

BARRAVENTO: O MESTRE DA CAPOEIRA
(Hitek, 1993 for Commodore Amiga)
This Brazilian game attempted to portray the elegant, dance-like martial art of Capoeira and failed spectacularly. A one-on-one fighting game with only one character and three attack moves, *Barravento* basically consists of two men waving their arms and legs. The controls frequently failed to respond and repeating the same kick was the only effective tactic. Still, at least the game was playable...
Grade: C-

ALIEN SIDESTEP
(Mr Computer, 1983 for Commodore Vic 20)
Widely considered the most pointless videogame ever, *Alien Sidestep* was essentially a version of *Space Invaders* in which an endless stream of enemies moved from left to right. However, these aliens had an extra trick up their sleeves as they could dodge bullets by stopping and moving back a bit. This made actually hitting them very difficult – the only way to land a blow was to shimmy your firing platform left and right while constantly firing, thus removing the point of aiming at all, and taking all of the fun of playing the game with it.
Grade: E+

COSMIC SHOCK ABSORBER
(Martech Games, 1987 for MSX)
This was supposed to be a space-themed first-person shooter, but the action revolved more around trying to dodge the big circles that filled the screen. It was often hard to tell if the directional controls were even working, and players usually died within 90 seconds of starting a game.
Grade: F

HUNTER
(Power Per Post, year unknown, for Atari 800XL)
Hunter attempted to bring all the thrills of hunting to videogames. Sadly, what it delivered was flat, blocky images of animals that slid across a landscape. Crucially, the animals all slid along exactly the same path, making the task of aiming your jittery machine gun largely unnecessary.
Grade: E

CANNOT BE COMPLETED DUE TO A PROGRAMMING ERROR

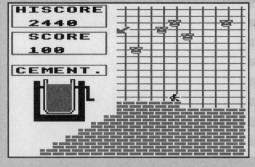

AUF WIEDERSEHEN, PET
(Tynesoft, 1984 for BBC Micro)
In the early 1980s, some people thought you could make a videogame out of anything. Then they tried one based on a British TV series about builders. Alexey Pajitnov's *Tetris* would make laying "bricks" fun, but in this title players were left desperately trying to control a tiny, sliding stick man who moved too fast to properly control. The slightest mistake, such as walking into an obstacle, resulted in an instant failure.
Grade: E-

SURF NINJAS
(MicroValue, 1994 for Commodore CD32)
Based on the 1993 movie of the same name, *Surf Ninjas* was a reasonably attractive scrolling beat-'em-up that fell flat on its collision detection, but that didn't matter much as players could simply walk past the stream of identical enemies. The lack of action was broken up by tedious tasks, such as fetching crates for an old man so he would stop blocking your path. It also featured some surprisingly gory death moves.
Grade: C

GRAFFITI MAN
(1987, Rainbow Arts for Atari ST)
A title that caused many gamers to weep hot, bitter tears of anger and frustration, *Graffiti Man* placed the player in a screen filled with grotesquely ugly freaks jerking around. The player soon learned that touching a freak caused their character to explode. Avoiding the freaks was no use, though, as the poor controls made it hard to judge the distances between objects on screen, and because players often exploded for no noticeable reason.
Grade: D-

COUNT DUCKULA 2
(Alternative Software, 1992 for Amstrad CPC)
Based on the British animated TV series of the same name, the Amstrad CPC version of *Count Duckula* was a simple platform game in which players had to travel across ledges that slowly flickered in and out of existence. Enemies trundled around at a similar pace and were easier to evade than to attack. The second screen on this version was so badly designed that it couldn't be completed.
Grade: D

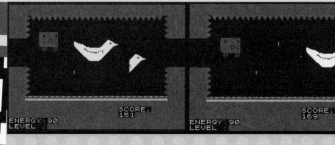

SQIJ!
(The Power House, 1987 for ZX Spectrum)
Move over *Angry Birds*, this is a bird-related game that just made players angry. At the start of the game, the player was presented with what appeared to be a huge pigeon that didn't do anything. Due to a programming oversight (and a lack of play-testing) none of the controls worked. Surprisingly, this fact didn't prevent the game from being published. Years later, clever gamers discovered that you could break into the game and fix the controls. Players could then make the pigeon move slowly across the screen to one of two exits. One exit did nothing, the other made the game crash. Who knows what kind of fun the original programmers expected this game to provide?
Grade: F

ACTION-ADVENTURE

BEST-SELLING 3DS GAME

Holder: *The Legend of Zelda: Ocarina of Time 3D*

(Grezzo/Nintendo, 2011)
With 800,000 copies sold in just six weeks, *The Legend of Zelda: Ocarina of Time 3D* was both the best-selling and fastest-selling 3DS title as of July 2011. With 3DS selling around 3 million by July 2011, close to one-in-five owners of Nintendo's latest handheld now have a copy of the game! However, the new 3D version has a long way to go to beat the N64 original's 7.6 million sales.

OVERVIEW

Action and adventure have been two of the key components of gaming since its very beginnings. And, as the medium evolves, so does this wide-ranging genre. An action-adventure game can – and regularly does – incorporate multiple elements, from shooting to platforming to puzzle-solving.

What connects these seemingly disparate games is how they bind together narrative and game mechanics, whether the player is creating their own story or following the path a developer has set out for them. Some series, such as the *Assassin's Creed* titles, allow for both, giving players the freedom to change the journey, if not the destination.

BIOGRAPHY

Chris Schilling has been writing about games for seven years, contributing reviews, previews and features to a wide variety of magazines and websites from *Edge* to Eurogamer.net. He will play just about any game once, but action-adventures are his speciality, with *Assassin's Creed: Brotherhood* and *Deadly Premonition* among his recent favourites.

CONTENTS

CRITICAL HIT!: *ASSASSIN'S CREED*	96
SANDBOX	98
NARRATIVE ADVENTURE	100
STEALTH	102
SURVIVAL HORROR	104
2D PLATFORMERS	106
3D PLATFORMERS	108
GRAPHIC ADVENTURE	110

ASSASSIN'S CREED

ASSASSIN'S CREED: BROTHERHOOD WAS THE FIRST GAME

BEST-SELLING MODERN FRANCHISE

Holder: *Assassin's Creed* **(Ubisoft, 2007–present)**
Having sold over 29 million units as of May 2011, the *Assassin's Creed* series is the best-selling modern console franchise, a record that is set to be extended even further upon the release of *Assassin's Creed: Revelations* (pictured).

The original *Assassin's Creed* is still the best-selling game in the series to date, shifting more than 9 million copies across the Xbox 360, PlayStation 3 and PC releases.

The series is publisher Ubisoft's second-biggest gaming brand overall, eclipsed only by the collective might of the diverse set of games bearing the name of thriller writer Tom Clancy. These titles have sold 55 million copies in total – although that figure accounts for more than 40 games issued over a period of 13 years.

MOST PLATFORMS SUPPORTED BY A STEALTH SERIES THIS CENTURY

Holder: *Assassin's Creed* **(Ubisoft, 2007–present)**
Since 2007, *Assassin's Creed* games have been made for a total of 13 different platforms. The four main games in the franchise have been made for PlayStation 3, Xbox 360 and PC, while less complex spin-off titles have been released for PSP, DS, Windows Phone 7, webOS and 3DS. There has even been a single-player game for Facebook called *Assassin's Creed: Project Legacy* (left).

HIGHEST KILL:DEATH RATIO ON *ASSASSIN'S CREED: BROTHERHOOD* MULTIPLAYER (XBOX 360)
Holder: ROCKY B 117 **(Canada)**
A gamer only known as ROCKY B 117 amassed an astonishing 75 kills per death from 2 days 15 hr 2 min of game time, as of 3 July 2011. The score is even more amazing when you discover that his nearest rival could only manage 27 kills per death.

IN THE SERIES TO FEATURE MULTIPLAYER FUNCTIONALITY ▶

LONGEST VIDEOGAME MARATHON

Holders: *Tony Desmet, Jesse Rebmann* and *Jeffrey Gammon* (all Belgium)

Masters of endurance Tony Desmet, Jesse Rebmann and Jeffrey Gammon spent an incredible 109 hours playing *Assassin's Creed: Brotherhood* (Ubisoft, 2010) at the GUNKtv World Record Gaming Event in Antwerp, Belgium, from 18 to 22 December 2010. The record attempt started with 20 participants, but the three record holders were the only ones with the willpower to stick it out to the bitter end.

LARGEST RANGE OF BOMBS IN A STEALTH VIDEOGAME

Holder: *Assassin's Creed: Revelations* (Ubisoft, 2011)

The "crafting" feature built into *Assassin's Creed: Revelations* enables players to create more than 300 different types of bomb to use on various in-game targets. Taking advantage of the game's "hookblade" weapon, which can be used to grapple on to ziplines, players can navigate cities smoothly and bomb them with devastating ease.

> "We like to surprise and shock the consumers and I think it's going to be the same with this game."
>
> UBISOFT'S ERIC GALLANT ON THE CLIFFHANGER ENDING OF *ASSASSIN'S CREED: BROTHERHOOD*

IT'S HOW UPLAY IT

Console manufacturers Microsoft and Sony both have their own systems for rewarding various in-game accomplishments, termed "Achievements" and "Trophies", respectively.

Starting with *Assassin's Creed II*, game publisher Ubisoft launched Uplay, a system to reward "Actions", their own term for in-game endeavours. Uplay also offers access to exclusive game content, including an additional tomb to explore.

TOP 10 ALL-TIME SCORERS ON *ASSASSIN'S CREED: BROTHERHOOD* MULTIPLAYER

RANK	PLAYER	SCORE
1	Chernzobog	33,572,125
2	i2elgN DoWn o	33,296,205
3	Vox Valentine	32,195,515
4	Xjjm420x	25,847,885
5	dcrossen	23,400,965
6	Wolf Appache	23,102,835
7	RaininStormwake	22,721,455
8	Swami Chuckles	22,611,320
9	L4ngeDuty	21,398,980
10	NAX PRIME	21,044,930

Source: in-game leaderboard

BONUS BOUNTY

Assassin's Creed games are renowned for their expansive, detailed playing environments, full of hidden nooks and crannies. What better way to tempt gamers to explore these rich environments than by seeding them with in-game items?

Assassin's Creed II, in particular, boasts a wealth of collectables, including codex pages, feathers, models and paintings – and that's before you start counting the standard gaming items, such as weapons and armour.

SHORTEST DEVELOPMENT PERIOD FOR A TRIPLE-A STEALTH SEQUEL

Holder: *Assassin's Creed: Brotherhood* (Ubisoft, 2010)

Released on 16 November 2010, a mere 364 days after *Assassin's Creed II*, *Assassin's Creed: Brotherhood* (right) has the shortest development period for a major stealth game sequel. Typically, successful high-profile games require at least two years to develop and often take even longer: rival stealth franchise *Metal Gear* has averaged 1,190 days between releases – over three times as long!

Fortunately for *Brotherhood*, the short time it took to develop and deliver didn't impact on the game's quality as it earned favourable reviews across all platforms and garnered Ubisoft over 1 million sales in the week of its release in Europe alone.

SANDBOX

AMIGA AND ATARI ACTION TITLE *HUNTER* (PAUL HOLMES, 1991)

SANDBOX OR OPEN WORLD?

Sandbox and open-world games are, to all intents and purposes, the same thing. They are non-linear games that allow users the freedom to explore and roam in numerous different ways, with no right or wrong way to play within the in-game world.

MOST VIEWED TRAILER FOR AN OPEN-WORLD HORROR VIDEOGAME

Holder: *Dead Island* **(Techland, 2011)**

The reveal trailer for first-person zombie adventure *Dead Island* has been watched by over 4.5 million people. The emotionally charged promo, produced by Glasgow-based Axis Animations, received 125,000 views in its first 16 hours, with the buzz quickly spreading on social networks.

BEST-SELLING INDEPENDENTLY DEVELOPED SANDBOX GAME

Holder: *Minecraft* (Mojang, 2009)

Minecraft has been an incredible success story for its small, independent developer, with more than 2.65 million users having paid to download it (as of June 2011). The game, which allows players to create various constructions using textured cubes in a three-dimensional world, was written by one man, Markus "Notch" Persson (Sweden), using software platform Java. *Minecraft* had no advertising to speak of yet quickly became a huge word-of-mouth success, allowing Persson to form his own videogame company and employ more staff to further the game's development.

IS CONSIDERED TO BE THE FIRST 3D SANDBOX GAME EVER RELEASED ▶

MOST FORMATS FOR A HANDHELD OPEN-WORLD TITLE

Holder: *Grand Theft Auto: Chinatown Wars* (Rockstar, 2009)
Grand Theft Auto: Chinatown Wars, developed by British companies Rockstar Leeds and Rockstar North, appeared on three different formats – the DS, PSP and iOS. The title is also the **most critically acclaimed 2D open-world game**, earning a Metacritic review average of 93% on DS, 91% on iOS and 90% on PSP. Indeed, it is the **highest-rated game on Nintendo's handheld** – with only the free animation app *Flipnote Studio* matching its impressive score.

FASTEST-SELLING XBOX LIVE INDIE GAME

Holder: *FortressCraft* (ProjectorGames, 2011)
Sandbox construction game *FortressCraft* sold 16,000 units on its launch day of 8 April 2011. The game, in which players use cubic blocks to build pretty much anything they like, was bought by 70% of those who downloaded the trial version.

MOST SUCCESSFUL VIDEOGAME BETA TEST

Holder: *Minecraft* (Mojang, 2009)
With more than 10 million registered users as of July 2011, block-builder *Minecraft* is the most successful game beta ever. It was launched on 17 May 2009 and entered beta testing on 20 December 2010, with an official release planned for late 2011. Different versions of the game were developed for iOS and Android smartphones, as well as the Xbox 360.

TOP 10 HIGHEST SCORERS ON *GRAND THEFT AUTO IV* MULTIPLAYER

RANK	PLAYER	SCORE
1	Black_Thunder07	1,592,587
2	S1MON3zZ_	1,160,676
3	peppone_2	350,537
4	biggee3005	248,248
5	NassMENASS	243,981
6	LUIS_DA_MONSTA	197,975
7	parisg	187,017
8	Wraptor	130,255
9	KrazyAqibNyC	129,516
10	Tibbe_Gamer	113,070

Source: Socialclub.rockstargames.com

REVERSE ZOMBIES

The "reveal" trailer for *Dead Island* gained instant notoriety for its dramatic backwards footage of a zombie attack on a holidaying family. The game's official Facebook page saw an influx of 100,000 fans in its first week. Even more remarkably, there were 3.2 million Tweets about the game within a week of its release. Some fans produced their own videos of the trailer's scenes in chronological order, while *Shaun of the Dead* director Edgar Wright created a video containing backwards footage of the film spliced with the trailer's soundtrack.

FIRST USER-GENERATED CONTENT CREATOR FOR AN OPEN-WORLD CONSOLE TITLE

Holder: *inFAMOUS 2* (Sucker Punch, 2011)
inFAMOUS 2, released on the PS3 in June 2011, has made open-world history with its user-generated content creator. Sucker Punch had been developing the feature for two years before its March reveal, having apparently been inspired by Media Molecule's *LittleBigPlanet*. In an interview with *Edge* magazine, the studio's co-founder, Brian Fleming, admitted that "[it] started with jealousy. We saw the presentation of UGC where they introduced *LittleBigPlanet* and were like: 'That is a great idea. I wish we'd thought of that.'"

NARRATIVE ADVENTURE

THE MUSIC SCORE FOR *CASTLEVANIA: LORDS OF SHADOW,* BY COMPOSER

HIGHEST-RATED 3D REMAKE

Holder: *The Legend of Zelda: Ocarina of Time 3D* **(Grezzo, 2011)**
The Legend of Zelda: Ocarina of Time 3D earned a mighty Metacritic average of 94%, making it the most acclaimed 3D remake to date. Developed by little-known Japanese company Grezzo, the game features a number of improvements on its N64 predecessor, with enhanced visuals, a revamped Master Quest mode, gyroscopic aiming and touch-screen item management. *Ocarina of Time 3D* is the 16th title in the *Zelda* series and sold 702,940 copies in its first three weeks.

A SERIES BUSINESS

Castlevania: Lords of Shadow (MercurySteam/Kojima, 2010) is one of the most critically successful franchise reboots in recent years. The adventure game was warmly received by reviewers, earning a Metacritic average of 85% on the PS3 and 83% on the Xbox 360. This was the highest-scoring entry in the series since *Castlevania: Symphony of the Night* (Konami, 1997) for the original PlayStation. Set in the Middle Ages, *Castlevania: Lords of Shadow* gives players control of elite knight Gabriel Belmont. British actor Robert Carlyle provides the voice of Belmont, while *Star Trek* and *X-Men* legend Sir Patrick Stewart narrates and voices the character of Zobek. With sales of 883,000 as of July 2011, *Lords of Shadow* represents an upturn in fortunes for Spanish developer MercurySteam. Their previous title, *Clive Barker's Jericho,* sold half that figure.

61 million The accumulated sales of *Zelda* games as of July 2011, making it the best-selling narrative adventure franchise so far.

GUINNESS WORLD RECORDS

OSCAR ARAUJO, WAS RECORDED BY A 120-PIECE ORCHESTRA ▶

BEST-SELLING SEVENTH-GENERATION PLAYSTATION 3 SERIES

Holder: *Uncharted* series (Naughty Dog, 2007-11)

Naughty Dog's *Uncharted* series, which shifted 8.33 million copies between November 2007 and July 2011, is the biggest-selling new franchise on the PS3. *Uncharted: Drake's Fortune* (2007) sold 3.65 million units, with successor *Uncharted 2: Among Thieves* (2009) selling 4.68 million worldwide. The sequel remains the most acclaimed PS3 exclusive ever, having garnered over 50 "game of the year" awards including four nods from BAFTA and an exceptional 10 from the Academy of Interactive Arts and Sciences.

MOST QUOTED NARRATIVE ADVENTURE VIDEOGAME ON TWITTER

Holder: *Superbrothers: Sword and Sworcery EP* (Capybara Games, 2011)
The iOS title *Superbrothers: Sword and Sworcery EP* inspired more than 200,000 tweets featuring the game's #sworcery hashtag between 27 March and 7 June 2011. The integration of Twitter functionality allows the player to connect to their Twitter account and simply tap a button on the touch-screen to relay any line of the game's witty dialogue to their followers. This promotional feature helped knowledge of the game spread throughout the social network, resulting in a total of 270,000 sales for the title between March and September 2011.

MOST CRITICALLY ACCLAIMED SUPERHERO VIDEOGAME

Holder: *Batman: Arkham Asylum* (Rocksteady Studios, 2009)
With average scores of 92% on the Xbox 360 and 91% on the PS3 and PC on Metacritic, *Batman: Arkham Asylum* is the top-rated superhero game. It has also notched up impressive sales of almost 5 million. Comic book writer Paul Dini crafted an all-new plot for the game, with Arkham Asylum re-envisioned as an Alcatraz-like island prison.

The only Batman comic book to be directly adapted into a videogame is *Batman: Dark Tomorrow* (HotGen, 2003). Unlike *Arkham Asylum*, it picked up almost universally negative reviews.

FIRST GAME TO USE THE LUNAR CYCLE

Holder: *Superbrothers: Sword and Sworcery EP* (Capybara Games, 2011)
In Session III of the game, two key items are only accessible during a new moon or full moon. The game is designed to make players wait, and it recognizes if the device's date is changed, making it impossible to cheat!

MOST PROLIFIC VOICE ACTOR (MALE)

Holder: Nolan North (USA)
Between 1997 and July 2011, Nolan North worked on 107 games, making him the most prolific male voice actor in videogames. North is best-known for his role as Nathan Drake in the *Uncharted* series, as well as Desmond Miles in Ubisoft's *Assassin's Creed* games. Jennifer Hale (USA, b. Canada) holds the record for the **most prolific voice actor (female)** with 129 games (see page 147).

TOP 10 *ZELDA* TITLES

RANK	GAME	TOTAL SALES
1	*Ocarina of Time*	7.6 million
2	*The Legend of Zelda* (original)	6.51 million
3	*Twilight Princess*	5.9 million
4	*Phantom Hourglass*	4.83 million
5	*A Link to the Past*	4.61 million
6	*The Wind Waker*	4.55 million
7	*The Adventure of Link*	4.38 million
8	*Link's Awakening*	3.83 million
9	*Majora's Mask*	3.36 million
10	*Spirit Tracks*	2.85 million

Source: VGChartz.com

HIDEO KOJIMA PLAYED THE VOICE OF GOD IN ONE OF HIS OWN GAMES,

FIRST HD STEALTH GAME REMAKES

Holder: *Tom Clancy's Splinter Cell Trilogy* **(Ubisoft, 2011)**
Giving classic games an HD makeover for their release on a modern platform is proving popular for gamers and publishers alike. In the stealth genre, the first titles to benefit from an HD re-release are the first three games in the *Splinter Cell* series – namely *Tom Clancy's Splinter Cell*, *Tom Clancy's Splinter Cell: Pandora Tomorrow*, and *Tom Clancy's Splinter Cell: Chaos Theory*.

At the time of going to press, the compilation, due for release in September 2011, seemed likely to beat rival stealth series *Metal Gear Solid* to the HD punch – the *Metal Gear Solid HD Collection* was due to hit the shops in November 2011.

FIRST GAME TO USE CAMOUFLAGE AS A MAJOR GAMEPLAY DEVICE

Holder: *Metal Gear Solid 3: Snake Eater* **(Kojima Productions, 2004)**
Camouflage is key in *Metal Gear Solid 3: Snake Eater* – the game's 10 types of camo gear offer different levels of protection in different environments – woodland camouflage for jungles, for example. If players don't select the appropriate gear (right), they increase their risk of being detected.

CAMOUF

Metal Gear Solid: Snake Eater 3D (Kojima Productions, 2011) may not have been the first 3D stealth game, but the game does have one particularly innovative feature. While the original version for the PSP provided Snake with 10 different types of camouflage, the 3D remake enables players to use photos taken with their 3DS as textures on Snake's fatigues. Pink flowers might not be the best choice, though.

METAL GEAR SOLID 4: GUNS OF THE PATRIOTS (KOJIMA PRODUCTIONS, 2008) ▶

TOP 10 DEATHMATCH POINT-SCORERS ON *METAL GEAR ONLINE*		
RANK	PLAYER	SCORE
1	:STAR:	218,957
2	solidus-scott	156,277
3	marlboro90	124,840
4	NICOLA CBR RR	123,271
5	0000?0000	104,065
6	SirHeymann	101,521
7	Whit3WidOw	89,022
8	DJDSNAKE	79,163
9	rapts	76,080
10	BigBear	72,970

Source: in-game leaderboard

MOST DIALOGUE OPTIONS IN A STEALTH VIDEOGAME

Holder: *Alpha Protocol* (Obsidian Entertainment, 2010)

An "Espionage RPG" that relies heavily on stealth gameplay, *Alpha Protocol* features a "Dialogue Stance System" to control how the player interacts with other characters in the game. The system allows players to select one of three different styles of response: "suave", "professional" or "aggressive". Developer Obsidian claimed this was based on "the three JBs": James Bond, Jason Bourne and Jack Bauer. Adopting different "stances" will lead to different reactions from the key non-player characters, and will cause the game's narrative to take off in different directions.

> "People go: 'Hey! I had this great idea last night about pushing a cop off a ledge', or whatever. Everyone's a closet hitman."
>
> **IO INTERACTIVE'S TORE BLYSTAD ON HIS STAFF'S IDEAS FOR *HITMAN: ABSOLUTION***

MOST CRITICALLY ACCLAIMED STEALTH VIDEOGAME

Holder: *Metal Gear: Ghost Babel* (Konami, 2000)

The Game Boy Color title *Metal Gear: Ghost Babel* has an average score of 95.92% on Gamerankings.com. Released in the West simply as *Metal Gear Solid*, the game employs an overhead perspective that gives the title a similar feel to the earliest games in the franchise.

FASTEST COMPLETION OF *HITMAN: BLOOD MONEY*

Holder: Mark "exploding cabbage" Amery (UK)

Using "pro", the most difficult setting for *Hitman: Blood Money* (IO Interactive, 2006), Mark Amery completed a segmented speed run (in which each section of the game is timed individually) in just 22 min 44 sec, posting his last segment to speeddemosarchive.com on 29 September 2009.

FIRST 3D STEALTH GAME ON PC

Holder: *Thief: The Dark Project* (Looking Glass Studios, 1998)

Released 10 months after the **first 3D stealth game** – *Tenchu: Stealth Assassins* (Aquire, 1998) – hit the PlayStation, *Thief: The Dark Project* became the first such game for PC in November 1998.

The game was hugely innovative in terms of the stealth genre on the PC platform, forcing players to make use of shadow and sound as key elements of its gameplay. It was also a big hit with the critics, with a score of 89.41% on Gamerankings.com.

FIRST DOWNLOADABLE STEALTH GAMES BASED ON A TV SHOW

Holder: *Doctor Who: The Adventure Games* (Sumo Digital, 2010)

An iconic TV science-fiction hero, the Doctor made his stealth-game debut in *Doctor Who: The Adventure Games*, a series of four titles distributed episodically, and for free for those in the UK, via the BBC's website from June to December 2010. *The Adventure Games* was a collaboration between the BBC, legendary adventure game creator Charles Cecil and Sheffield-based developer Sumo Digital, and featured the Time Lord and his assistant Amy Pond sneaking around to avoid being discovered by Daleks and other monsters.

SURVIVAL HORROR

A CGI *RESIDENT EVIL* MOVIE, DUBBED *RESIDENT EVIL: DEGENERATION* IN THE USA,

BEST-SELLING SURVIVAL HORROR GAME

Holder: *Resident Evil 4* **(Capcom, 2004)**

Outselling *Resident Evil 5* by a mere 40,000 copies in terms of total sales across all formats, *Resident Evil 4* still sits atop the mound of seething tentacled flesh that is the survival horror sales chart. The game, widely regarded as the high point of the series, had sold 7.03 million copies worldwide as of July 2011, and with an HD re-release due in late 2011, *Resident Evil 4* is likely to retain its position for some time to come.

MOST EXPENSIVE XBOX 360 GAME SOLD AT AUCTION

Holder: *Dead Space Ultra Limited Edition* **(EA, 2008)**

When he bought his copy of the *Dead Space Ultra Limited Edition*, Damian Fraimorice (Israel) paid its original retail price of $149 (£80). However, this dedicated videogame fan proved he was also a shrewd businessman when he managed to sell the package to an anonymous eBay buyer in New York for $2,999 (£1,864) on 2 February 2011. Only 1,000 copies of the Ultra Limited Edition of *Dead Space* were manufactured and, in addition to a copy of the game, they included a bonus DVD, a lithograph illustrated and signed by comic artist Ben Templesmith, a 97-page *Dead Space* art book, a 160-page graphic novel and an insignia patch of the main spaceship in the game, the USG *Ishimura*.

MOST LIVE-ACTION FILM ADAPTATIONS OF A VIDEOGAME

Holder: *Resident Evil*

With four films already released and a fifth planned for September 2012, the slavering beast that is the *Resident Evil* franchise is the most successful movie series to be based on a videogame. The films have grossed over $600 million (£360 million) worldwide to date, with each film making more money than the last.

1,332 The number of crew aboard the USG *Ishimura* in *Dead Space* (EA Redwood Shores, 2008). No one survives the necromorph horrors to make it to the end of the game.

RECEIVED A LIMITED CINEMA RELEASE IN THE USA AND JAPAN IN 2008 ▶

TOP 10 BEST-SELLING *RESIDENT EVIL* GAMES BY FORMAT

SALES IN MILLIONS	GAME (FORMAT)
5.82	*Resident Evil 2* (PS)
5.05	*Resident Evil* (PS)
4.03	*Resident Evil 5* (PS3)
3.52	*Resident Evil 3: Nemesis* (PS)
3.40	*Resident Evil 4* (PS2)
2.96	*Resident Evil 5* (Xbox 360)
2.07	*Resident Evil – Code: Veronica X* (PS2)
1.94	*Resident Evil 4* (Wii)
1.69	*Resident Evil 4* (GameCube)
1.45	*Resident Evil: The Umbrella Chronicles* (GameCube)

Source: VGChartz.com

MOST CRITICALLY POLARIZING SURVIVAL HORROR GAME

Holder: *Deadly Premonition* **(Access Games, 2010)**
With review scores ranging from 10/10 from reviews website Destructoid to 2/10 from rival site IGN, *Deadly Premonition* has split critical opinion. According to the former, the survival horror is "a game that consistently surprises and amazes and leaves jaws hanging", while the latter was less complimentary, describing it as "awful in nearly every way... Terrible controls. Terrible pacing. Terrible sound effects. Terrible visuals." Scary stuff!

FIRST CO-OP MODE IN A SURVIVAL HORROR VIDEOGAME

Holder: *Resident Evil: Outbreak* **(Capcom, 2003)**
Capcom's 2003 survival horror *Resident Evil: Outbreak* introduced a new element to its gameplay: co-operation between players through the introduction of an online multiplayer mode. Players with broadband internet access for their PS2 could connect with up to four players and team up against the hordes infected by the T-virus. Players without fast internet access just had the single-player campaign.

FASTEST COMPLETION OF *CONDEMNED: CRIMINAL ORIGINS*

Holder: Adrian Feiertag (USA)
An early title for the Xbox 360, *Condemned: Criminal Origins* (Monolith Productions, 2005) tasked players with investigating a series of grisly murders. Gamer Adrian Feiertag solved the case, and shot dead the game's serial killer, in just 1 hr 56 min 25 sec. His attempt was cut into 10 sections, and although he avoided collecting all the clues, Adrian was still forced to sit through the game's unskippable cutscenes.

"I'd say the fear and the ecstatic feelings after you overcome the fear are essential functions in order for humans to live."

SIREN WRITER/DESIGNER KEIICHIRŌ TOYAMA ON THE APPEAL OF SURVIVAL HORROR GAMES

MOST EXCLUSIVE SPECIAL EDITION

Holder: *Enemy Zero* **(WARP, 1996)**
Just 20 units of the Sega Saturn survival horror game *Enemy Zero Limited Edition* were produced. Coming in a small crate crammed full of *Enemy Zero* merchandise, including a leather costume and replica gun, each copy cost 200,000 yen (£1,000; $1,700) and was hand-delivered by the game's designer, Kenji Eno.

FIRST DOWNLOAD-ONLY SURVIVAL HORROR GAME

Holder: *AMY* **(Lexis Numerique, 2011)**
While *Siren: Blood Curse* (Japan Studio, 2008) was the **first survival horror made available via the PlayStation Network**, Sony also released the game at retail on a single Blu-Ray disc. By contrast, Lexis Numerique's latest title, *AMY*, was developed for download only. Created by a team headed by French game-designing maestro Paul Cuisset, it charges players with escorting an eight-year-old autistic girl named Amy through a city overrun with demonic creatures.

2D PLATFORMERS

FIRST SIMULTANEOUS FOUR-PLAYER MODE IN A 2D PLATFORMER

Holder: *'Splosion Man*
(Twisted Pixel Games, 2009)

On 22 July 2009, Xbox 360 title *'Splosion Man* became the first ever 2D platformer to feature a simultaneous four-player mode. Although not as successful as the better-known four-player *New Super Mario Bros. Wii* (Nintendo EAD, 2009), it beat Nintendo's game to the accolade by four months. *'Splosion Man*, part of the 2009 Xbox Live Summer of Arcade promotion, had sold 400,000 copies by January 2011, and was voted Best Original XBLA Game of 2009 by Xbox Live players. It also spawned a sequel, *Ms. Splosion Man*.

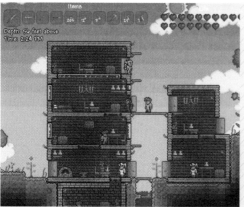

FASTEST-SELLING OPEN-WORLD 2D PLATFORMER

Holder: *Terraria* **(Re-Logic, 2011)**

Released on 16 May 2011, independent PC title *Terraria* sold 200,000 copies in its first week, making it the fastest-selling 2D open-world adventure game to date. Positioned as a 2D alternative to blockbuilder game *Minecraft* (Mojang, 2009), but with exploration elements akin to the *Metroid* series, *Terraria* sold 50,000 copies on its first day, with a peak of 17,000 users simultaneously online. The game outsold higher-profile titles such as *The Witcher 2: Assassins of Kings* (CD Projekt RED, 2011) and *Portal 2* (Valve Corporation, 2011) to top the chart on download service Steam during its launch week. *Terraria* also achieved an impressive Metacritic average of 83%.

MOST IN-HOUSE LEVELS IN A 2D PLATFORMER

Holder: *Super Meat Boy* **(Team Meat, 2010)**

Featuring 307 different stages, *Super Meat Boy* boasts the most levels of any 2D platformer. While *LittleBigPlanet* (Media Molecule, 2008) has more user-created levels, those included in *Super Meat Boy* were all created by developer Team Meat. The game, based on 2008 Flash title *Meat Boy*, was originally released for the Xbox Live

$7.5 million The revenue (equivalent to £4.8 million) brought in by *Limbo* (Playdead, 2010), making it the highest-grossing Xbox Live Arcade title in 2010.

SUPER 2D

Does *New Super Mario Bros. Wii* prove that 2D is better than 3D when it comes to platformers? Whatever your preference, it is comfortably the biggest-selling platformer of its generation, having outsold both *Super Mario Galaxy* titles put together. With sales of 22 million copies and counting, it's the third biggest-seller of all time in its genre, beaten only by *New Super Mario Bros.* (Nintendo EAD, 2006) on the DS and the original *Super Mario Bros.* (Nintendo, 1985) on the NES. The 2D vs 3D debate goes on...

FIRST USE OF COMPUTER-CONTROLLED "HELP" FEATURE

Holder: *New Super Mario Bros. Wii* **(Nintendo, 2009)** *New Super Mario Bros. Wii* offers a computer-controlled "help" feature called the Super Guide, whereby the player is guided to complete a level they are struggling with. The system is the brainchild of Mario creator Shigeru Miyamoto, and can be activated if a player dies eight times on a single level. In *New Super Mario Bros. Wii*, a green block appears, with a computer-controlled version of Mario's brother Luigi automatically completing tricky parts of the level. The player is free to jump in and take over whenever they want. *New Super Mario Bros. Wii* has been a huge success for Nintendo, with its record sales matched by an excellent Metacritic average of 87%.

allowing users to connect to the LBP.me website to find new community levels, which they can queue up to play the next time they connect their console to the PlayStation Network. The website also allows users to check level statistics, and even generate QR codes for their self-created levels. The codes send the player directly to the level in question when scanned with the PlayStation Eye camera, also a first for a videogame.

HIGHEST-RATED 2D PLATFORMER ON XBOX LIVE INDIE GAMES
Holder: *The Impossible Game* **(FlukeDude, 2009)**
As of 18 July 2011, *The Impossible Game* has a four-star-plus average from a total of 15,761 ratings, making it the highest-rated 2D platformer on Xbox Live Indie Games. It is also the best-selling platformer on the service. The game's creator, Edward Bentley, confirmed that the game had been purchased 39,000 times in its first six weeks, with an impressive purchase/trial ratio of 29%.

> ## "I knew that it was going to sell like hot cakes... I'm kidding!"
SHIGERU MIYAMOTO ON *SUPER MARIO BROS.*, STILL THE BIGGEST-SELLING PLATFORMER EVER

Arcade platform, but has since been ported to the PC and Mac. As well as the existing levels, *Super Meat Boy* features additional user-generated content under the moniker "Teh Internets".

FIRST GAME TO FEATURE A BROWSER-BASED LEVEL SEARCH
Holder: *LittleBigPlanet 2* **(Media Molecule, 2011)**
Puzzle platformer *LBP 2* led the way for browser-based level searches,

TOP 10 MOST "HEARTED" *LITTLEBIGPLANET* LEVELS

RANK	LEVEL	HEARTS
1	Little Dead Space	214,445
2	Bora Bora Island Water Sports	151,163
3	LittleBIG Ninja Warrior	127,905
4	SPEED ROLLER COASTER	124,172
5	Distress in Ocean	119,721
6	The Bunker	109,601
7	Super Sack Bro Rescue Mission: Pink Princess NOBODY's L4	104,435
8	Motorstorm	96,261
9	The World's Fastest Sackboy!	93,263
10	TITANIC The Ship of Dreams	85,637

Source: LBP.me

3D PLATFORMERS

AMONG ITS CAST, *EPIC MICKEY* FEATURES OSWALD THE LUCKY RABBIT,

LARGEST DEVELOPMENT TEAM FOR A 3D PLATFORMER

Holder: *Epic Mickey* (Junction Point Studios, 2010)

A bold game that justifies its title for its scope alone, *Epic Mickey* returns the iconic mouse to his earliest mischievous roots at Disney. Designed by *Deus Ex* (Ion Storm Inc., 2000) creator Warren Spector and a crew of around 700 staff at Texas-based firm Junction Point Studios, *Epic Mickey* was originally planned for release on Xbox 360 and PlayStation 3, but the versions for these formats were eventually abandoned, with the team shifting their focus to developing the title as a Wii exclusive.

FIRST STEREOSCOPIC 3D PLATFORM GAME

Holder: *The Sly Collection* (Sanzaru Games)

Usually, the "3D" in "3D platformers" refers to the perspective from which players view the action, but *The Sly Collection* uses stereoscopy (the method used to create the illusion of depth in 3D movies) to bring extra depth to the concept. As its title suggests, *The Sly Collection* is a compilation of three titles from the *Sly Cooper* series, each originally released on the PS2, with added HD stereoscopy to provide the appearance of depth. Released in November 2010, it predates *Rayman 3D* (Ubisoft, 2011) on the 3DS by four months, making it the first platform game with full 3D functionality.

MOST PIRATED 3D PLATFORMER

Holder: *Super Mario Galaxy 2* (Nintendo, 2010)

According to downloading news site Torrentfreak.com, which collates data annually from all public BitTorrent trackers, *Super Mario Galaxy 2* was downloaded over 1.4 million times from its release on 23 May 2010 to the end of December the same year. This beat the 1.1 million times *New Super Mario Bros. Wii* (Nintendo, 2009) was downloaded.

1.3 million The impressive first-month sales for *Epic Mickey* in the USA. This success was not reflected in the game's sales in Europe and Asia.

A CHARACTER WHO HAD NOT APPEARED IN A DISNEY CARTOON SINCE 1928! ▶

TOP 10 BEST-SELLING 3D PLATFORMERS

RANK	GAME	SALES IN MILLIONS
1	Super Mario 64	11.89
2	Super Mario Galaxy	9.46
3	Super Mario 64 DS	9.15
4	Crash Bandicoot 2: Cortex Strikes Back	7.57
5	Crash Bandicoot 3: Warped	7.12
6	Crash Bandicoot	6.80
7	Super Mario Galaxy 2	6.43
8	Super Mario Sunshine	6.28
9	Donkey Kong 64	5.27
10	Crash Bandicoot: The Wrath of Cortex	4.97

Source: VGChartz.com

BEST-SELLING THIRD-PARTY Wii PLATFORMER
Holder: *Sonic and the Secret Rings* **(Sonic Team, 2010)**
By June 2011, *Sonic and the Secret Rings* had sold an amazing 2.43 million copies worldwide. A Wii-exclusive published by Sega, who exited the console-building business after the poor performance of the Sega Dreamcast (launched in late 1998 and discontinued in early 2001), *Sonic and the Secret Rings* added experience points and increasing abilities to Sonic's standard ring-gathering gameplay. The title also has the best sales for a modern single-format Sonic title, although *Sonic Unleashed* (Sonic Team, 2009) hit sales of 3.96 million copies across multiple platforms.

FIRST ONLINE FOUR-PLAYER MODE IN A 3D PLATFORMER
Holder: *Ratchet & Clank: All 4 One* **(Insomniac, 2011)**
When it comes to online play, *Ratchet & Clank: All 4 One* is the first to bring it. The game enables "drop-in and drop-out" casual online co-operative play as well as local multiplayer play, with Ratchet and Clank joined by Captain Qwark and the series' antagonist Doctor Nefarious as playable characters.

"**I want to see people going out there and saying, 'I want to be Mickey Mouse'.**" JUNCTION POINT STUDIOS' WARREN SPECTOR

FIRST SPLITSCREEN FOUR-PLAYER MODE IN A 3D PLATFORMER
Holder: *Donkey Kong 64* **(Rare, 1999)**
Released for the N64 in 1999, *Donkey Kong 64* brought platform gamers together for shared gaming in a four-player mode. Made by British developer Rare, the 3D platformer was the first title to require the N64's "Expansion Pak", which offered additional RAM for better graphics and larger playing environments.

FIRST EPISODIC 3D PLATFORM SERIES
Holder: *Ratchet & Clank Future: Quest for Booty* **(Insomniac Games, 2008)**
Following the 2007 retail release of *Ratchet & Clank Future: Tools for Destruction*, Insomniac Games opted for an episodic digital launch for the spin-off story, *Ratchet & Clank Future: Quest for Booty*. The game sees the eponymous heroes hunting for a pirate who might help Ratchet recover Clank from the mysterious energy beings, the Zoni. The four-hour adventure was well-received, but for the 2009 follow-up game, *Ratchet & Clank: A Crack in Time*, Insomniac reverted to a standard retail release.

GRAPHIC ADVENTURE

THE GRAPHIC ADVENTURE STAR NAMED STRONG BAD BEGAN LIFE AS A CHARACTER

MOST EXPENSIVE DEVELOPMENT FOR A GRAPHIC ADVENTURE

Holder: *L.A. Noire*
(Team Bondi, 2011)
With over 200 employees at Sydney-based developer Team Bondi having worked on the game, the budget on the police procedural game *L.A. Noire* is estimated at over $50 million (£31 million). The game was originally funded by Sony and intended to be a PS3 platform exclusive, but delays and spiralling development costs led to the developer partnering with Take-Two Interactive and Rockstar Games to release *L.A. Noire* on PS3, Xbox 360 and PC.

MOST CAMERAS USED TO CAPTURE FACIAL ANIMATION FOR A VIDEOGAME

Holder: MotionScan (Australia)
The MotionScan equipment used by Team Bondi in *L.A. Noire* required a rig of 32 HD cameras to capture the facial expressions of the game's various actors. These expressions are key to the most important facet of *L.A. Noire*'s gameplay, with players tasked with trying to gauge whether or not suspects and witnesses are telling the truth. The motion-capture recording was a time-consuming process; actor Aaron Staton, who plays lead character detective Cole Phelps, spent over 80 hours in MotionScan filming.

/// "CAPTURES ALL THE INTENSITY, EMOTION AND EXCITEMENT OF A REAL-LIFE TENNIS MATCH" ///

26 million The total number of cases solved by *L.A. Noire* (Team Bondi, 2011) players around the world in the game's first six weeks of release.

IN THE *HOMESTAR RUNNER* WEB ANIMATIONS ▶

TOP 10 GRAPHIC ADVENTURES RATED ON STEAM

RANK	GAME	RATING
1	*The Longest Journey*	91%
2	*Monkey Island 2: LeChuck's Revenge Special Edition*	87%
3	*The Secret of Monkey Island Special Edition*	86%
4=	*Machinarium*	85%
4=	*Nancy Drew: The Haunted Carousel*	85%
6	*Time Gentlemen, Please! & Ben There, Dan That!* (Double Pack)	84%
7	*Riven: The Sequel to MYST*	83%
8=	*Broken Sword 3: The Sleeping Dragon*	82%
8=	*Syberia*	82%
8=	*Strong Bad's Cool Game for Attractive People* (Season 1)	82%

Source: Steam

NEVER-ENDING NOIRE

At over 2,200 printed pages, the script for *L.A. Noire* (Team Bondi, 2011) is the longest written for a graphic adventure, beating *Heavy Rain* (Quantic Dream, 2010) by more than 200 pages. The game features 200 characters and multiple missions, with additional dialogue options to cover all playable narrative possibilities, plus incidental speech that crops up repeatedly throughout the adventure. The script, which is close to 20 times longer than the average film script, was written by Team Bondi founder Brendan McNamara, who also scripted the more contemporary crime drama game *The Getaway* (Team Soho, 2002).

MOST PROLIFIC GRAPHIC ADVENTURE PUBLISHER

Holder: **Telltale Games (USA)**
Telltale Games has proved itself to be the most prolific publisher of graphic adventure titles, and is responsible for creating a total of 16 games between September 2005 and June 2011. The most successful of these are the episodic *Sam & Max* series and *Strong Bad's Cool Game for Attractive People* (2008). The company was started by a small group of ex-employees from LucasArts, the hugely influential developer that pioneered the graphic adventure form, and their latest series – *Back to the Future: The Game* (2010, right) – is another popular film tie-in.

LARGEST VOICE CAST IN A VIDEOGAME

Holder: *L.A. Noire* **(Team Bondi, 2011)**
L.A. Noire wasn't just labour-intensive in terms of its script and motion-captured visuals; the game also featured 364 credited actors in its voice cast. Among the recognizable voices (and faces) are John Noble, best known as Walter in sci-fi series *Fringe*, and Greg Grunberg, better known as police officer Matt Parkman from *Heroes*.

FIRST GRAPHIC ADVENTURE TO SUPPORT THE PLAYSTATION MOVE CONTROLLER

Holder: *Heavy Rain* **(Quantic Dream, 2010)**
Billed by Sony senior vice president Michael Denny as an "interactive drama", *Heavy Rain* places players in the middle of a hunt to stop the "origami killer". The game was originally designed to be played through a standard Sixaxis controller and used on-screen prompts informing players how to use the device to progress through the narrative. Soon after the September 2010 release of Sony's motion-sensing Move controller, a patch was released for the game to enable gamers to play it using the Move.

FIRST BLIND-FRIENDLY GRAPHIC ADVENTURE

Holder: *Real Sound: Kaze no Regret* **(WARP, Inc., 1997)**
Originally created for the Sega Saturn, *Real Sound: Kaze no Regret* is an unusual graphic adventure in that it was created by game designer Kenji Eno to be playable by the visually impaired. Players were required to listen to a story, and a chime sound to indicate when narrative-altering decisions could be made. In exchange for exclusive rights to the game, Sega offered to donate 1,000 Sega Saturns to blind people.

Real Sound was remade for the Dreamcast in 1999 with a "Visual Mode" that displayed still photos as the story unfolded.

"Getting the likenesses was our first really important step..."

TELLTALE GAMES' DENNIS LENART ON THE LOOK OF THE NEW *BACK TO THE FUTURE* GAME

FIGHTING GAMES

FIGHTING IN THE STREETS!

In a one-off double-header event for *Gamer's 2012*, we brought together two very different pro *Street Fighter* players, each with their own records. On the left, dressed as Ryu, we have Ryan Hart (UK). Winning over 450 *Street Fighter* events in 13 different countries from 1998 to 2011, Ryan claims the record for the **most international *Street Fighter* competition wins**.

On the right, dressed as Chun-Li, we have Marie-Laure Norindr (France). With an incredible 42 top-three finishes in competitions over her playing career from 2001 to 2011, Marie-Laure holds the record for the **most podium placements in a fighting game (female)**.

OVERVIEW

Whether you're fighting to save the world, get the girl or just to win a shiny trophy, there's one thing you have to come to terms with – simple punches and kicks will only get you so far in fighting games. To take down a pro and really kick butt, you need to learn how to invoke each character's "special moves" and "combos".

BIOGRAPHY

Dan Bendon has been throwing dragon punches since the days of the Super Nintendo and currently owns more arcade sticks than pairs of shoes. As founder of ready-up.net, Dan has hosted various fighting game tournaments and launch events in the UK, but even *he* would think twice before getting into the ring for real.

GUINNESS WORLD RECORDS

CONTENTS

CRITICAL HIT!:
  CAPCOM CROSSOVERS   **114**
2D FIGHTERS   **116**
3D FIGHTERS   **118**
BEAT-'EM-UPS   **120**
COMBAT SPORTS   **122**

CHINESE RESTAURANT

CAPCOM CROSSOVERS

CAPCOM'S FIRST PRODUCT WAS 1983'S PINBALL-LIKE COIN-OPERATED

WANNA FIGHT?

Combat crossovers pitch fighters from various different publishers against each other. Although Capcom didn't invent the genre, they now dominate it, which is why this celebration of their games is one of our Critical Hits!

MOST CRITICALLY ACCLAIMED CROSSOVER FIGHTING GAME

Holder: *Marvel vs. Capcom 2* **(Capcom, 2000)**

A true classic of the genre, *Marvel vs. Capcom 2* received a score of 90% for its Dreamcast version on the reviews site Metacritic. Even its 2009 ports for Xbox Live Arcade and the PlayStation Network scored high, with 82% and 85% respectively – not bad for a game that was, by then, nine years old! Shown here is the follow-up game, *Marvel vs. Capcom 3: Fate of Two Worlds*.

THE **DATA EAST** ARCADE HIT!
KARNOV

Commodore 64 "128"
5¼" DISKS
Joysticks Required

DATA EAST

Moby

FIRST VIDEOGAME "GUEST STAR"

Holder: Karnov

Although derivative of its genre, *Fighter's History* (Data East, 1993) boasted one key innovation – in its final bout, the player faced off against Karnov, the protagonist from Data East's 1987 platform title of the same name (pictured left), thus making Karnov the first guest star in any videogame. Capcom was so unimpressed by similarities between *Fighter's History* and its own smash-hit *Street Fighter* that it took legal action against Data East. Ironically, Capcom now produces many combat crossovers filled with guest stars.

MOST CONSECUTIVE ONLINE WINS ON *MARVEL vs. CAPCOM 3*

Holder: Zidane_shinigami (USA)

Playing on the PS3 version of *Marvel vs. Capcom 3* (Capcom, 2011), American PSN user Zidane_shinigami tore his way through 1,003 consecutive opponents without losing a match, placing him firmly at the top of the PSN leaderboard. This feat easily beats the 308 consecutive wins of the highest-ranking player on the Xbox 360 version.

FIRST FIGHTING GAME TO FEATURE AN "EASY OPERATION" MODE

Holder: *Capcom vs. SNK 2* (Capcom, 2001)

The GameCube version of *Capcom vs. SNK 2* introduced a mode that allowed players to execute complex special moves by pressing a single button and a direction on the C-Stick instead of a lot of buttons. Although some gamers thought this made the game too easy, the mode is now a common feature in many crossover titles.

27 The number of different manga series whose characters feature in crossover fighting title *Jump Ultimate Stars* (Ganbarion, 2006).

CRITICAL HIT!

LITTLE LEAGUE, BUT ITS FIRST ARCADE GAME WAS *VULGUS* (1984)

MOST REUSED CHARACTER SPRITE IN A FIGHTING GAME

Holder: Morrigan Aensland
Making her debut in the horror-themed *Darkstalkers* (Capcom, 1994), the sprite for Capcom's sultry succubus Morrigan was used in 10 different brawling titles before being retired after seven years with *Capcom vs. SNK 2* (Capcom, 2001). By this time, she clashed somewhat with the updated look of the other characters, so Morrigan received a much-deserved makeover (pictured) for *Tatsunoko vs. Capcom* (Capcom, 2008) on the Wii.

TOP 10 REQUESTED MARVEL COMICS CHARACTERS FOR *MARVEL VS. CAPCOM 3*

RANK	CHARACTER	VOTES
1	Venom	2,243
2	Gambit	2,010
3	Carnage	1,444
4	Ghost Rider	1,380
5	Ms. Marvel	1,230
6	Psylocke	1,225
7	Cyclops	1,067
8	Dr. Strange	1,056
9	Nightcrawler	1,038
10	Squirrel Girl	895

Source: Capcom website poll

ALL MIXED UP

Crossover fighting game *Fighters Megamix* (Sega, 1996) features some pretty odd unlockable characters (available only when players have completed certain in-game tasks). Aside from its main cast, predominantly from *Virtua Fighter*, the unlockables included a palm tree inspired by the developer's logo, Bark the Polar Bear and Hornet, a stock car from the *Daytona USA* racing series.

MOST EVOLUTION CHAMPIONSHIP SERIES TITLES HELD ON A SINGLE GAME

Holder: Justin Wong (USA)
In his competitive fighting game career, Justin Wong has won the *Marvel vs. Capcom 2* (Capcom, 2000) event at the Evolution Championship Series (EVO) five times, in 2003, 2004, 2006, 2008 and 2010. Japanese fighting legend Daigo Umehara has won a total of six solo EVO titles, but they are across a variety of different games.

OLDEST CHARACTER IN A FIGHTING GAME

Holder: Superman
Although not a Capcom title, an honorary mention must go to *Mortal Kombat vs DC Universe* (Midway Games, 2008). Inspired by Capcom's combat crossovers with Marvel, Midway, the developer behind *Mortal Kombat*, agreed a deal with Marvel's rivals, DC Comics, to release *Mortal Kombat vs DC Universe* in 2008. The game boasted a colourful cast that included Superman, who, having debuted 70 years earlier in *Action Comics* No.1 from 1938, is the earliest character in such a fighting game. The title was not enough to save Midway from bankruptcy, and Time Warner – DC Comics' parent company – has since bought many of Midway's assets.

2D FIGHTERS

STARTED IN 2002, THE EVOLUTION CHAMPIONSHIP SERIES (EVO) IS ONE OF THE

LONGEST ONLINE WINNING STREAK IN *MORTAL KOMBAT*

Holder: Futant462 (USA)

Xbox Live user Futant462 lacerated, decapitated and eviscerated his way through an impressive 378 online matches without a single loss on *Mortal Kombat* (NetherRealm Studios, 2011), the latest release in the violent 2D fighting series. Futant462 tops the in-game leaderboard for the Xbox 360 version, and his score also beats the highest-ranking player on the PS3 game.

MOST ANIMATION FRAMES IN A 2D FIGHTER

Holder: *Street Fighter III: 3rd Strike* (Capcom, 1999)

In 2D fighters, the game's graphics usually come in two parts: luscious backgrounds and sprites (all the moving characters). These sprites all need to be animated frame-by-frame. With a total of 23,039 in-game character animation frames, *Street Fighter III: 3rd Strike* has the most detailed animation of all 2D fighters, even a decade on from its initial release.

MOST EVOLUTION CHAMPIONSHIP SERIES TITLES HELD

Holder: Daigo "The Beast" Umehara (Japan)

Daigo Umehara has won a total of six "EVO" titles; for *Super Street Fighter II Turbo* (Capcom, 1994) in 2003 and 2009, *Guilty Gear XX* (Arc System Words, 2002) in 2003 and 2004, *Guilty Gear X2* (Arc System Words, 2002) in 2009 and *Super Street Fighter IV* (Capcom, 2010) in 2010. Perhaps surprisingly, Daigo's day job is as a nurse for the elderly.

WORLD'S MOST PRESTIGIOUS FIGHTING GAME TOURNAMENTS ▶

BEST-SELLING FIGHTING GAME

Holder: *Super Smash Bros. Brawl* **(Game Arts, 2008)**
Super Smash Bros. Brawl had sold 10,381,960 copies worldwide as of July 2011, overtaking its GameCube predecessor *Super Smash Bros. Melee* (HAL Labs, 2001) as the best-selling fighting game of all time. The game unites heroes and villains from throughout the Nintendo universe, as well as some special guests – including Sonic the Hedgehog and Metal Gear's Snake.

TOP 10 BEST-SELLING VIDEOGAMES ON THE NEO GEO CONSOLE

SALES	GAME
250,000	Samurai Shodown II
230,000	The King of Fighters '95 (CD)
200,000	The King of Fighters '95
200,000	Samurai Spirits (CD)
140,000	The King of Fighters '94 (CD)
120,000	The King of Fighters '94
80,000	Samurai Shodown III
70,000	Samurai Shodown
60,000	The King of Fighters '96
40,000	Art of Fighting 3: The Path of the Warrior

Source: VGChartz.com

PRINCE'S RAIN

RAIN WINS

Mortal Kombat's ninja, Rain, wears a purple costume and is said to be the "Prince of Edenia". These are all references to the 1984 song "Purple Rain" by the pop star Prince. He was made a playable character in the retail release of *Ultimate Mortal Kombat 3* (Midway, 1995).

HIGHEST SCORE IN *SUPER STREET FIGHTER IV* ARCADE MODE

Holder: Rob "desk" Seymour **(UK)**
On 5 December 2010, Rob Seymour racked up 2,587,000 points on the PlayStation 3 version of *Super Street Fighter IV* (Capcom, 2010), more than doubling the previous record. He used high-scoring combos to pile on the points and deliberately lost one round per fight to allow the maximum scoring opportunities across all three rounds in a bout.

FIRST 2D FIGHTER FOR A HANDHELD

Holder: *Fist of the North Star* **(Shouei Systems, 1989)**
Just eight months after the original Game Boy was first released in Japan, the revolutionary handheld saw its first 2D fighting game in the form of *Fist of the North Star*. Based upon the popular manga and anime series of the same name, the game featured an impressive 11 playable characters, each of whom could perform high, low and special attacks.

LONGEST FIGHTING-GAME MARATHON

Our very own Gaming Editor Gaz Deaves (centre) was on hand to certify that Melissa Estuesta, Cristopher Bryant, Paul Chillino and J Lance Moose (left to right, all USA) each played *Mortal Kombat* (NetherRealm Studios, 2011) on the PS3 for 32 hr 5 min 47 sec at the Electronic Entertainment Expo (E3) in Los Angeles, USA, on 7–8 June 2011.

3D FIGHTERS

FIRST RETAIL GAME TO INCLUDE "ZERO POINT" ACHIEVEMENTS

Holder: *Dead or Alive 4* **(Team Ninja, 2005)**

Most in-game "achievements" in Xbox 360 games add points to the player's "gamerscore". *Dead or Alive 4*, however, contains four achievements that add nothing to this score. Players gain these dubious achievements by losing five, 10 or 20 matches in a row, or for dropping below a "C" rank in online combat matches.

BEST-SELLING SEGA SATURN GAME

Holder: *Virtua Fighter 2* **(Sega, 1995)**

Sega's home console conversion of its own arcade classic *Virtua Fighter 2* made use of the Saturn's dual CPUs and memory expansion modules to give a fantastic fighting experience. This helped the game become the platform's most popular title, and it sold 1,929,807 units worldwide – about a fifth of the total sales of the Saturn itself.

FIRST PAID-FOR DOWNLOADABLE CHARACTERS IN A FIGHTING GAME

Holder: *SoulCalibur IV* **(Namco, 2008)**

When *SoulCalibur IV* was first released, guest characters Yoda and Darth Vader from *Star Wars* were exclusive to the Xbox 360 and PlayStation 3 versions respectively. Three months later, the same two characters were offered as paid-for downloads on whichever system they had not already been offered on for free.

1,634,936 The total sales of *Dead or Alive 3* (Team Ninja, 2001). Exclusive to the Xbox and a launch title for the console, it was the first game in the series not to be released on an arcade.

MOST CRITICALLY ACCLAIMED 3D FIGHTER

Holder: *SoulCalibur* (Namco, 1999)

With a score of 98% on reviews site Metacritic, gamers and reviews alike rank *SoulCalibur* as the best of the best – not just in relation to 3D fighters, but also in terms of games available for Sega's Dreamcast. The sequel to *SoulEdge*, *SoulCalibur*'s key innovation was "eight-way run", which allowed players to move in eight different directions, whereas previous games in the genre had a more limited field of movement.

MOST DOWNLOADED 3D FIGHTER TRAILERS

DOWNLOADS	GAME
12,997,717	Tekken 6
8,813,731	SoulCalibur IV
4,777,287	Naruto: Ultimate Ninja Storm
3,849,056	Dissidia: Final Fantasy
2,669,375	Virtua Fighter 5
2,343,799	Naruto Shippuden: Ultimate Ninja Storm
2,093,359	Def Jam: Icon
1,072,435	Mortal Kombat: Armageddon
960,838	Naruto: Ultimate Ninja Heroes
932,374	Bleach: Shattered Blade

Source: Game Trailers.com   Accurate at 25 July 2011

VAMPIRE BACKFIRE?

Never released outside of Japanese arcades, *Fighting Layer* (Arika, 1998) is a game that needs to be seen to be believed. At first glance it might appear to be a below-average 3D fighter, but it offers some bafflingly unusual opponents, such as a shark!

The game's final battle pits the player against a vampire/werewolf hybrid that can swap places with the player's character, firing any attacks the player had prepared right back at them.

FIRST 3D FIGHTING GAME PLAYABLE IN FIRST-PERSON MODE

Holder: *Tekken 2* (Namco, 1996)

Many games have "Easter eggs" – hidden features that are like gifts from the game's designers. *Tekken 2* contains an Easter egg that allows gamers to play the game from a first-person perspective by holding down the L1 and L2 buttons while selecting their character. For this trick to work, however, players must first unlock all of the playable characters on the game's roster.

FASTEST-SELLING 3D FIGHTING GAME

Holder: *Tekken 3* (Namco, 1997)

With worldwide sales of 1.175 million units in its first week of release, *Tekken 3* outclasses all of its opponents in terms of speedy sales. The game went on to shift 6.91 million copies, also making it the **best-selling 3D fighting game** across all platforms.

FASTEST *TEKKEN 6* "TIME ATTACK"

Holder: gekkanokihaku (Japan)

In "Time Attack" mode on *Tekken 6* (Namco Bandai, 2009), players must win nine standard two-round matches on the game's default settings and defeat the demonic "Big Boss" Azazel in the fastest possible time. The Japanese PlayStation Network user gekkanokihaku holds the record for this feat, having blitzed his way through in just 1 min 45.95 sec, playing as the giant bear Kuma (right).

BEAT-'EM-UPS

SCOTT PILGRIM vs. THE WORLD: THE GAME (UBISOFT, 2010) FEATURES

BEST-SELLING BEAT-'EM-UP ON PLAYSTATION 3

Holder: *God of War 3*
(Santa Monica Studios, 2010)
With 3,942,100 copies sold worldwide as of 20 July 2011, the critically acclaimed *God of War 3* is not only the best-selling game of its genre on the PlayStation 3, but also the biggest seller in the *God of War* series. Since Kratos first slashed his way on to the PlayStation 2 in 2005, the total sales figure for the entire series across all platforms is just under 17 million units.

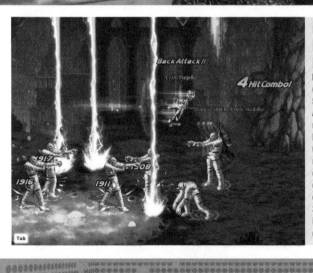

MOST CONCURRENT PLAYERS IN AN MMO BEAT-'EM-UP

Holder: *Dungeon Fighter Online*
(NeoPle, 2005)
Side-scrolling MMO beat-'em-up *Dungeon Fighter Online* has more than 300 million registered users worldwide. The PC game became a massive success throughout China, Taiwan, Japan and South Korea, reaching a record peak of 2.4 million concurrent players. Publisher Nexon organized a *Dungeon Fighter Online* celebration video when the game reached 300 million users, before launching the title in North America in 2010. An anime version of the game aired on Japanese TV in 2009.

FIRST BEAT-'EM-UP CHARACTER IN A 2D FIGHTING GAME
Holder: Guy – *Final Fight* **(Capcom, 1989)**
Guy, the hero of *Final Fight*, was the first playable character to make the genre transition from beat-'em-up to 2D fighting in *Street Fighter Alpha* (Capcom, 1995). He was later joined by his jailbird partner Cody in *Street Fighter Alpha 3* (Capcom, 1998), and both characters appear in *Super Street Fighter IV* (Capcom, 2010). Several *Final Fight* enemies have also featured.

/// "UNCOVER SECRET TRUTHS HIDDEN WITHIN A GRIPPING TALE OF INTRIGUE, BETRAYAL, HERESY, LOVE AND HEROISM" ///

6,524,612 The total number of princesses logged online as having been saved by the heroic quartet of knights in the first two years of *Castle Crashers* (The Behemoth, 2008).

REFERENCES TO *STREET FIGHTER, SUPER MARIO BROS.* AND *PAC-MAN* ▶

HACK AND SLASH OR BEAT-'EM-UP?

Hack and slash titles and beat-'em-ups share a common purpose: they are both combat genres in which players must beat their opponents into submission. But hack and slash games such as *Bayonetta* and *God of War* tend to be more gory than their beat-'em-up brothers.

HIGHEST SCORE ON *SCOTT PILGRIM* vs. *THE WORLD: THE GAME*

Holder: hungryman88 (Canada)

Fighting his way through Ramona's seven evil exes, PS3 user hungryman88 racked up a top score of 196,583.51 on the PlayStation 3 version of *Scott Pilgrim vs. The World: The Game*, putting him at the top of the PlayStation Network leaderboard. Along the way he knocked out 12,081 enemies, considerably fewer than the second-placed user, proving that you need to fight smart, not just hard, to win the heart of the one you love.

BEST-SELLING XBOX LIVE ARCADE GAME

Holder: *Castle Crashers* (The Behemoth, 2008)

This mystical, medieval beat-'em-up previously held the record for best-selling Xbox Live Arcade (XBLA) title in its year of launch. As of September 2011, *Castle Crashers* is at the top of Microsoft's chart of all-time best-selling XBLA games, ahead of

Family Game Night. At least 2 million XBLA players each paid to download the game, which was released for the PS3 in 2010.

TEN GODLY POSSESSIONS IN *GOD OF WAR 3*

POSSESSION	FUNCTION
Zeus' Eagle	Grants infinite "Rage"
Hades' Helm	Maxes out "Health", "Magic" and "Item" bars
Helios' Shield	Increases combo timer
Hermes' Coin	Multiplies "Red Orbs"
Hercules' Shoulder Guard	Decreases damage by one third
Poseidon's Conch Shell	Grants infinite "Magic"
Aphrodite's Garter	Unlocks "Athena's Blades"
Hephaestus' Ring	Automatically completes "Quick Time Events"
Daedalus' Schematics	Grants infinite "Item" use
Hera's Chalice	Drains "Health" over time

HIGHEST XBOX 360 *FAMITSU* SCORE

Holder: *Bayonetta* (PlatinumGames, 2009)

Known as the definitive source of review scores in Japan, weekly magazine *Famitsu* gave the Xbox 360 version of the action-packed *Bayonetta* (below right) a perfect 40/40 score. In the history of the magazine, *Famitsu* has only given 15 games a perfect score, and of those 15 *Bayonetta* is the first and only Xbox 360 game. The PlayStation 3 version of the game scored a slightly lower 38/40, due to some minor frame-rate issues. *Bayonetta* has sold 1.69 million copies on both formats worldwide.

> "I don't think film can ever replicate the unique thrill of gaming. Perhaps James Cameron will figure out a way we can all be in *Avatar* for real."
>
> **EDGAR WRIGHT, DIRECTOR OF THE FILM *SCOTT PILGRIM* vs. *THE WORLD***

THE WWF HAD TO BE RENAMED   THE WWE AFTER A COPYRIGHT

FIRST MMA GAME WITH FEMALE FIGHTERS

Holder: *Supremacy MMA*
(Kung Fu Factory, 2011)
Bringing the girls to the Mixed Martial Arts (MMA) party, *Supremacy MMA* features digital representations of real-life female MMA fighters Felice "Lil Bulldog" Herrig and Michele "Diablita" Gutierrez headlining the game's female roster opposite the male MMA superstars Jens Pulver and Shane Del Rosario (all USA).

MOST CRITICALLY ACCLAIMED COMBAT SPORTS GAME

Holder: *WWF SmackDown! 2: Know Your Role*
(Yuke's, 2000)
As they produce more games for a particular console, developers become more adept at getting the most out of it. Consequently, games released towards the end of a console's lifespan are often the most critically acclaimed. The last WWF game to be released on the original PlayStation, *WWF SmackDown! 2: Know Your Role* was just that, and garnered a score of 90% on reviews site Metacritic and a perfect score from the US *Official PlayStation Magazine*.

FIRST OFFICIALLY LICENCED UFC FIGHTING GAME
Holder: *Ultimate Fighting Championship*
(Anchor Inc., 2000)
Seven years after it was founded as a Mixed Martial Arts promotion company in 1993, the Ultimate Fighting Championship (UFC) saw the release of a self-titled game on the Dreamcast and PlayStation. THQ acquired the UFC licence in 2007 and brought in games developer Yuke's to successfully revive the series.

55 million The number of officially licenced World Wrestling Federation/Entertainment (WWF/E) games sold worldwide, as of July 2011.

DISPUTE WITH THE *OTHER* WWF – THE WORLD WIDE FUND FOR NATURE ▶

> "This is our chance to finally show gamers that female fighters can hold their own."

FELICE "LIL BULLDOG" HERRIG
ON *SUPREMACY MMA*

WHACKO JACKO

If you've ever wanted to see pop star Michael Jackson fight basketball legend Shaquille O'Neal or former US President Bill Clinton, then cartoon boxing game *Ready 2 Rumble Boxing: Round 2* (Point of View, 2000) is the one for you. Clearing the game's arcade mode 10 times unlocks all these and a host of other "secret" playable characters, giving gamers new reasons to keep on fighting.

MOST ONLINE WINS IN *FIGHT NIGHT CHAMPION*

Holder: mdkrafis (USA)
The Xbox Live user known as mdkrafis racked up 1,259 wins with his own fighter in the "Online World Championship" mode in *Fight Night Champion* (EA Canada, 2011), putting him at the top of the Xbox 360 leaderboard. An impressive 1,229 of those fights were won by knock-out, putting him at the top of the KO leaderboard as well.

FIRST OFFICIAL UFC FACEBOOK GAME

Holder: *UFC Undisputed Fight Nation* (Zuffa, 2011)
The first game to expand the UFC series into social network gaming, *UFC Undisputed Fight Nation* tasks players with managing the career of their fighter, placing importance not just on winning bouts, but also on earning "cred" as they fight. Players gain bonuses for the number of "friends" they have, and can gift each other energy-giving items such as a "Can of Whoopass".

FIRST FIGHTING GAME TO FEATURE "BONUS STAGES"
Holder: *Karate Champ* (Data East, 1984)
A commonplace component in 2D fighter games, bonus stages vary the gameplay players require to succeed in fighting games by focusing on a specific task, such as smashing a car, rather than pounding another opponent. *Karate Champ* was the first to bring in this innovation with challenges to dodge thrown objects, break wooden boards and face off against a charging bull on a beach!

HIGHEST SCORE ON *PUNCH-OUT!!* (ARCADE)
Holder: Sean Sandnes (Canada)
On 13 July 2010, Twin Galaxies verified DVD footage of Sean Sandnes scoring 18,999,970 points on the arcade cabinet version of *Punch-Out!!* (Nintendo, 1984). The series had one arcade sequel before becoming a home-console franchise.

FIRST WWE GAME WITH ONLINE MULTIPLAYER
Holder: *WWE SmackDown! vs. Raw* (Yuke's, 2004)
While somewhat limited in its functionality, *SmackDown! vs. Raw* used the PlayStation 2's Network Adaptor to allow players to compete online in "One-on-One" or "Bra and Panties" matches. The latter challenge had gamers playing the role of female wrestlers competing to be the first to strip their opponent down to their underwear!

TOP 10 BEST-SELLING COMBAT SPORTS GAMES

SALES IN MILLIONS	GAME
6.87	*WWE SmackDown! vs. Raw 2008*
4.83	*Fight Night Round 3*
4.69	*WWF War Zone*
4.54	*WWE SmackDown! vs. Raw 2010*
4.42	*WWE SmackDown! vs. Raw 2009*
3.69	*WWE SmackDown! vs. Raw 2007*
3.54	*UFC 2009 Undisputed*
3.47	*WWE SmackDown! vs. Raw 2006*
3.20	*WWF SmackDown! 2: Know Your Role*
3.11	*WWF SmackDown!*

Source: VGChartz.com

PUZZLE GAMES

MOST INTERNET MEMES IN A PUZZLE GAME

Holder: *Super Scribblenauts*
(5th Cell, 2010)

Super Scribblenauts is an action puzzler that allows players to interact with the game by writing or typing words to conjure up objects. Among the 30,000-plus entries understood in the vocabulary are 48 internet memes – well-known in-jokes that have spread via social networks, emailing and SMS – such as "ROLFcopter", "Ninja Shark", "Orly Owl", "Keyboard Cat" and even "your mom" (which conjures up a zombie!).

OVERVIEW

Few pleasures in gaming are more satisfying than cracking a well-designed puzzle. Sure, one can save galaxies, rescue princesses or become a champion of the realm, but very little beats that "a-ha!" rush that comes with saving the day (or at least the level) with good ol'-fashioned brain smarts.

These days, puzzles are ingrained in nearly every modern videogame; however, pure puzzle games are still popular in their own right. Provided you've got the skills – or the patience – playing around with puzzle games can be both enjoyable and rewarding.

BIOGRAPHY

Matthew Bradford is a freelance writer for websites, radio and magazines. He has been penning his thoughts about gaming since before there were things like "the internet" and "decent computers". Over the years, he has had the pleasure of working with websites such as GamesRadar.com and Canoe.ca, and serves as editorial director for Twin Galaxies International.

CONTENTS

CRITICAL HIT!: *ANGRY BIRDS*	126
BLOCK PUZZLES	128
SPATIAL PUZZLES	130
PHYSICS-BASED PUZZLES	132
LOGIC PUZZLES	134

ANGRY BIRDS

GAME DEVELOPERS MIKAEL AND NIKLAS HED DEVELOPED 51 GAMES BEFORE

"When you see one screenshot of the game you know what you have to do. *Angry Birds* is simple, but it still has depth."

MIKAEL HED, CEO OF ROVIO,
MAKERS OF *ANGRY BIRDS*

BEST-SELLING MOBILE SERIES

Holder: *Angry Birds* **(Rovio, 2009)**
On 18 May 2011, Rovio's Peter Vesterbacka announced that in all its different varieties, paid for and free, *Angry Birds* had reached a combined download total of 200 million games. In June 2011, the game surpassed the 250 million combined download mark, and with its regularly updated *Angry Birds Seasons* (Rovio, 2010), sales of the series show no signs of calming down any time soon.

MOST DAYS SPENT AS THE BEST-SELLING APP IN iTUNES STORE

Holder: *Angry Birds* **(Rovio, 2009)**
On 24 May 2011, *Angry Birds* ended its 275 consecutive-day run as the best-selling app in the US Apple App Store – the longest period any app had spent in the coveted top position in Apple's mobile phone gaming marketplace. The birds were finally flung from first place by the puzzle game *The Heist* (MacHeist, 2011), which sold more than 25,000 copies in its first day on sale.

MOST WATCHED *ANGRY BIRDS* **YOUTUBE VIDEO**
Holder: *Angry Birds* **Cinematic Trailer**
It's only fitting that a game that owes much of its success to social media and word-of-mouth promotion is also the subject of some of the most watched YouTube videos. The most popular *Angry Birds* clip on the online video-sharing site is the 1-min 31-sec *Angry Birds* Cinematic Trailer, which was posted on 3 February 2010 and had been viewed 32,864,235 times as of 13 July 2011.

200 million The number of minutes gamers spend playing *Angry Birds* each day, according to Rovio's Peter Vesterbacka.

GUINNESS WORLD RECORDS

THEY FINALLY STRUCK IT RICH WITH *ANGRY BIRDS* ▶

TEN *ANGRY BIRDS* MILESTONES

DATE	MILESTONE
9 Dec 2009	*Angry Birds* debuts in the App Store with "Poached Eggs", a set of levels referring to the birds' stolen eggs
Feb 2010	*Angry Birds'* first major update and levels pack "Mighty Hoax" is released
Apr 2010	Golden Egg special levels are added
22 Oct 2010	The problem-solving "Mighty Eagle" character debuts on *Angry Birds* for Nokia's Symbian smartphones
23 Nov 2010	*Angry Birds* hits 36 million downloads across all versions with 10 million in Apple's App Store alone
15 Mar 2011	*Angry Birds* hits 100 million downloads across all available versions
22 Mar 2011	*Angry Birds Rio* is released and garners a total of 10 million downloads in just 10 days
11 Apr 2011	*Angry Birds* wins "Best Game App" and "App of the Year" at the first ever Appy Awards, an event honouring mobile phone and tablet apps, held in London, UK
9 Jun 2011	Rovio announces the in-house development of an *Angry Birds* animated movie
15 Jun 2011	As *Angry Birds* hits 250 million downloads, Rovio announces plans for a game entitled *Angry Birds Magic*, a location-based addition to the series

HIGHSCORE 80540 SCORE 510

HIGHEST SCORE ON *ANGRY BIRDS RIO*

Holder: geauxtiger44wh

As of 30 June 2011, a gamer known only by his tag geauxtiger44wh held the highest score on *Angry Birds Rio*, with a tally of 2,938,700 points. Tied into the 2011 computer-animated movie of the same name, the game stars the blue bird Rio, who enlists the help of the Angry Birds to free a variety of caged exotic birds from various locations in and around Rio de Janeiro, Brazil.

MOST PEOPLE IN A MOBILE PHONE GAME RELAY

To help promote the launch of the Nokia N8, the mobile phone manufacturer Nokia staged a massive gaming relay at their "Angry Birds Playground" in Kuala Lumpur, Malaysia, on 11 June 2011. Passers-by were invited to participate by each playing a single level of *Angry Birds* on the Nokia handset. Over the course of 10 hours, a total of 2,030 players took turns at attempting a level of the game.

LARGEST GAME OF *ANGRY BIRDS*

To welcome Finnish viewers to his show, and in a reference to the Finnish nationality of *Angry Birds'* developer Rovio, the 3 March 2011 edition of the American talkshow hosted by Conan O'Brien featured a man-sized real-life version of *Angry Birds* in his studio set. The game was recreated by the show's production staff and featured obstacles made from furniture, while inflatable balls were used to represent the game's birds and pigs.

SICK AS A PIG

"What's the deal with the green pigs?" That's the question curious gamers have pondered as they flicked their birds at the swindling swine. When Rovio was developing *Angry Birds* in 2009, swine flu was making headlines in North America and beyond. Rovio's Ville Heijari claims they were intrigued by the idea of a literal "sick pig", and were inspired to colour the game's pigs green.

FIRST USE OF AN EMBEDDED IMAGE IN A SUPER BOWL AD

Holder: *Angry Birds* Super Bowl advert

Rovio and Fox Entertainment scored a Super Bowl first on 6 February 2011 when an advert for the animated feature film *Rio* (USA, 2011) aired during Super Bowl XLV. The trailer contained an image that indicated a level on the original *Angry Birds* on which *Rio*-themed *Angry Birds* content could be unlocked. Rovio and Fox teamed-up again to produce a special *Rio* version of *Angry Birds*. As Rovio's Chief Executive Mikael Hed (right) said in an interview, a deal that linked the two bird-related products was "a natural fit".

BLOCK PUZZLES

BEST KNOWN FOR HIS PLATFORM GAMES, PLUMP PLUMBER MARIO HAS ALSO

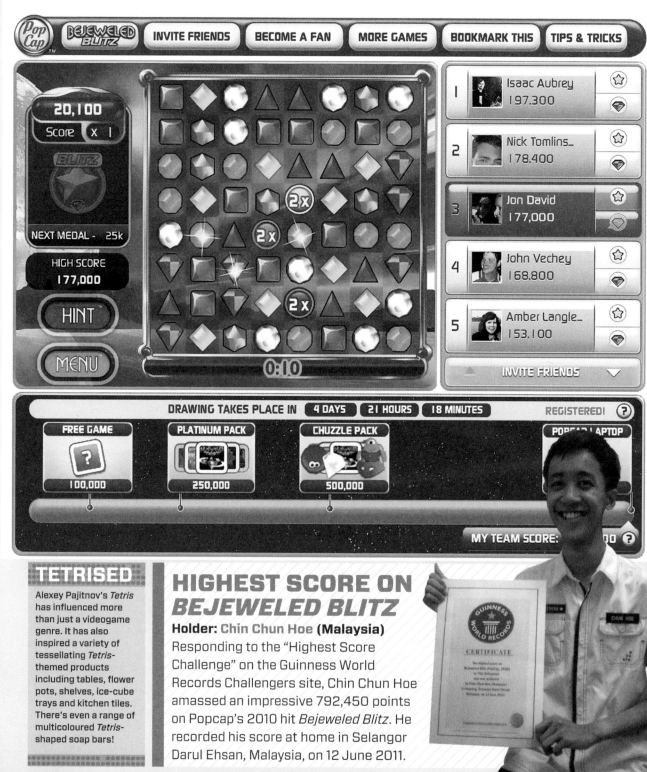

TETRISED

Alexey Pajitnov's *Tetris* has influenced more than just a videogame genre. It has also inspired a variety of tessellating *Tetris*-themed products including tables, flower pots, shelves, ice-cube trays and kitchen tiles. There's even a range of multicoloured *Tetris*-shaped soap bars!

HIGHEST SCORE ON *BEJEWELED BLITZ*

Holder: Chin Chun Hoe (Malaysia)
Responding to the "Highest Score Challenge" on the Guinness World Records Challengers site, Chin Chun Hoe amassed an impressive 792,450 points on Popcap's 2010 hit *Bejeweled Blitz*. He recorded his score at home in Selangor Darul Ehsan, Malaysia, on 12 June 2011.

$1,220 The price fetched on 5 May 2011 for a Nintendo Game Boy and *Tetris* game used in space by Russian cosmonaut Aleksandr Serebrov.

BEST-SELLING PSP PUZZLE GAME
Holder: *Lumines* **(Q Entertainment, 2004)**
Selling more than a million copies worldwide, *Lumines* is the PlayStation Portable's most financially successful puzzle game. Upon its release, *Lumines* earned accolades from critics and fans alike for infusing music and colour elements to the standard block puzzle formula. Tetsuya Mizuguchi – the creator of *Lumines* – has a long history of employing music as a game mechanic, starting with *Rez* (United Game Artists, 2001) and then continuing with *Every Extend Extra* (Q Entertainment, 2006) and his subsequent title, *Child of Eden* (Q Entertainment, 2011).

HIGHEST SCORE ON *ART STYLE: CUBELLO* (WiiWARE)
Holder: William Willemstyn III (USA)
A 3D colour-matching block game, *Cubello* (Skit Ltd, 2009) is one of the seven titles in the downloadable *Art Style* series. The aim of the game is to deconstruct a complex block structure (the cubello of the game's title) until only a single core block remains. Matching four or more coloured blocks causes the group to fall off the structure. Cutting swiftly to the core time and again, American William Willemstyn III scored 32,650 points on the game's "endless" mode on 28 December 2009.

MOST HIGH SCORES ON *CHIME*
Holder: Erica "Fang Aili" Henson (USA)
As of 30 June 2011, record-breaking gamer Erica Henson holds eight out of the 15 high scores on *Chime*'s (Zoë Mode, 2010) leaderboards.

> "The basic rule for gameplay is quick-simple. There is no intention to change the format or rules to the game."

TETSUYA MIZUGUCHI, DEVELOPER OF *LUMINES*, ON CONVERTING HIS PSP CLASSIC FOR PLAY ON THE XBOX LIVE ARCADE

TOP 10 *KLAX* RECORD SCORES BY PLATFORM

RANK	PLAYER	VERSION	SCORE
1	Todd Rogers (USA)	TurboGrafx-16	9,999,990
2	Dennis Gee (USA)	M.A.M.E [Set 1]	2,201,269
3	Tom Votava (USA)	NES	2,021,025
4	Roger Gray (USA)	Game Boy	1,978,420
5	Roger Gray (USA)	PS2 (Midway Arcade Treasures)	1,875,145
6	Roger Gray (USA)	Sega Mega Drive	1,333,735
7	Brian Mundo (USA)	Game Cube (Midway Arcade Treasures)	894,091
8	Kelly Flewin (Canada)	Game Boy Advance	871,380
9	Ryan Sullivan (USA)	PSP (Midway Arcade Treasures: Extended Play)	804,655
10	Ron Corcoran (USA)	Atari Lynx	533,330

Source: TwinGalaxies.com

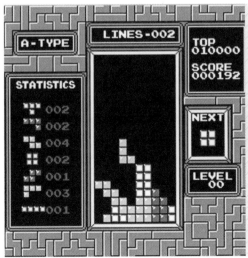

MOST LINES ON *TETRIS* (NES NINTENDO VERSION)
Holder: Ben Mullen (USA)
Stacking up an impressive 296 lines, Ben Mullen took the title for the most lines scored on the Nintendo version of *Tetris* on 22 July 2008. When it comes to the record on the NES platform overall, however, Ben has to get in line. Because of a dispute between Atari and Nintendo over who held the licence to adapt Alexey Pajitnov's *Tetris* for gaming platforms outside of Soviet Russia, there are two different versions of *Tetris* for the NES. Ultimately – and after several lawsuits – Nintendo prevailed, but not before Atari's home-console division Tengen had released their own version of the game.

The **most lines on the NES Tengen version of** *Tetris* – and on *Tetris* for the NES platform overall – is 1,502 lines, slotted together by Thor Aackerlund (USA) on 12 August 2010.

HIGHEST SCORE ON *DR. MARIO* (NES)
Holder: Will P Nichols (USA)
The objective of the *Tetris*-inspired *Dr. Mario* (Nintendo, 1990) is to destroy viruses inside a medicine bottle, and a great many viruses met their match in Jackson, Mississippi, USA, on 18 February 2011 when Will Nichols scored 2,922,600 points on the game's high-speed setting. Will is also listed on the Twin Galaxies scoreboard as having the highest score on *Dr. Mario*'s medium-speed setting, with a total of 2,010,400 points set on 12 March 2010.

KEITA TAKAHASHI, THE CREATOR OF *WE LOVE KATAMARI*, ALSO DESIGNED

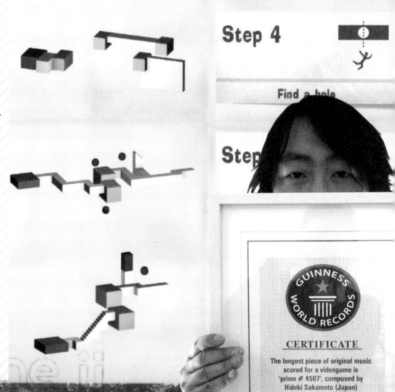

LONGEST VIDEOGAME SOUNDTRACK COMPOSITION

Holder: *echochrome ii*
(Sony, 2010)

Lasting 1 hr 15 min 7 sec, "prime # 4507", composed by Hideki Sakamoto (Japan, right) for spatial puzzler *echochrome ii*, is the longest original soundtrack for a videogame. Unlike most videogame scores, which are composed on a level-by-level basis or use pre-existing music, "prime # 4507" is one continuous arrangement that plays throughout the game, regardless of a player's progress. Sakamoto says he wanted "a piece of background music for a particular situation, i.e., while 'playing with puzzles', which would play continuously, just like how background music at formal events and parties is provided continuously".

HIGHEST LEVEL SCORE ON *MERCURY MELTDOWN REVOLUTION* (Wii)

Holder: Matt "packattack" Flees **(USA)**

A spiritual successor to all marble-rolling games, Ignition Entertainment's 2007 title tasks players with using the Wii's motion-sensing controller to coax a glob of mercury through an increasingly complex series of labyrinths. The highest score recorded for a single level on this mad maze game is 227,594 points in the VR Lab (World 10), on level 13, set by Matt Flees under his gamer tag of "packattack", on 2 August 2009.

HIGHEST LEVEL SCORE ON *MARBLE MADNESS* (NES VERSION)

Holder: Scott Kessler **(USA)**

On 15 August 2006, Scott Kessler skilfully teetered and tottered his way into the record books by achieving a score of 177,570 points on the NES version of *Marble Madness* (Rare, 1989) in Monroe, North Carolina, USA. As of July 2011, he sits in top place on the Twin Galaxies scoreboard, but his position is precarious – he is just 300 points ahead of his closest competitor, a fellow American named Travis Reisch.

/// "ALL HEARTS CAN BREAK, BUT NOT WITHOUT A FIGHT" ///

1,000,000 The number of roses required to construct the "Rose Nebula" bonus challenge in *We Love Katamari* (Namco, 2005).

A PLAYGROUND FOR NOTTINGHAM CITY COUNCIL IN THE UK ▶

TOP 10 FASTEST TOTAL COMPLETIONS OF *BRAID* ON XBOX LIVE

RANK	PLAYER	TIME*
1	AfewGoodTaters	27:54.08
2	oBAKAAo	28:19.47
3	SprintGod	28:56.98
4	cwolf2012	29:05.90
5	BahamoBK	29:20.82
6	Ardonite	29:22.43
7	Chumwit	29:37.65
8	Alex1st	29:50.27
9	TaCo Monster209	29:59.07
10	TPR BBoyle	30:01.77

Source: in-game leaderboard   ** Times in minutes and seconds*

HIGHEST SCORE ON *SOLOMON'S KEY* (NES)
Holder: Tom Votava (USA)
Solomon's Key (Tecmo, 1987) is a notoriously difficult puzzle game due to its lack of a "save" function and the ability for players to sabotage their own progress in the game. Undaunted by its toughness, American Tom Votava spent years researching and practising the best way to complete each level for his record attempt, starting his preparations in 2002. After a lot of hard work he finally pulled off a score of 16,765,120 points on 31 October 2008, having successfully mastered the 50 rooms of the game's "constellation space".

SPATIAL OCCASION

The mind-bending levels in *echochrome* (Game Yarouze, 2008) and its 2010 sequel were inspired by the "impossible" architectural designs of Swedish artist Oscar Reutersvärd, known as "the father of impossible figures". He is credited for creating the Penrose Triangle, an image of a "3D" triangle that can be drawn, but not built, and was a major inspiration for Dutch abstract artist M C Escher.

FASTEST SINGLE-SEGMENT COMPLETION OF *WE LOVE KATAMARI*
Holder: Tom "slowbro" Batchelor (USA)
A keen fan of Namco's 2005 planet-building title *We Love Katamari*, Tom Batchelor completed all 26 stages of the game in a single session lasting 1 hr 5 min 31 sec on 25 December 2005.

BOUND BY SOUND

Saving all 300 slaves in *Oddworld: Abe's Exoddus* (Oddworld Inhabitants, 1998) is taxing for most players, but Terry Garrett took the challenge further by using the game's audio as his only guide.

Completely blinded at the age of 10, Terry spent the next decade-and-a-half learning to play games based on their audio cues alone.

In April 2011, he demonstrated his ability to play a near-perfect game of *Abe's Exoddus* to *Wired* magazine, and was lauded by the game's developer for his idiosyncratic gaming style.

FIRST 2D/3D HYBRID PUZZLE GAME
Holder: *Crush* (Zoë Mode, 2007)
The first puzzle game to use interchangeable 2D and 3D perspectives was *Crush* for Sony's PlayStation Portable. The game required players to navigate an insomniac's dreamscapes by "crushing" them back and forth between 3D environments and 2D platforming planes, effectively squishing enemies and creating new paths. Although the game's crushing mechanic was compared to that of *Super Paper Mario* (Intelligent Systems, 2007), Zoë Mode's executive producer Paul Mottram claimed *Crush*'s core idea was one the studio had been tinkering around with since 2002.

PHYSICS-BASED PUZZLES

ZEPTOLAB'S *CUT THE ROPE* WAS INSPIRED BY THE ROPE-CUTTING MECHANIC

FIRST APP STORE GAME TO WIN A BAFTA AWARD

Holder: *Cut the Rope* **(Zeptolab, 2010)**
Cut the Rope became the first game created for iOS (the operating system for Apple's touch-screen mobile devices) to win a British Academy of Film and Television Award, on 22 May 2011. The app tasks players with feeding candy to a ravenous creature named Om Nom. The candy is suspended by ropes and often surrounded by various hazards that can destroy Om Nom's treats. The trick is knowing which rope to cut and when to cut it.

RAREST ACHIEVEMENT IN *PORTAL 2*

Holder: "Still Alive"
By 30 June 2011, only 2.6% of PC players of *Portal 2* (Valve, 2011) had obtained the title's "Still Alive" achievement, making it the rarest trackable challenge in the game. To get this badge of honour, partners must buddy up in "co-op" mode and solve all nine chambers on Course Four, Excursion Funnels, without either player dying. With so many easier challenges, co-op teams often skip this task.

HIGHEST-RANKED PLAYER IN *CUT THE ROPE*

Holder: EmTenTeo
A gamer known only as EmTenTeo is *Cut the Rope*'s (Zeptolab, 2010) most prolific high-scorer overall, appearing in the top three positions for four out of the game's seven level leaderboards. As of June 2011, EmTenTeo ranked first in the Foil Box and Gift Box leaderboards, second in the Cardboard Box leaderboard and third in the Fabric Box leaderboard. His Om Nom is surely very full.

/// "AFTER A DECADE OF DEMAND... GAMING'S GREATEST CROSSOVER CONTINUES" ///

0.3 The percentage of PC players of *World of Goo* (2D Boy, 2008) who have earned all the Obsessive Completion Distinction flags for perfecting each level.

OF THE DEVELOPER'S PREVIOUS GAME, *PARACHUTE NINJA* ▶

FIRST CROSS-PLATFORM MULTIPLAYER PUZZLE GAME

Holder: *Portal 2* **(Valve, 2011)**
Because bending the laws of physics is better with a friend, Valve designed *Portal 2*'s co-op mode to allow PS3, PC and Mac gamers to play together using the studio's online gaming service Steam as a bridge between the systems. This was the first time a puzzle game allowed such robust cross-platform integration, and also the first time Steam was made available to PS3 owners. Sadly, Xbox 360 players missed the party and could only play with other gamers using the same console.

FASTEST SINGLE-SEGMENT COMPLETION OF *TRINE*

Holder: Eirik "clux" Albrigtsen (UK)
Speedrunner Eirik "clux" Albrigtsen set the fastest verified completion time for the physics-based platform puzzler *Trine* (Frozenbyte, 2009) with a time of 23 min 41 sec on 2 April 2010.
Eirik used a number of time-saving tricks to whip through the PC version of the game, skipping all the cutscenes and making cunning use of his rope to power through the levels more quickly. What prompted him to go after the record? Eirik claims "This is what happens when you allocate too much time for exams."

MOST CRITICALLY ACCLAIMED PUZZLE GAME ON XBOX 360

Holder: *Peggle Deluxe* / *Peggle Nights* **(PopCap Games, 2009)**
Tied at an aggregate review score of 89% on Metacritic, both *Peggle Deluxe* and *Peggle Nights* are the most popular puzzle games on Xbox 360 among critics. The two games were released together as *Peggle: Duel Shot* on the DS, but this combo wasn't as well regarded, and scored 84%.

FASTEST COMPLETION OF *THE MISADVENTURES OF P.B. WINTERBOTTOM*'S "CHALLENGE" LEVELS

Holder: Calmly Frenetic (Australia)
The puzzle element of *The Misadventures of P.B. Winterbottom* (The Odd Gentlemen, 2010) comes from the way in which players must manipulate time and create clones to successfully gather pies. Australian gamer Calmly Frenetic cleared all 25 of the "challenge" levels of the game in a breathtaking time of 6 min 25.47 sec. His fastest level clearance, of the Blue Brothers level in Baked Blue Follies, took just 3.51 seconds.

FIRST ROBOT PERIPHERAL

Holder: R.O.B. (Nintendo, 1985)
Nintendo's R.O.B. (Robotic Operating Buddy) was the first commercially available robot designed to give players an extra hand with videogames. It came packaged with *Gyromite* (Nintendo, 1985), a physics-based puzzler wherein R.O.B. and the player teamed up to help Professor Hector navigate his lab while avoiding evil lizards called Smicks. R.O.B. has since made cameos in other Nintendo games including *Mario Kart DS* (2005) and *WarioWare: Smooth Moves* (2007).

TOP 10 CRITICALLY ACCLAIMED PHYSICS-BASED PUZZLE GAMES

GAME	VERSION	SCORE
Portal 2 (2011)	PC	95%
Portal 2 (2011)	X360	94%
World of Goo (2008)	Wii	94%
Portal 2 (2011)	PS3	93%
World of Goo (2008)	PC	92%
Peggle Nights (2005)	X360	89%
Peggle Deluxe (2010)	X360	89%
Armadillo Run (2006)	PC	88%
Art of Balance (2010)	X360	88%
Critter Crunch (2005)	PS3	87%

Source: GameRankings.com

LOGIC PUZZLES

AS WELL AS HIS GAMES, PROFESSOR LAYTON ALSO STARRED IN THE 2009

HIGHEST SCORE ON DR. KAWASHIMA'S BODY AND BRAIN EXERCISES

Holder: Victoria Norval (UK)

The highest score achieved in the Balloon Buster challenge on *Dr. Kawashima's Body and Brain Exercises* was 7,850 points, achieved by Victoria Norval, on 22 February 2011. The attempt took place in the Coryton branch of the ASDA superstore in Cardiff, UK, as part of the launch of the 2011 *Gamer's* book.

MOST POPULAR LOGIC PUZZLE GAME ON FACEBOOK

Holder: *Mahjong Trails* (MegaZebra GmbH, 2010)

Attracting more than 3,279,000 monthly active users (people who played the game at least once in a month), *Mahjong Trails* is the most popular logic puzzle game on Facebook. The game offers a globe-trotting slant on the classic Chinese tile-matching game, taking players through a string of levels set in exotic locales across the world. As well as being a popular game, *Mahjong Trails* also stood as the 97th most popular Facebook application overall as of 30 June 2011.

FIRST HANDHELD PUZZLE GAME

Holder: *Mindbuster* (Milton Bradley, 1979)

Released in 1979, Milton Bradley's Microvision was the first handheld system to use interchangeable cartridges, one of which was the puzzle game *Mindbuster*. The game posed players various tests that could be solved by pressing buttons in the correct sequence. Unfortunately, lack of industry support and poor systems sales led to the demise of the Microvision as a viable gaming platform.

456 The number of puzzles in the first three games in the *Professor Layton* series, excluding the various downloadable challenges.

JAPANESE FILM *PROFESSOR LAYTON AND THE ETERNAL DIVA* ▶

MOST COINS IN *EteRNA*

Holder: *Mathew "mat747" Zada* (Australia)

Crafted by Carnegie Mellon University/Stanford University (both USA), *EteRNA* is a free-to-play PC "game" in which players are challenged with folding the basic building blocks of ribonucleic acid (RNA) into sustainable structures. They are rewarded with coins for successful construction. *EteRNA* is also an online crowd-sourcing experiment that provides scientists with a steady stream of RNA data for analysis. The scientists sometimes even replicate RNA from the "game" in their real-world labs.

In January 2011, Mathew Zada from Port Augusta, Australia, became *EteRNA*'s top player – a position he retained as of 30 June 2011 with 410,0188 coins.

FIRST CARTRIDGE-BASED CONSOLE PUZZLE GAME

Holder: *Maze* (Fairchild Semiconductor, 1976)

Developed in 1976 by Gerald Anderson Lawson for the American electronics firm Fairchild Semiconductor, the Channel F was the first console to use interchangeable games cartridges. Among the titles available for the console was a simple, self-explanatory puzzle game called *Maze*.

TOP 10 BEST SCORES IN *BIG BRAIN ACADEMY: Wii DEGREE*'S BRAIN QUIZ

RANK	PLAYER	SCORE*
1	saugfuchs	157
2	axel	144
3	johnny	123
4	jumjum	121
5	aleolivia86	114
6	affzbr	109
7	cook94	99
8	provriguy	92
9	thiago	88
10	ako	82

Source: in-game leaderboard   * Accurate at 28 June 2011

HEAVIEST BRAIN IN *BIG BRAIN ACADEMY: Wii DEGREE*

Holder: *Gerard "GerardRub" Roodhorst* (Netherlands)

Big Brain Academy: Wii Degree calculates players' "brain weight" with a catch-all IQ quiz that drills players on their mental skills across all its puzzle categories. On 24 September 2007, Gerard Roodhorst proved he had the heaviest digital brain with a verified weight of 2,513 g (5.54 lb) – roughly twice as heavy as the average human brain.

FIRST LOGIC GAME FOR THE 3DS

Holder: *Professor Layton and the Mask of Miracle* (Level-5, 2011)

Debuting as a launch title for the Japanese release of Nintendo's 3DS on 26 February 2011, *Professor Layton and the Mask of Miracle* is the first logic game for the 3D handheld. As with all the releases in the *Professor Layton* series, the latest instalment teams the gentleman-sleuth with his faithful sidekick Luke as they (and the player) are confronted with over a hundred new puzzles on their way to uncovering a greater secret. However, this time there is an added third dimension to the problem-solving. The game proved to be an instant hit, selling a total of 119,591 copies on its first day.

STAR WARS

LEGO STAR WARS ALLOWS PLAYERS

THESE ARE THE GAMES YOU'RE LOOKING FOR

E3 2011 saw the release of "Return", a new trailer for *Star Wars: The Old Republic* (left), the latest game – and the second major MMORPG – to be set in the ever-expanding *Star Wars* universe. Exciting and impressive as the trailer was, it simply left gamers craving the final game, which – at the time of going to press – was set to be unveiled in December 2011. LucasArts and BioWare had been tight-lipped at E3 about offering advance information on *The Old Republic*, but gamers no longer need to wait for this much-anticipated release...

To mark 30 years of *Star Wars* games, we at *Gamer's* thought it was a good time to look back at some of the very best videogames that had their origins a long time ago in a galaxy far, far away...

FIRST GAME WITH VIRTUAL LIGHTSABERS

Holder: *Lego Star Wars: The Complete Saga* **(Traveller's Tales, 2007)** The Nintendo Wii version of *Lego Star Wars: The Complete Saga* used the motion-sensing capabilities of the Wii Remote to enable players to engage in lightsaber duels by swinging their controllers. Their actions were then replicated on screen. VWOORM!

IS THERE MORE TO THIS RECORDING?

Star Wars: The Old Republic constitutes the **largest entertainment voice-over project** ever. More than 200,000 lines of recorded dialogue was performed by several hundred voice actors for the MMORPG, making this a far more ambitious recording project than any undertaken for a feature film.

STAR WARS GALAXIES

Launched in 2003, and due to be shut down at the end of 2011, *Star Wars Galaxies* (Sony, 2003) was one of the more ambitious MMORPGs. Steeped in *Star Wars* lore, its sandbox covered vast areas of space and a rich variety of planets.

Players could choose to become a virtuous Jedi or a villainous Sith, or even a less powerful character with a more mundane career within the *Star Wars* universe, be it an antiques dealer or an architect, a trader or a smuggler.

Whole user-generated cities sprang up in addition to the better-known space ports, such as Mos Eisley on Tatooine. In these hives of scum and villainy social interactions soon came to mimic real life, with the creation of socio-economic guilds, and even localized systems of government.

It's inevitable that such an enormous MMO would have problems and *Galaxies* certainly had its fair share, particularly with its initial combat mechanics, which were refined in one of two significant technical overhauls in 2005. MMOs are designed to evolve, however, and over eight years *Galaxies* grew from being "just" an MMO to becoming a significant online community.

The news that the game's servers were to be closed down was received with lamentation by its most ardent fans, and indeed all those who love *Star Wars*.

/// "YOUR SMALLEST DECISIONS CAN CHANGE EVERYTHING" ///

TO MIX AND MATCH THE HEADS, TORSOS AND LEGS OF ALL ITS CHARACTERS

THE GALAXY'S BEST STAR WARS VIDEOGAMES

The **first *Star Wars* videogame** was based on the second film made in the series, *The Empire Strikes Back* (Parker Brothers, 1982), and was for the Atari 2600 and Intellivision. Here are our picks of the games that followed.

WHO SAYS?

A Padawan learner and seasoned gamer, Charlie Peacock has been playing *Star Wars* videogames since he was a youngling. Now The Force is strong with him, he shares his assessment of the many titles in the ever-growing *Star Wars* canon.

10. THE FORCE UNLEASHED II

Released in 2010, *Star Wars: The Force Unleashed II* (LucasArts) is the most recent entry in our list of top picks. The game's impressive physics engine enabled players to feel The Force in various lightsaber duels and also by grabbing and hurling around both characters and vehicles.

9. STAR WARS ARCADE

Wrongly believed by many to be the first *Star Wars* videogame, this 1983 vector-graphics first-person space sim from Atari was the **first arcade game to feature digitized speech from a movie**.

8. REPUBLIC COMMANDO

Set in the wake of the Clone Wars, as seen in the movie *Star Wars Episode II: Attack of the Clones*, *Star Wars: Republic Commando* (LucasArts, 2005) allowed the player to take the role of one of the Galactic Republic's elite clone warriors through three campaigns. Although the game as a whole could be considered a little short for some fans' tastes, many of the missions rewarded repeated play. A must for any true *Star Wars* fan.

7. SUPER STAR WARS

Out of the three games based on the classic trilogy that were created for the Super Nintendo, *Super Star Wars: The Empire Strikes Back* (Sculptured Software/LucasArts, 1993) is perhaps the best loved. Released in the dark days between the release of the classic *Star Wars* film trilogy and the prequels, the *Super Star Wars* games were renowned for an almost ridiculous level of difficulty. The password system introduced in *Super Star Wars: The Empire Strikes Back* at least ensured players would not have to start each mission again whenever they "died". Many frustrating, but fun, hours have been spent playing this platformer.

6. JEDI OUTCAST

The third in a series of four first-person-shooter *Dark Forces* games and the final instalment in which players can take control of Kyle Katarn (right), a former Stormtrooper turned Jedi disciple. In the game, players work to develop Katarn's Force abilities and martial skills in order to eventually defeat a particularly nasty Sith named Desann and foil his dastardly plans. The game's intuitive controls – and its engaging combat and puzzles formula – quickly found favour with a large number of *Star Wars* fans.

5. ROGUE SQUADRON

Essentially a flight sim, *Star Wars: Rogue Squadron* (Factor 5/LucasArts, 1998) was originally developed for the N64 but was later adapted for a PC release. The game followed the elite X-Wing squadron around the *Star Wars* universe. The high spot for this title has to be the thrilling re-enactment of the Battle of Hoth.

4. EMPIRE AT WAR

This well-loved real-time strategy game came out in 2006 and is notable for splitting its battles between planet surfaces and space. Starting in space, attackers try to secure landing points while defenders attempt to prevent them gaining a foothold. Epic in scope, *Star Wars: Empire at War* (Petroglyph Games) allows fans to relive the pivotal battles of the *Star Wars* universe.

3. X-WING vs TIE FIGHTER

Developed by Totally Games and released in 1997, the third game in the X-Wing series of space combat simulators was the most advanced of the three, and had amazing multiplayer capabilities for its time. Whether as a Rebel or as a member of the Imperial Navy, the game's dogfights are a great challenge.

2. LEGO STAR WARS: THE COMPLETE SAGA

Since Traveller's Tales produced the first *Lego Star Wars* adaptation in 2005, the series has blossomed into a sub-brand under the *Star Wars* umbrella. This wordless, light-hearted and highly entertaining take on the franchise has opened up the series to new gamers of all ages.

1. KNIGHTS OF THE OLD REPUBLIC

Widely regarded as the best *Star Wars* game so far, *Knights of the Old Republic* (BioWare, 2003) featured a cast of memorable characters, such as T3 M4 (right). The game was pioneering in the freedom it gave players to choose between the way of the Jedi or the dark path of the Sith. And then there's an amazing plot twist – so *don't* turn to page 184 if you want to remain spoiler-free!

ROLE-PLAYING GAMES

OVERVIEW

Role-playing games are as varied as they are numerous, spanning everything from giant post-apocalyptic open worlds (*Fallout*) to high fantasy (*Elder Scrolls*), from epic tales (*Final Fantasy*) to tactical strategy games set inside colourful versions of hell (*Disgaea*). You might play as a plucky hero, a queen, a prisoner, a pauper, a warrior or a wizard. Sometimes your character is a blank canvas you can delineate and colour at will. Fundamentally, RPGs are all about *you*: who do you want to be? Where do you want to go? What do you want to become?

CONTENTS

CRITICAL HIT!: *POKÉMON*   **140**
ACTION RPGs   **142**
JAPANESE RPGs   **144**
WESTERN RPGs   **146**
STRATEGY RPGs   **148**

BIOGRAPHY

Keza MacDonald is the UK Games Editor for the IGN website, and has a passion for role-playing games that encompasses everything from the barren wastes of *Fallout* to the colourful collect-o-mania of *Pokémon*. She previously spent six years writing about games for *Edge*, *Eurogamer*, *Official Nintendo Magazine* and *The Observer*, among others. She expects to emerge from *The Elder Scrolls V: Skyrim* sometime in 2013.

LARGEST COMPETITIVE *POKÉMON* VIDEOGAME FAMILY

Holder: The Arnold family (USA)

Pokémon's family-friendly charm is confirmed by the record-breaking five members of the Arnold family from Frankfort, Illinois, USA, who take part in official *Pokémon* videogame world championships. They are (left to right) Ryan, mum Linda, Ryan's twin David, dad Glenn and youngest child Grace. Their most recent tournament took place in California in August 2011.

POKÉMON

POKÉMON IS BEHIND ONLY *MARIO* IN THE ALL-TIME BEST-SELLING GAME

BEST-SELLING HANDHELD RPGs

Holder: *Pokémon Red*, *Green* **and** *Blue* **(Game Freak, 1996)**
Pokémon Red, *Green* and *Blue*, the first games in the series, became the most successful RPGs on any handheld console after being released on the Game Boy in 1996 (two years later in the USA and Europe). They sold 31,366,863 copies between them, and, behind *Tetris*, are the second best-selling handheld games ever.

PROKÉMON

In July 2008, biologists from the Osaka Bioscience Institute in Japan discovered a protein that enables visual information to be transmitted to the brain. They named it pikachurin, after Pikachu!

/// "BRINGS YOU CLOSER THAN EVER TO THE FURY OF COMBAT" ///

225,000,000+ The total number of *Pokémon* games sold across the 45 titles released in the series.

FRANCHISES CHART, AND THE PLUMBER HAD A 15-YEAR HEAD START ▶

TOP 10 BEST-SELLING *POKÉMON* GAMES

GAME (FORMAT)	SALES
Red/Green/Blue (Game Boy)	31.36 million
Gold/Silver (Game Boy)	23.1 million
Diamond/Pearl (DS)	17.81 million
Ruby/Sapphire (Game Boy Advance)	15.38 million
Yellow (Game Boy)	14.64 million
Black/White (DS)	11.7 million
FireRed/LeafGreen (Game Boy Advance)	10.49 million
HeartGold/SoulSilver (DS)	10.35 million
Plàtinum (DS)	7.38 million
Crystal (Game Boy)	6.39 million

Source: VGChartz.com

SMALLEST POKÉMON

Holder: Joltik
The tiny, bug-like Pokémon Joltik – introduced in *Pokémon Black* and *White* – is the smallest Pokémon at a mere 10 cm (4 in) in height. The sparrow-sized creature can cling to the bodies of larger monsters, absorbing static electricity and storing it in an electric pouch. Joltik evolves into the much larger and more threatening Galvantula, a hairy yellow and blue spider.

FASTEST-SELLING DS GAME

Holder: *Pokémon Black* and *White* (Game Freak, 2010)
Between 31 July and 22 August 2010, *Pokémon Black* and *White* (above) racked up a massive 1.08 million pre-orders in Japan, making them the fastest pre-ordered DS games in history. They went on to sell 5 million units in Japan by mid-January 2011, thereby becoming the fastest-selling DS games ever. As of July 2011, they had sold 11.7 million copies around the world.

LONGEST-RUNNING TV SHOW BASED ON A VIDEOGAME

Holder: *Pokémon* TV series
The first episode of the *Pokémon* TV series aired in Japan in 1997 and – now into its 14th series – is still running. Translated into English, it has been broadcast on US, Australian and UK TV since 1998. The 700th episode went out on Japanese channel TV Tokyo in August 2011.

HIGHEST-GROSSING ANIMATED MOVIE BASED ON A VIDEOGAME

Holder: *Pokémon: The First Movie: Mewtwo Strikes Back*
Grossing $163,644,662 (£101,200,000) in cinemas worldwide, the first *Pokémon* film, released in 1999, was a chart-topping sensation. There have been 13 films based on the games since, but not one has come close to replicating the success of the first. The **highest-grossing non-animated film based on a videogame** is 2010's *Prince of Persia: The Sands of Time*, which made $326,813,000 (£211,841,000) in box-office receipts during its theatrical run from May 2010.

FIRST CONSOLE GAME TO TRANSFER DATA FROM A HANDHELD

Holder: *Pokémon Stadium* (HAL Laboratory, Inc., 1999)
The Nintendo 64's *Pokémon Stadium* was the first game to allow players to use data from a portable cartridge on a home console. Characters from the Game Boy titles *Pokémon Red* and *Blue* could be transferred to the N64, thus allowing them to do battle in glorious 3D.

BUG CHUG

The original Pokémon was created by Satoshi Tajiri, who imagined tiny creatures chugging along the Game Boy's Link Cable, giving him the inspiration for Pokémon. As a child, Satoshi was keen on collecting bugs.

HEAVIEST POKÉMON

Holder: Groudon
At 950 kg (2,094 lb), "Ground-type Legendary" Pokémon Groudon is the heaviest monster in the Pokédex to date. It weighs so much that its movements have the ability to expand whole continents and make volcanoes erupt. Groudon was the mascot for *Pokémon Ruby*, the eighth game in the main *Pokémon* series, which launched in 2002.

ACTION RPGs

IN JAPAN, *MONSTER HUNTER PORTABLE 3RD* (2010) WAS RELEASED ALONGSIDE

PLAYER

HITPOINT ❤ 000300

STRENGTH ⚔ 000500

EXP. ? 000000

GOLD 💰 000200

MAGIC ✦ 000000

CROWN 👑

MONSTER

FIRST ACTION RPG

Holder: *Dragon Slayer* **(Nihon Falcom, 1984)**
Released for the NEC PC-88, an early home computer sold only in Japan, *Dragon Slayer* is the first true action RPG. The game has the hallmarks of the genre, such as an emphasis on combat and a limited inventory that forces players to choose carefully what they carry.

BEST-SELLING Wii RPG
Holder: *Monster Hunter Tri* **(Capcom, 2009)**
Just a few months after its Western launch in April 2010, *Monster Hunter Tri* became the best-selling RPG game on the Wii, shifting a total of 1,873,753 units worldwide. Most popular in Japan, where gamers bought over 1 million copies, the game tasks players with capturing or killing a slew of beasts, some of which are so tough that they are best tackled in "multiplayer" mode as part of a team.

MOST EXPENSIVE VIDEOGAME DEVELOPMENT PER UNIT
Holder: *Too Human* **(Microsoft, 2008)**
According to figures compiled by games news website digitalbattle.com, the action RPG game *Too Human* cost more than $60 million (£32 million) to develop. The game sold fewer than 700,000 copies worldwide, meaning that each copy would have had to have been sold at $90 (£62) just to cover its immense development costs.

/// "I THINK WE CAN PUT OUR DIFFERENCES BEHIND US FOR SCIENCE... YOU MONSTER" ///

A THEMED PSP WITH A SPECIAL ANALOGUE STICK TO MAKE IT EASIER TO PLAY ▶

LONGEST DEVELOPMENT TIME FOR AN RPG

Holder: *Diablo 3* (Blizzard, unreleased)

The long-planned sequel to the massively popular action RPG *Diablo 2* (Blizzard, 2000) has been in development for 10 years and counting, as of July 2011. Such delays are not unusual for Blizzard – 12 years passed between the releases of the company's RTS titles, *Starcraft* (1998) and *Starcraft II* (2010).

BEST-SELLING PSP SERIES

Holder: *Monster Hunter* (Capcom, 2004–present)

When it comes to the PSP, the *Monster Hunter* series is clearly the biggest beast, boasting 13.5 million units sold from four games. Before even gaining a worldwide release, Capcom's 2010 sequel, *Monster Hunter Portable 3rd*, had already sold 4.4 million units in Japan. What's more, this record is unlikely to be beaten as the series' nearest rival, the *Grand Theft Auto* series, has sold "just" 11.4 million units on the PSP, and the handheld will soon be superseded by the PlayStation Vita.

FASTEST SINGLE-SEGMENT COMPLETION OF *FABLE*

Holder: David Arnold (USA)

Fable (Lionshead Studios, 2004) is a sprawling epic action RPG in which gamers play their character from childhood to adulthood. However, gamer David Arnold was able to whizz through it in just 1 hr 37 min on 2 August 2010. The secret of his success? Using "assassin rush" character traits and rolling around to move more quickly. An added advantage of this technique is that characters cannot be hurt when rushing or rolling.

FASTEST COMPLETION OF *DEMON'S SOULS*

Holder: alternalw

A gamer known only as alternalw completed *Demon's Souls* (From Software, 2009) in a record time of just 54 min 54 sec. As with *Fable*, invulnerability when rolling is the key to swift progress, as well as being a good method to avoid being crushed by the game's falling boulders.

> **"The main thing we're focusing on in development is creating a game that is enjoyable."**
> **RYOZO TSUJIMOTO ON *MONSTER HUNTER*'S FUTURE**

TOP 10 BEST-SELLING ACTION ROLE-PLAYING GAMES

RANK	GAME	SALES
1	Kingdom Hearts	5.5 million
2	Diablo 2	5.33 million
3	Monster Hunter Freedom Unite	5.14 million
4	Pokémon Mystery Dungeon: Explorers	4.8 million
5	Monster Hunter Freedom 3	4.44 million
6	Fable II	3.97 million
7	Kingdom Hearts II	3.89 million
8	Diablo	3.46 million
9=	Pokémon Mystery Dungeon: Blue Rescue Team	3.11 million
9=	Fable III	3.11 million

Source: VGChartz.com

FIRST RPG ON A 128-BIT CONSOLE

Holder: *Eternal Ring* (From Software, 2000)

Released as a PlayStation 2 launch title, first-person action RPG *Eternal Ring* was the first of the genre for a seventh-generation console. It pipped *Grandia II* (Game Arts, 2000) to the post by five months, even though *Grandia* was developed for Sega's ill-fated Dreamcast, which was released in 1998 as the **first 128-bit console**.

JAPANESE RPGs

THE DEMONIC TECHNOLOGY *SHIN MEGAMI*   *TENSEI* GAMES ARE BASED

MOST PROLIFIC ROLE-PLAYING GAME SERIES

Holder: *Final Fantasy*
(Square Enix, 1987–present)

As of July 2011, Square Enix's *Final Fantasy* series boasts a record total of 54 games in its franchise with 14 main entries (two of which were MMORPGs) and 40 spin-off titles featuring characters and elements from the main series.

MOST ENDINGS IN A JAPANESE RPG

Holder: *Chrono Trigger DS* (Square, 1995)

With 14 distinct ways for the game's story to end, *Chrono Trigger* has a greater variety of possible outcomes than any other Japanese RPG. The DS version beats the original SNES game because it features a new secret boss, the "Dream Devourer" (pictured left).

Beating this final enemy gives players an extra possible ending, but to stand a chance against the beast, players need to grind their character up to at least level 60. Defeating this monster also provides players with the ultra-powerful Dreamseeker weapon.

MOST PROLIFIC JAPANESE RPG DEVELOPER

Holder: Square Enix

With a total of 65 releases in the genre under its belt, Square Enix dominates the world of Japanese RPGs like a videogaming giant.

The company, which both develops and publishes games, was formed in 2003 through a merger of Square, who made the *Dragon Quest* series, and Enix, the company behind the *Final Fantasy* titles.

/// "FIVE UNIQUE ABILITIES! VENGEANCE AGAINST THE PIGS!" ///

57 million The number of games sold to date in the *Dragon Quest* franchise. The series, which started in 1986, has now been going for a quarter of a century!

TOP 10 BEST-SELLING JAPANESE RPGs

RANK	GAME	TOTAL SALES
1	*Final Fantasy VII*	9.72 million
2	*Final Fantasy X*	7.95 million
3	*Final Fantasy VIII*	7.86 million
4	*Final Fantasy XII*	5.74 million
5	*Dragon Quest IX*	5.51 million
6	*Final Fantasy IX*	5.30 million
7	*Final Fantasy X-2*	5.21 million
8	*Dragon Quest VIII*	5.00 million
9	*Final Fantasy XIII*	4.66 million
10	*Dragon Warrior VII*	4.33 million

Source: VGChartz.com

LARGEST XBOX 360 GAME

Holder: *Lost Odyssey* (Mistwalker, 2007)

One of only three Japanese RPGs exclusive to the Xbox 360 – along with *Blue Dragon* (Mistwalker, 2006) and *The Last Remnant* (Square Enix, 2008) – *Lost Odyssey* had an unwanted attribute that set it apart from these titles; it came on four discs. Because of the limited amount of data that can be squeezed on to a single DVD, certain Xbox 360 games have required more than one disc. The sprawling *Lost Odyssey*, whose lead character is a long-lived amnesiac, needed more than any other game for the console.

> "The JRPG is intended for younger players because the journey of the character leaving the village to conquer the world resonates with them."

YOSHINORI KITASE, *FINAL FANTASY* **PRODUCER**

LONGEST-RUNNING SCI-FI RPG SERIES

Holder: *Phantasy Star* (Sega, 1987–present)

With a total of 20 years and 79 days between its first release in 1987 and the most recent online RPG version for Xbox 360, Sega's *Phantasy Star* has been around for longer than any other sci-fi RPG series.

MEGURO'S MEGAMIX

Widely regarded as the last great game for the PS2, the European and North American releases of the *Shin Megami Tensi* game *Persona 4* (Atlus, 2008) came complete with an added bonus in the form of a soundtrack CD. Mainly composed by Atlus staffer Shōji Meguro, the soundtrack was developed at the same time as the game, with the composer basing his work on an outline of the plot.

LONGEST RELAY ON A JAPANESE RPG

Holder: TheSpeedGamers (USA)

Raising money for autism charity ACT Today, charity group TheSpeedGamers (founded by American Britt LaRivere) spent 168 hours playing *Final Fantasy* games back-to-back in July 2009. Starting with the first game, TheSpeedGamers crew managed to complete the first nine games in the series and get part of the way through *Final Fantasy X*, raising $50,734 (£30,840) for their chosen charity in the process.

FIRST RPG PLAYABLE ACROSS HANDHELD AND HOME CONSOLES

Holder: *Final Fantasy: Crystal Chronicles* (Square Enix, 2003)

Connecting to the GameCube via link cables, *Final Fantasy: Crystal Chronicles* enabled up to four players at a time to control their characters on screen via their Game Boy Advances.

The main action still appeared on the screen hooked up to the GameCube, but players used their GBAs to view their inventories and stats.

WESTERN RPGs

THE VOICE CAST OF *MASS EFFECT 2* INCLUDES TWO

TOP 10 BEST-SELLING CONSOLE WESTERN RPGs

SALES*	GAME
6.11 million	*Fallout 3*
5.48 million	*The Elder Scrolls IV: Oblivion*
4.54 million	*Fallout: New Vegas*
3.42 million	*Dragon Age: Origins*
3.01 million	*Mass Effect 2*
2.75 million	*Mass Effect*
2.01 million	*Knights of the Old Republic*
1.84 million	*The Elder Scrolls III: Morrowind*
1.33 million	*Knights of the Old Republic II: The Sith Lords*
0.77 million	*Dragon Age II*

Source: VGChartz.com   * Accurate at 11 August 2011

FASTEST COMPLETION OF *BALDUR'S GATE*

Holder: Benjamin "beenman50" Culley (UK)
Sword and sorcery RPG *Baldur's Gate* (BioWare, 1998) is a game that can take upwards of 100 hours to fully explore. Benjamin Culley managed to complete it in just 18 min 29 sec on 6 May 2009. To achieve his feat, Benjamin made use of glitches that enabled him to generate plenty of potions, particularly "oils of speed", and teleport glitches to cut out much of the game. Away from the glitches, his other key secret was hiding in shadowy areas instead of engaging in lengthy battles that would have otherwise slowed him down.

MOST PROLIFIC WESTERN RPG SERIES

Holder: *Ultima* (Origin Systems, 1980–99)
Excluding online titles, a total of 17 games and expansion packs have been released in the *Ultima* series since 1980. The brainchild of the British-American game designer turned astronaut Richard Garriott, the *Ultima* story came to an end in 1999 with *Ultima IX*, in which the player's character is forced to ascend to a higher plane of existence.

800 The number of workers employed by game-development company BioWare across four different sites in North America.

CYLONS: MICHAEL HOGAN AND TRICIA HELFER FROM *BATTLESTAR GALACTICA* ▶

Menu
LIMITLESS RANDOMLY-GENERATED DUNGEONS & FOES EACH QUEST...
HITS: 518/1001   10000   LVL: 22

MOST PROLIFIC VOICE ACTOR

Holder: Jennifer Hale (USA)

Between 1994 and July 2011, Jennifer Hale (pictured below) worked on 129 videogames, making her both the **most prolific voice actor (female)** and the most prolific vocal artist in the field overall. Her game tally surpasses that of Nolan North (USA), the **most prolific voice actor (male)**, who worked on 107 games between 1997 and July 2011. Jennifer's most acclaimed recent role is in the *Mass Effect* series, in which she voices the female version of Commander Shepard (left).

MOST CRITICALLY ACCLAIMED "ROGUELIKE" FOR IOS

Holder: *Sword of Fargoal* (Fargoal, 2009)

Taking their name from *Rogue*, a dungeon-exploring game created in 1980 by Michael Toy, Glenn Wichman and Ken Arnold (all USA), "Roguelikes" are notoriously difficult role-playing games in which players explore randomly generated levels. The goal with such games is often simply to survive as long as possible. *Sword of Fargoal* has withstood the attacks of critics to score 85% on reviews site Metacritic, but with many games in this genre being released for IOS, how long will its record survive?

> **"I've always been intrigued by the concept of a hero's journey. A role-playing game is really well-suited to showing that."**
>
> RAY MUZYKA, CO-FOUNDER OF BIOWARE, THE MAKERS OF *MASS EFFECT*

FIRST RPG

Holder: *dnd* (Gary Whisenhunt and Ray Wood, 1975)

A simple text-only game based on the pencil and paper role-playing game *Dungeons & Dragons*, the first RPG was *dnd*, created by American students Gary Whisenhunt and Ray Wood on a PLATO, an early computer system, at the University of Illinois, USA, in 1975.

MOST UNIQUE NPCs IN A VIDEOGAME

Holder: Obsidian Entertainment (USA)

There are exactly 900 named non-player characters in *The Elder Scrolls IV: Oblivion* – more than in any other game. Each has his or her own name and distinctive facial features, although some lines of dialogue and voice actors are shared by the less important characters.

MOST PROLIFIC DEVELOPER OF RPG SEQUELS

Holder: Obsidian Entertainment (USA)

California-based developer Obsidian has carved out an impressive CV in producing sequels to other companies' role-playing games. As of July 2011, Obsidian has developed sequels for four RPG franchises with *Star Wars: Knights of the Old Republic II* (2004), *Neverwinter Nights 2* (2006), *Fallout: New Vegas* (2010, see right) and *Dungeon Siege III* (2011).

STRATEGY RPGs

PS3 STRATEGY RPG *VALKYRIA CHRONICLES* (SEGA, 2008) SPAWNED A 2009

LONGEST-RUNNING STRATEGY RPG SERIES

Holder: *Fire Emblem*
(Intelligent Systems, 1990–present)

Fire Emblem is a series of fantasy strategy RPGs created by Shouzou Kaga, which now numbers 12 titles. The first entry appeared on the NES in 1990, and the latest one was released for the Nintendo DS on 15 July 2010. It is closely followed by the *Shining Force* titles, which were first released in 1992.

KING KAGA

The *Fire Emblem* series was created by Shouzou Kaga, the same designer and developer who worked on *Advance Wars* (Intelligent Systems, 2001). This was a successful and critically acclaimed turn-based strategy series for the Game Boy Advance. The first game garnered a Metacritic average of 92% and a perfect 10 from Eurogamer, among several excellent reviews. Its release did not go smoothly, however: the game arrived in US shops just a day before the 11 September 2001 attacks, and its Japanese debut was subsequently delayed by three years. Two follow-up games were released for the Nintendo DS in 2005 and 2008. Kaga, meanwhile, left Intelligent Systems to set up his own company.

FASTEST COMPLETION OF *FIRE EMBLEM: PATH OF RADIANCE*
Holder: Stephen "SMK" Kiazyk (USA)
Fire Emblem: Path of Radiance (Intelligent Systems, 2005) for the Nintendo GameCube was the first game in the venerable *Fire Emblem* series to be released since 2000. On 23 December 2006, Kiazyk managed all 28 chapters of the game in 2 hr 30 min 1 sec. The run took him 158 turns.

HIGHEST-RATED STRATEGY RPG
Holder: *Shining Force II* (Camelot, 1993)
With a Gamerankings rating of 89.25%, Sega classic *Shining Force II* on the Megadrive/Genesis remains the most critically acclaimed strategy RPG. It narrowly beats *Fire Emblem* at 88.57% on the Game Boy Advance, while PSP game *Final Fantasy Tactics: The War of the Lions* (Square Enix, 2007) aggregated a score of 88.26%.

MOST CRITICALLY ACCLAIMED SRPG ON A CURRENT-GENERATION HOME CONSOLE
Holder: *Valkyria Chronicles* (Sega, 2008)
With a Metacritic average of 86%, *Valkyria Chronicles* – a sweeping epic set in an alternate-history World War I – is the highest-rated strategy RPG on a modern console. The genre is under-represented on the PS3, Xbox 360 and Wii – most SRPGs are released on portable platforms.

/// "PEOPLE LIKE TIM SEEM TO LIVE OPPOSITELY FROM THE OTHER RESIDENTS OF THE CITY. TIDE AND RIPTIDE, FLOWING AGAINST EACH OTHER" ///

999,999,999 The maximum attack stat for a character in a *Disgaea* (Nippon Ichi, 2003) party at level 9,999. They can do "several billion damage".

Flonne
I can only do this once, because I need to use this item I got from the Seraph!

How may I help you?
· Buy weapons
· Buy armor
· Buy accessories
· Buy items
· Sell

ATK 724
DEF 607
INT 621
RES 1009
SPD 565
STEAL 10
GUARD 10%
Marona
Lv 100
HP 1509/1509
Default Chroma
EQUIP
HP 0
ATK +36
DEF 0
INT +62
RES +100
SPD -56
to Switch
Equipment

"We wanted it very realistic in that sense – if you lose a person in war, they are not going to come back."

***VALKYRIA CHRONICLES'* PRODUCER RYUTARO NONAKA ON PERMANENT CHARACTER DEATH**

TOP 10 BEST-RATED STRATEGY RPGS ON THE PSP

%	GAME
88	*Final Fantasy Tactics: The War of the Lions* (Square Enix, 2007)
87=	*Tactics Ogre: Let Us Cling Together* (Square Enix, 2010)
87=	*Disgaea: Afternoon of Darkness* (Nippon Ichi, 2007)
87=	*Jeanne D'Arc* (Level 5, 2006)
83=	*Valkyria Chronicles 2* (Sega, 2010)
83=	*Disgaea 2: Dark Hero Days* (NIS America, 2009)
67	*Blazing Souls Accelate* (Idea Factory Neverland, 2010)
66	*PoPoLoCrois* (SCEI, 2005)
65	*Phantom Brave: The Hermuda Triangle* (Nippon Ichi, 2011)
64	*Lord of the Rings: Tactics* (Amaze, 2005)

Source: Metacritic.com

MOST STRATEGY RPGs ON A SINGLE SYSTEM

Holder: Sony PlayStation 2

With 56 strategy RPGs to its name, the PS2 (below) is home to the most tactical RPGs of any console in history (the original PlayStation is close behind, at 46). The games include *Disgaea, Tactics Ogre, Wild Arms* and *Phantom Brave*, with a good mix of ports and re-releases along with original titles. The PSP has the most of any modern console, with 21.

SONY

FIRST STRATEGY RPG TO INCLUDE DATING SIM ELEMENTS

Holder: *Langrisser III* (CareerSoft, 1996)

In *Langrisser III* on the Sega Saturn, there is an open-ended relationship system whereby the main character's relationships with his female allies affect both the story and the eventual outcome of the game. The player's character ultimately ends up with whichever lady likes him the most. Subsequent games to adopt this system include *Riviera: The Promised Land* (Sting, 2002).

BIGGEST SRPG PARTY SIZE

Holder: *Final Fantasy Tactics Advance* (Square, 2003)

With up to 24 members on the field at a time, *Final Fantasy Tactics Advance* (right) is at the top of the party-size table. Other SRPGs have hundreds of units, but usually only a few accompany players on to the battlefield. *Final Fantasy Tactics Advance* is the second SRPG in the FF series – the first was *Final Fantasy Tactics* (Square, 1997).

MMO GAMES

BIGGEST MMO HACK

Holder: Sony Online Entertainment (2011)

Following a huge online hack attack on Sony in April 2011, the firm revealed that user details from 24.6 million accounts in its MMO arm, Sony Online Entertainment (SOE), may have been stolen. Games included in this were *Everquest I & II*, *Free Realms*, *Vanguard*, *Clone Wars Adventures* and *DC Universe Online* (right). Approximately 12,700 credit or debit card numbers and expiration dates, plus 10,700 direct debit records, could have been compromised as part of the hack, leading to SOE taking all of its MMOs offline for 12 days.

OVERVIEW

Where once "MMO" meant paying £10 a month to attack respawning orcs with a big sword, lately the genre has been splintering off into all kinds of weird and wonderful forms. Recent developments include the free-to-play trend, which sees subscriptions ditched in favour of a "pay as you play" arrangement, whereby players can buy new content or virtual clothes as they proceed through a game. There has also been a surge in social network games, which let bands of players work together to build bigger and better farms or engage in turn-based battles. It's a vast and ever-changing field to cover.

BIOGRAPHY

Alec Meer has worked as a videogames journalist for 10 years. He is the co-founder of Rock, Paper, Shotgun, the PC games site on which he is regularly amazed, confused and horrified at the seemingly endless torrent of new MMOs announced on a daily basis.

CONTENTS

CRITICAL HIT!: *ULTIMA ONLINE*   152
FANTASY MMORPGs   154
SCI-FI MMORPGs   156
SOCIAL NETWORK GAMING   158

ULTIMA ONLINE

BORN IN SEPTEMBER 1997, *ULTIMA* REMAINS

FIRST GLOBAL MMO CONVENTION

Holder: World Faire 2000

The inaugural *Ultima Online* World Faire was held in Austin, Texas, USA, on 10–11 November 2000. The event, at Origin Systems' HQ, saw some 800 players enjoy more than 50 panels and workshops, as well as tournaments, demos and merchandise stalls. The World Faire in Austin was also the first time an MMO expansion was unveiled at a convention.

FIRST MMO ZOMBIE INVASION

Holder: *Ultima Online: The Second Age*

Zombie-themed events are par for the course in MMOs, but *Ultima Online* was the first virtual world to suffer an undead uprising. After ruler Lord British vanished in February 2000, an enormous undead army seized the peaceful city of Trinsic. Banding together, *UO*'s industrious players were able to fend off the supernatural invaders and

reclaim Trinsic – paving the way for the game's second expansion, *Renaissance*.

FIRST GAME SUED BY ITS PLAYERS

Holder: *Ultima Online* (Origin Systems/EA, 1997)

As well as playing a major role in creating modern MMOs, *Ultima Online* set a rather less happy precedent on 3 March 1998: it was sued by its players on the grounds that it didn't live up to its promises. This revolved around publisher EA's claim

that *UO* could be played "24 hours a day, everyday", when in fact its servers were down for several hours daily. The

case was settled, with each side paying their own fees and EA donating money to a San Diego museum.

> "They staged a sit-in at Lord British's castle. They had a civil disobedience uprising."
>
> **RICHARD GARRIOTT, LORD BRITISH, ON *ULTIMA ONLINE* IN-GAME PLAYER REBELLIONS**

/// "WAKE UP TO A NEW BREED OF SUPERHERO!" ///

6,006,313 Lines of code in *Ultima Online* by 2008. This works out at a gargantuan 25,103,295 words.

FIRST RETAIL MMO EXPANSION PACK

Holder: *Ultima Online: The Second Age* **(Origin, 1998)**

While both *Meridian 59* (Archetype Interactive, 1995) and the original *Neverwinter Nights* (BioWare, 1992) had already released expansions by 1998, they were free to subscribers. *Ultima Online* was the first to market an add-on pack in its own box with its own price tag. *The Second Age* was the first of eight expansions, and although the added cost was divisive at first, it proved so beloved that player-run servers dedicated to that version of the game can still be found today.

MISSING!

The kingdom's ruler, Lord British, is currently missing, lost in an ethereal realm. This may or may not have something to do with *Ultima* creator Richard Garriott having kept the rights to the Lord British persona when he departed from publisher EA in 2000.

FIRST PLAYER HOUSING

Holder: *Ultima Online*

Ultima Online invented player housing so that players could build houses almost anywhere in the world, even turning them into shops with non-player characters acting as salesmen when the owner was offline. Soon after launch, the various worlds of *Ultima* were covered by rampant house-building schemes, with some players building just the walls of houses to claim the territory for themselves. The *Age of Shadows* expansion in 2003 allowed players to customize their homes in a variety of shapes, sizes and colours.

10 WAYS TO KILL THE "INVINCIBLE" LORD BRITISH

GAME	METHOD OF DEATH
Ultima	Persistent hitting; Lord British is not truly invincible, he just has high hit points
Ultima III	Lure him into your boat's cannon fire
Ultima IV	Surround him with lava repeatedly
Ultima IV	Use the Skull of Mondain, the sheer evil of which can kill instantly
Ultima V	Fail to rescue him – this will lead to his death from starvation
Ultima VI	Surround him with barrels of gunpowder, then light them
Ultima VI	Drag a poison trap to his throne while he's sitting on it
Ultima VI	Wait for Lord British to fall asleep, then stab him with a glass sword
Ultima VII	Look at the gold plaque with "Lord British" written on it when he's standing beneath it – this will fall and kill him
Ultima IX	Trick him into eating a poisoned loaf of bread

Source: Computerandvideogames.com

FIRST IN-GAME ECOSYSTEM

Holder: *Ultima Online* **(Origin Systems/EA, 1996)**

During *Ultima Online*'s closed beta, the developers worked very hard to create a working ecosystem. For example, the dragons in the game ate the deer, but if there were no deer left (as a result of players hunting them), the dragons would then attack towns for food.

At the time of launch, however, over-zealous players killed the creatures in the game's world so quickly that the ecosystem collapsed. It was promptly scrapped, making this the **first in-game ecosystem to become extinct**.

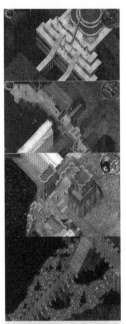

MMO WITH THE MOST CANCELLED SEQUELS

Holder: *Ultima Online*

Firstly, there was *Ultima Online 2*, announced in 1999, which then changed direction to become *Ultima Worlds Online: Origins*. This steampunk-themed sequel ran aground in 2001 when EA got cold feet about harming *UO* subscriptions. Next was *Ultima X: Odyssey*, a hybrid of the single-player and MMO *Ultimas*, which ended in 2004 when its developer dissolved. Yet another *UO* sequel, created solely for the Chinese market, was announced in 2009, but it has not been talked about since and all mentions of it appear to have vanished from developer Netdragon's website. Finally, 1997's abortive *UO* remake, *Kingdom Reborn*, was pulled in 2009 in favour of another new game client.

FANTASY MMORPGs

THE FIRST CROSS-PLATFORM MMORPG WAS *FINAL FANTASY XI* (SQUARE ENIX,

FASTEST-SELLING PC GAME

Holder: *World of Warcraft: Cataclysm* **(Blizzard, 2010)**
The third expansion pack for *World of Warcraft* became
the simultaneous holder of three records: **fastest-selling
MMO**, **fastest-selling MMO expansion** and **fastest-
selling PC game**. This was down to it shifting some
4.7 million copies within a month of release – 3.3 million
of which were on its first day. It takes these records
from the previous *WoW* expansion, *Wrath of the
Lich King*, which sold 2.8 million on its first day.

/// "A BEAUTIFUL AND DISTINCTIVE ARTWORK STYLE GIVES
THE APPEARANCE OF A WATERCOLOUR PAINTING IN MOTION" ///

$1 million The amount made by sales of iPhone MMORPG *Order & Chaos* (Gameloft, 2010) in its first 20 days. That's 140,000 copies in under three weeks.

2002), RELEASED ON THE XBOX 360, PLAYSTATION 2 AND PC ▶

TOP 10 MOST-SUBSCRIBED MMO GAMES

PLAYERS	GAME
11,400,000	World of Warcraft
3,400,000	Aion
1,300,000	Runescape
750,000	Lineage
750,000	Lineage II
520,000	Dofus
350,000	Eve Online
350,000	Final Fantasy XI
210,000	Lord of the Rings Online
125,000	City of Heroes/Villains

FIRST FREE-TO-PLAY CONSOLE MMO
Holder: *Free Realms* (SOE, 2011)
This virtual-world kids' MMO was initially exclusive to PC and Mac gamers, managing to amass over 17 million registered users. On 29 March 2011, it made the jump to the PlayStation network. In so doing, it became the first free-to-play MMO on a console, thus breaking a decades-long trend of consumers paying up-front for console games. Others quickly followed, including *Magic: The Gathering* (Stainless Games, 2010).

FIRST PLAYER TO REACH LEVEL 85 IN *WORLD OF WARCRAFT: CATACLYSM*
Holder: Athene, aka Forescience
This human "paladin character" – assisted by guildmates – was the first to "beat" the world's biggest MMO in its current form, managing to reach the hallowed level 85 within less than six hours of the release of latest expansion pack *Cataclysm*. For the average player, achieving this takes around a week-and-a-half of regular play.

MOST USERS SIMULTANEOUSLY ONLINE IN AN MMORPG
Holder: *Fantasy Westward Journey* (Netease, 2005)
World of Warcraft might be the world's biggest subscription MMO, with 11.4 million users, but of that global populace only a fraction are online at any one time. It's a different matter for the most popular Chinese online game, *Fantasy Westward Journey*. Some 1.66 million players were logged on concurrently on 2 March 2008.

LONGEST TIME PLAYING A VIDEOGAME WHILE TRAVELLING IN A CRATE
Holder: Jordan Wayne Long (USA)
One of this year's oddest gaming records took place from 1 to 8 July 2011, when performance artist Jordan Wayne Long spent seven days travelling 2,000 miles across the USA locked inside a tailor-made crate on a flatbed trailer. His only company was a laptop running *Lord of the Rings Online* (Turbine, 2007). Long took a set of clothes, 28 protein bars and four gallons of water. The only form of communication he had throughout the trip was in-game with another player documenting Long's *Lord of the Rings Online* activities on a public blog.

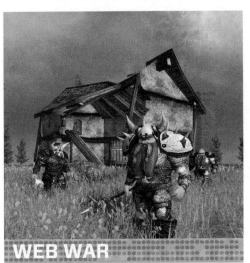

WEB WAR
More than 200 guilds within fantasy MMO *Darkfall* (Aventurine SA, 2009) "declared war" on games website Eurogamer.net in May 2009 after what fans perceived was an unfair review of the game. Eurogamer scored *Darkfall* 2/10, which led to outraged players creating a new guild called "EUROGAMER NET" and persuading almost every other guild on the game's server – comprising around 10,000 players – to activate a command which proclaimed it their sworn enemy. These events were in keeping with *Darkfall*'s gameplay, in which allied clans declare war upon both their own race and their allies.

Eurogamer later reconsidered their verdict, and, in re-reviewing the game, raised its score to 4/10.

SCI-FI MMORPGs

SHORTEST-LIVED MMO

Holder: *APB* **(Realtime Worlds, 2010)**
The much-anticipated online cops-and-robbers MMO *APB* collapsed just 79 days after it was launched on 29 June 2010. The game was rumoured to have a budget of $50 million (£32 million), but was criticized for its poor gameplay and failed to attract a sufficient number of paying subscribers. Realtime Worlds pulled the plug on *APB* on 16 September 2010, but it has since been reported that K2 Network has bought the rights to the game and has plans to redevelop it under the title *APB Reloaded*.

TOP 10 SHORTEST-LIVED SCI-FI AND FANTASY MMOs

LIFESPAN	GAME
79 days	*APB* (see above)
149 days	*SEED*
294 days	*Fury*
428 days	*Face of Mankind*
457 days	*Tabula Rasa*
507 days	*Auto Assault*
638 days	*Chronicles of Spellborn*
751 days	*Earth and Beyond*
1,134 days	*Asheron's Call 2*
2,120 days	*Time of Defiance*

Source: publishers' press releases

MOST USER-GENERATED MISSIONS IN AN MMO

Holder: *Star Wars Galaxies* **(Sony, 2003–2011)**
Released on 1 October 2009, the "Chronicle Master" update for *Star Wars Galaxies* enabled players to build their own quests within the game for others to play. The pack was a huge hit with the game's fans and within a month of its launch they had built over 3 million missions. One particularly dedicated gamer created more than 6,000 missions all on his own!

500,000 The number of regular subscriptions the upcoming *Star Wars* MMO *The Old Republic* will need to become profitable, according to publisher EA.

MOST EXPENSIVE VIRTUAL PROPERTY
Holder: SEE Virtual Worlds (USA)
On 20 December 2010, entertainment company SEE Virtual Worlds paid $6 million (£3,860,000) for Planet Calypso, a virtual planet within the online game *Entropia Universe* (MindArk, 2003). The virtual real-estate was purchased directly from the game's developers and – in a separate transaction – some of MindArk's in-house development team also joined SEE Digital. The company subsequently announced plans to build a Michael Jackson-themed planet in the MMO.

BIGGEST THREATENED PLAYER WALKOUT IN AN MMO
Holder: *Eve Online* **(CCP, 2003)**
As part of a protest against the "Incarna" update pack, 5,833 players claimed they had cancelled their subscriptions to sci-fi MMO *Eve Online*. Incarna allows players to finally leave their spaceships and introduces new charges for various aspects of gameplay including high-priced "vanity items" (in-game objects that offer no benefits except prestige). If the protesting players stay away from the game, its developer could be set to lose out on $87,203 (£54,432) in monthly subscription revenues.

MOST FREE MMO CONTENT UPDATES
Holder: *City of Heroes and Villains* **(NCsoft, 2004–present)**
In June 2010, NCsoft announced plans for the 21st free major update to its core superhero MMO. The update is planned to coincide with the game abandoning subscription charges, as it becomes a free-to-play game with optional paid-for content.

LARGEST VOICE CAST IN AN MMO
Holder: *DC Universe Online* **(Sony, 2011)**
The Non-Player Characters (NPCs) in MMOs usually communicate with players through on-screen text-based "speech", but Sony's superhero MMO *DC Universe Online* has opted to allow their NPCs to speak. A total of 236 actors recorded lines of dialogue for the MMO in advance of its launch on 11 January 2011, with many famous voices among them, including Mark Hamill (who played Luke Skywalker in the classic *Star Wars* trilogy) and Dwight Schultz (*The A-Team*'s Captain H.M. "Howling Mad" Murdock). Additional dialogue for future expansions will require new recordings from the actors.

SOCIAL NETWORK GAMING

THE MICROSOFT BING PAGE ON FACEBOOK GAINED 400,000 FRIENDS IN ONE

811,483   1   More in 3.26   11   0   3,950   36663   68

ADD COINS & CASH

FASTEST-GROWING SOCIAL GAME

Holder: *CityVille* **(Zynga, 2010)**
The follow-up to Zynga's smash hits *FarmVille* (2009) and *FrontierVille* (2010) had a lot to live up to, but *CityVille* turned out to be even more successful than its predecessors. The urban-building game claimed a staggering 26 million players within 12 days of its launch, and 290,000 users on its first day alone. After just a week, players had built 2.7 million homes, 500,000 bakeries and 5 million sections of road.

Welcome to Gardens of Time
● Locate Hidden Objects across Time
⚔ Collect Artifacts to Display in your Garden
🛡 Protect History from Sinister Forces!

Let's Get Started!

MOST EXPENSIVE SOCIAL GAME DEVELOPER ACQUISITION

Holder: Playdom
The Walt Disney Company made a clear statement of intent as regards social gaming when it purchased developer Playdom for $563 million (£350 million) in July 2010. This dwarfed EA's $275-million (£171-million) acquisition of rival firm Playfish in November 2009. Playdom's games, such as *Gardens of Time* (left) and *Mobsters*, "only" boasted 38 million monthly players at the time of the sale, compared with 60 million for Playfish, creators of *Pet Society*.

FIRST SOCIAL GAME BENEFICIAL TO THE ENVIRONMENT

Holder: *Ecotopia* **(Talkie, 2011)**
Ecotopia introduced environmental awareness to social gaming by offering in-game rewards for real-world achievements, such as recycling and composting. Players have to demonstrate their eco-achievements using the game's photo and video features. Its creators have also pledged to plant 25,000 real trees in São Paulo, Brazil.

750 million The number of active users on the world's most popular social networking website, Facebook, home to most major social MMO games.

DAY WHEN IT WAS ADVERTISED ON *FARMVILLE* (ZYNGA, 2009) ▶

Hello Cow
Cost: 200 Mooney
You need more mooney

Bacon Cow
Cost: 200 Mooney
You need more mooney

Oil Cow
Cost: 200 Mooney
You need more mooney

Longhorn Bull
Cost: 500 Mooney
You need more mooney

Mao Cow
Cost: 500 Mooney
You need more mooney

Bling Cow
Cost: 10,000 Mooney
This is your cow

TOP 10 MOST POPULAR SOCIAL NETWORK GAMES

RANK	GAME	MONTHLY ACTIVE USERS
1	*CityVille* (Zynga)	80,102,161
2	*Empires & Allies* (Zynga)	44,952,433
3	*FarmVille* (Zynga)	35,751,468
4	*Texas Hold 'Em Poker* (Zynga)	34,416,467
5	*Gardens of Time* (Playdom)	15,670,102
6	*FrontierVille* (Zynga)	12,393,042
7	*Monster Galaxy* (Gaia Online)	11,469,117
8	*CaféWorld* (Zynga)	11,292,852
9	*Bejeweled Blitz* (PopCap Games)	10,702,237
10	*Diamond Dash* (Wooga)	9,989,797

Source: Appdata.com   *Accurate at July 2011*

FIRST SATIRICAL SOCIAL NETWORK GAME
Holder: *Cow Clicker* (Ian Bogost, 2010)
American videogame designer Professor Ian Bogost describes *Cow Clicker* as "a Facebook game about Facebook games". This social network MMO satirizes titles such as *FarmVille*, and involves clicking on a picture of a cow every six hours. It drew an all-time monthly high of 54,245 users, and spawned a puzzle game, an iPhone game and an alternate reality game, making it the most successful satirical social MMO to date. It also sells new cow pictures to be clicked on, the most expensive of which, the "Roboclicker", had an asking price of 5,000 "Mooney", or £208 ($340).

MOST EXPENSIVE VIRTUAL ANIMAL
Holder: Pheasant from *FarmVille* (Zynga, 2009)
The priciest creature sold within a videogame is this high-prestige pheasant. Buying it costs players 2,000,000 *FarmVille* coins, or £835 ($1,300) if purchased with real money. The pheasant generates so few *FarmVille* coins that it would take 119 years to pay for itself, but it provides plenty of XP points.

BIGGEST SOCIAL GAME COMPANY
Holder: Zynga
Despite having only existed for three years, San Francisco firm Zynga has rapidly become one of the biggest fish in the gaming pond. A high of 280 million players per month makes it the biggest company of its kind. Its purchase of mobile game development start-up Newtoy added to Zynga's value, and in 2010, Zynga was valued at $5.5 billion (£3.5 billion). By June 2011, this figure had risen sharply to $20 billion (£12.5 billion), ahead of a stock exchange flotation.

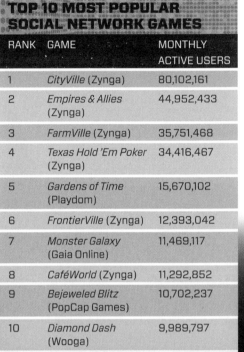

> " I did every horrible thing in the book just to get revenues right away."
> **ZYNGA CEO AND FOUNDER MARK PINCUS**

FIRST ALBUM TO DEBUT IN A SOCIAL NETWORK GAME
Holder: *Born This Way* (Lady Gaga, 2011)
Flamboyant pop star Lady Gaga decided on an eye-catching and original launch for her second album in May 2011. In collaboration with Zynga, she arranged for a special, glitzy modification of *FarmVille*, known as *GagaVille*, which contained quests to unlock individual *Born This Way* tracks a week before the album's release. By 20 May, three days before the album went on sale in the UK, it could be unlocked and heard in its entirety in *GagaVille*. Upon retail release, *Born This Way* went straight to No.1 in 23 countries, including the UK and the USA, where it sold 1.1 million copies in its first week alone.

STRATEGY & SIMULATION

OVERVIEW

Whether you're harvesting resources and building bases, executing hundreds of commands a minute or plotting the conquest of a long-lost civilization over the course of a leisurely Sunday afternoon, strategy and simulation games require some serious thought. *The Sims* and the *Civilization* series have dominated the simulation genre for well over a decade, a lifetime in videogame years, and both franchises are still going strong today. Meanwhile, the recent release of new episodes of *StarCraft II* (Blizzard, 2010) have reinvigorated the premier game in the strategy genre.

MOST USB PERIPHERALS FOR ONE GAME

Holder: Saitek "Procedure Trainer"

Designed to integrate with *Microsoft Flight Simulator X* (Microsoft, 2006), the peripherals manufacturer Saitek produces 18 different USB devices to mimic a variety of aeroplane cockpits. These devices range from display panels to steering yokes, simulating both combat and commercial aircraft. The company has even brought some of its products together into a demonstration rig it dubs the "Procedure Trainer" (pictured).

BIOGRAPHY

Eurogamer news editor Wesley Yin-Poole's love of virtual strategy began with *Sid Meier's Civilization* (MicroProse, 1991) on the Amiga 20 years ago. So enamoured was he with its depth and accuracy that he claims to have learnt more about history from the game's bulging manual than he ever did at school!

CONTENTS

CRITICAL HIT!: *STARCRAFT*   162
TURN-BASED STRATEGY   164
REAL-TIME STRATEGY   166
SIMULATION ROUND-UP   168
LIFE SIMULATORS   170

STARCRAFT

THERE ARE THREE PLAYABLE RACES IN *STARCRAFT*: THE HUMANOID TERRANS,

BEST-SELLING PC GAME OF 2010

Holder: *StarCraft II: Wings of Liberty* **(Blizzard, 2010)**
On 1 September 2010, Blizzard announced that
StarCraft II had outsold all other PC games released in
that year, shifting over 3 million copies in its first month
alone. By the end of December, it had sold 4.5 million
units, but the game has a long way to go to beat the
best-selling PC game ever – *The Sims*, which has
shipped over 16 million copies since 2000.

" I think we've
come up with the
ultimate real-time
strategy game in
StarCraft II."
**CARL CHIMES, LEAD SOFTWARE
ENGINEER ON *STARCRAFT II***

THE INSECTOID ZERG AND THE TECHNOLOGICALLY ADVANCED PROTOSS ▶

MOST POPULAR *STARCRAFT* PLAYER
Holder: Lim "SlayerS_BoxeR" Yo-Hwan (South Korea)
Boasting a fan club of a million-plus members, *StarCraft*'s best-known player is Lim Yo-Hwan. Known as "The Emperor of *StarCraft*", Lim has been the subject of a documentary film, and in June 2009 this two-time World Cyber Games champion was voted the all-time best *StarCraft* player by readers of TeamLiquid.net. He has even penned an autobiography, *Crazy Like Me* – compulsory reading for all pro-gamers.

FASTEST COMPLETION OF PROTOSS MISSION SEVEN IN *STARCRAFT*
Holder: Bryan Wilson (USA)
Throwing any sense of caution to the wind, Bryan Wilson completed the seventh mission in the Protoss campaign on *StarCraft* (Blizzard, 1998) in just 1 min 3 sec on 18 April 2010. His speedy time was due to the "suicide route" he took his five Templar units straight through an enemy base on the way to his destination. Bryan predicts that his incredible time could still be bettered, but only with "insane luck".

TOP 10 HIGHEST-RANKING PROFESSIONAL *STARCRAFT* PLAYERS

RANK	GAMER	GAMER TAG	RACE	POINTS
1	Lee Young-Ho	Flash	Terran	2,411
2	Lee Jae-Dong	n.Die_Jaedong	Zerg	2,377.5
3	Won Shin-Dong	hydra	Zerg	2,238.8
4	Jung Myung-Hoon	By.FanTaSy	Terran	2,190
5	Song Byung-Goo	stork	Protoss	1,980.8
6	Kim Taek-Yong	Bisu[Shield]	Protoss	1,929
7	Kim Myung-Woon	MenSol[Zero]	Zerg	1,703.3
8	Kim Yoon-Hwan	Inter.Calm	Zerg	1,626.8
9	Yum Bo-Sung	Sea[Shield]	Terran	1,406.3
10	Kim Gu-Hyun	GooJila	Protoss	1,253.3

Source: South Korean eSports Association KeSPA

MOST GAME DATA ILLEGALLY DOWNLOADED
Holder: *StarCraft II: Wings of Liberty* (Blizzard, 2010)
Illegal copies of most PC games can usually be found lurking around the darker corners of the internet, but *StarCraft II: Wings of Liberty* has proven especially popular on websites hosting illicit "torrents" of various games. One *StarCraft II* torrent weighing in at 7.19 GB was downloaded 2.3 million times in the three months after its official release. This amounts to 15.77 Petabytes of illegally distributed data – more than any single data warehouse in the world could store.

FASTEST COMPLETION OF ZERG MISSION SEVEN ON *STARCRAFT: BROOD WAR*
Holder: Blake "Spider-Waffle" Piepho (USA)
On 23 November 2005, Blake Piepho finished the seventh Zerg mission on *StarCraft: Brood War* (Blizzard, 1998) in 4 min 23 sec. The hallmarks of Zerg strategy are speed and overwhelming numbers – the "Zerg rush" – but Blake struggled to successfully employ such tactics on this level. In fact, he found it so hard-going that he only managed to complete it twice in five hours of attempts. Even after passing a key part of the mission, involving crossing a bridge with full health, Blake estimates he only had a 35% chance of completing the level.

FIRST VIDEOGAME TO BE INVOLVED IN A MATCH-FIXING SCANDAL
Holder: *StarCraft: Brood War* (Blizzard, 1998)
On 13 April 2010, the South Korean eSports scene was rocked with a series of match-fixing revelations in the popular *StarCraft: Brood War* league. At the time of going to press, 16 people had been implicated in the scandal, a figure that includes a gaming academy owner, a South Korean footballer and an alleged gangster as well as 11 professional players. The pro-gamers were accused of deliberately losing matches between September 2009 and February 2010, pocketing up to 6.5 million Korean Won ($5,400; £3,500) in bribes. Some gamers had also made as much as 35 million Won ($29,000; £19,000) from illegal bets. All 11 were handed lifetime bans by the Korean eSports Players Association KeSPA, effectively ending their professional careers.

In addition, the ex-players faced fines of up to 12.5 million Won ($10,000; £6,700), community service and suspended sentences that could mean jail if they commit further crimes.

FRUITFUL EXPERIENCE
Life as a professional *StarCraft* player is notoriously tough. Most pros typically train at the game for 10 hours a day, six days a week. So when pro-gamer Kim Won-Gi, then known as "Cool[fOu]", announced he was cutting down to a mere four hours a day to help his mother in the family fruit-selling business, some suggested he change his tag to "FruitDealer". Despite this, his Zerg army finished top in the final of the first Global *StarCraft II* League tournament. Along with the prize of 100,000,000 Korean Won ($83,000; £54,000), he was presented with a piece of personalized art depicting a trio of fruit-themed Zerg, in recognition of his respect for family duty.

TURN-BASED STRATEGY

IN 2011, *CIVILIZATION* LANDED ON FACEBOOK WITH *CIVILIZATION*

FIRST VIDEOGAME THEME TO WIN A GRAMMY AWARD

Holder: "Baba Yetu" from *Civilization IV* **(Firaxis, 2005)**

The Grammy Awards are recognized the world over as the "Oscars" of the music industry. On 13 February 2011, *Civilization IV* became the first game to feature a Grammy-winning theme song. Composer Christopher Tin (USA) won in the Best Instrumental Arrangement Accompanying Vocalist(s) category with "Baba Yetu", some six years after the song gained acclaim and attention as the opening theme of *Civilization IV*. Tin included the song on his 2009 album, *Calling All Dawns*, which is how it became eligible for a Grammy in 2011. The piece features the Soweto Gospel Choir and the Royal Philarmonic Orchestra.

FASTEST COMPLETION OF *CIVILIZATION IV: COLONIZATION*

Holder: Derek "Tentacle Monster" Zhang **(USA)**

On 19 March 2010, gamer Derek Zhang completed the epic *Civilization IV: Colonization* (Firaxis, 2008) in an incredible time of 14 min 38 sec. He achieved his record time on the "pilgrim difficulty", using the Dutch civilization. Derek said he wasn't "satisfied" with his running time, modestly admitting that "the luck in treasure drops were more responsible for the fast time than my execution, which was rather sloppy".

MOST CRITICALLY ACCLAIMED HOME CONSOLE TURN-BASED STRATEGY GAME

Holder: *Civilization Revolution* **(Firaxis, 2008)**

The highest-rated turn-based strategy game for a home console is the seventh in the *Civilization* series – the first for a console and not for the PC – which has an average score of 85% on Metacritic. The game was acclaimed upon release because of its intuitive user interface, slick control scheme and "one more turn" addictiveness. It was so good that some *Civilization* fans have said they prefer it to the usual PC version.

/// "COLLABORATION, CREATIVITY, LOCAL INSIGHT, COURAGE... 10 MISSIONS, 10 WEEKS" ///

745,890 The total sales of *Empire: Total War* (The Creative Assembly, 2009) as of August 2011, more than double those of follow-up *Napoleon: Total War*.

WORLD, IN WHICH PLAYERS JOIN WITH FRIENDS TO FORM NATIONS ▶

MOST ON-SCREEN UNITS IN A TURN-BASED STRATEGY GAME

Holder: *Total War: Shogun 2* **(The Creative Assembly, 2011)**

The battle engine in *Total War: Shogun 2* supports an enormous 56,000 soldiers in a single conflict. This is significantly higher than predecessor *Napoleon: Total War*'s best of 10,000, and 11 times higher than the first game in the series, *Shogun: Total War*, which had 5,000. Skirmishes between armies occur on land and sea, and siege battles often involve charging vast wall defences.

FIRST STRATEGY GAME TO WIN AN IVOR NOVELLO AWARD

Holder: *Napoleon: Total War* **(The Creative Assembly, 2010)**

The prestigious Ivor Novello Awards have been rewarding British musicians and songwriters since 1955. On 19 May 2011, strategy game *Napoleon: Total War* scooped the award for Best Original Videogame Soundtrack. Collecting the prize, lead composer Richard Beddow (UK) rubbed shoulders with the likes of Kylie Minogue and Plan B. The videogame category first appeared at the 2010 award ceremony.

ONE IN THE EYE

Brad Wardell, the CEO of development company Stardock, admitted that troubled PC turn-based strategy game *Elemental: War of Magic* (Stardock, 2010) gave the company a "black eye" following its "disastrous" launch. After poor reviews and disappointing sales, the company made lay-offs.

MOST SPECIES OF TREE IN A STRATEGY GAME

Holder: *Total War: Shogun 2* **(The Creative Assembly, 2011)**

Taking the phrase "attention to detail" to a whole new level, the latest title in the *Total War* series features the most different species of tree in a strategy game – a grand total of 80 – yet there are only 30 different types of combat unit!

The trees were realistically modelled by designers, who spent a year studying Japanese art. The game's developers painstakingly recreated buildings, units and weapons to accurately reflect feudal Japan and make sure that the game environment was as detailed as possible to simulate real-world warfare. The incredible detail isn't limited to trees: there are mountains and hills inspired by ancient Japanese art, and if players zoom in on the ground, they will see blades of grass and flowers swaying in the wind.

TOP 10 *CIVILIZATION V* PLAYER RANKINGS

PLAYER	POINTS*	MEDALS
Crafty1	126	60
lawofqr	59	31
Mallow	39	9
vexing	29	7
Firvulag	27	9
KungFuMonkey52	20	14
Peets	14	6
khrax	13	3
Kamist Reloe	12	2
hphazrd	9	1

Source: Hof.CivFanatics.net   * Accurate at 2 August 2011

MOST POST-RELEASE DOWNLOADABLE CONTENT FOR A TURN-BASED STRATEGY GAME

Holder: *Civilization V* **(Firaxis, 2010)**

Since its launch in September 2010, Firaxis' turn-based strategy hit *Civilization V* has seen the release of no fewer than six additional civilizations, adding to the 18 included with the game. These are Babylonia, Mongolia, Spain, the Inca Empire, the Polynesian Empire and the Danish civilization. Four new map packs were also made available.

PSP GAME *PATAPON* WAS THE FIRST RTS TITLE IN WHICH GAMERS COULD

BEST-SELLING RTS SERIES

Holder: *Command & Conquer*
(Westwood Studios, 1995–2003)
The most commercially successful RTS series to date is *Command & Conquer*, which had sold more than 30 million units as of July 2011. The last game in the series, *Command & Conquer 4: Tiberian Twilight* (EALA, 2010), concluded the saga, which began 15 years previously. In 2011, Electronic Arts announced plans to launch another title, to be developed by new strategy studio Victory Games.

MOST CRITICALLY ACCLAIMED REAL-TIME STRATEGY GAME

Holder: *Company of Heroes*
(Relic Entertainment, 2006)
Company of Heroes is the highest-rated game in the RTS genre to date, with an average review score of 93.82% according to the Gamerankings.com website. The game expands on the system of control points as an in-game resource. This system was popularized with the developer's earlier title, *Warhammer 40,000: Dawn of War* (Relic Entertainment, 2004), which dispensed with worker units in favour of a more combat-oriented, tactical experience.

FIRST RTS GAME
Holder: *Cytron Masters*
(Ozark Softscape, 1980)
In 1980, American Dan Bunten Berry created the game that started it all. *Cytron Masters* for the Atari and Apple II featured many elements found in modern examples of the genre, including real-time tactics that required players to build up their forces to win. Generators produced energy, which had to be harvested before being spent to produce robot warriors called Cytrons, which gamers controlled.

FIRST 3D RTS GAME
Holder: *Total Annihilation*
(Cavedog, 1997)
This ground-breaking PC title is powered by a physics engine that determines how projectiles, explosions and wreckage work on the battlefield. The terrain contains height values, which make its 2D surface appear three-dimensional. Hills, for example, obstruct fire or enhance visual and firing ranges. Various moving units are rendered in 3D, too. The game was released on the Microsoft Windows and Mac OS platforms.

/// "JACK BLACK IS EDDIE RIGGS. FROM ROADIE TO ROCK GOD" ///

700,000,000 Won The value (equivalent to £354,000; $502,570) of the three-year contract given to Jang "Moon" Jae Ho of South Korea by eSports team WeMade FOX in 2009.

GUINNESS WORLD RECORDS

DETERMINE ACTIONS BY INPUTTING SEQUENCES OF RHYTHMIC BEATS ▶

FASTEST COMPLETION OF *WARCRAFT III: REIGN OF CHAOS*
Holder: Philipp "Stupid" H (Germany)

It took *Warcraft* fan Philipp H a remarkably speedy 4 hr 26 min 4 sec to complete *Warcraft III: Reign of Chaos* (Blizzard, 2002) on 27 July 2007. This is the combined time for the Human, Undead, Orc and Night Elf campaigns (the prologue is not included). Philipp uses cutscene teleporting and level-cap management to speed through the game. *Reign of Chaos* is the second sequel to *Warcraft: Orcs & Humans*, following *Tides of Darkness*.

FASTEST COMPLETION OF *WARCRAFT III: THE FROZEN THRONE*
Holder: Juri Rosenkilde (Denmark)

On 3 September 2010, gamer Juri Rosenkilde set the record for the fastest completion of *Warcraft III: The Frozen Throne* (Blizzard, 2003). It took him just 2 hr 8 min, and was completed in Vallensbæk, Denmark. Like fellow speed runner "Stupid" (see above), Juri was able to teleport as a way of minimizing wasted time. He claims that expansion pack *The Frozen Throne* is more "speed-run friendly" than *Reign of Chaos* because there are no survival chapters.

TOP 10 *WARCRAFT III: THE FROZEN THRONE* PLAYERS

RANK	GAMER*	GAMER TAG
1	Kim Sung-Sik (South Korea)	ReMinD
2	Manuel Schenkhuizen (Netherlands)	Grubby
3	Park June (South Korea)	Lyn
4	Nikita Pomadov (Russia)	Nicker
5	Weiliang Lu (China)	Fly100%
6	Zhuo Zeng (China)	TED
7	Xiang Huang (China)	th000
8	Dmitry Kostin (Russia)	Happy
9	Thomas Glinski (Denmark)	GaB-ThomasG
10	Eom Hyo-Seop (South Korea)	FoCuS

* Finalists at World Cyber Games 2010

MOST CRITICALLY ACCLAIMED CONSOLE RTS
Holder: *Plants vs. Zombies* (PopCap, 2010)

The highest-rated console real-time strategy title is tower-defence game *Plants vs. Zombies* (below), which has an average review score of 89% on Metacritic. The multi-platform game's Xbox 360 release followed huge success on the PC and iPhone. The game's creator, George Fan (USA), was inspired by a popular *Warcraft III* modification called *Defense of the Ancients*.

MOST TOURNAMENT WINS ON *WARCRAFT III*
Holder: Jang "Moon" Jae Ho (South Korea)

Prolific *Warcraft III* (Blizzard, 2002) player Jang "Moon" Jae Ho has won eight World Championships and nine televised championships in Korea – the most tournament wins achieved by any player, as of 8 September 2011. The 25-year-old, whose Night Elf strategy is admired throughout the pro scene, won the eSports Player of the Year award in 2008, and his exploits were captured in the pro-gaming documentary film *Beyond the Game*.

SIMULATION ROUND-UP

IN 2007, EA RELEASED *RAIL SIMULATOR* FOR THE PC, WHICH ALLOWED GAMERS

launch detected

MOST DEATHS IN A SIMULATION GAME

Holder: *Defcon* (Introversion, 2006)

In *Defcon*, the player can cause the virtual deaths of billions of people through the use of nuclear weapons. This wargames simulator allows players to plot the destruction of rivals with carefully placed nuclear warheads. These are then deployed to devastating effect from ground units, aircraft and ships. *Defcon* also has the dubious "honour" of being described by its creators as "the world's first genocide-'em-up".

LONGEST DEVELOPMENT PERIOD FOR ANY VIDEOGAME

Holder: *Elite IV* (Frontier Developments, 1997–present)

Space sim *Elite IV* has been in development longer than any other game, even longer than *Duke Nukem Forever* (Gearbox Software, 2011), which launched after 13 years in production. At the Game Developers Conference in 2011, programmer David Braben confirmed that *Elite IV* was still in the works.

MICROFLY

Microsoft's closure of *Microsoft Flight Simulator* developer ACES caused a fan uproar. But in August 2010, Microsoft announced *Microsoft Flight*, a new flight sim intended to replace the discontinued franchise. The developer is an internal team at Microsoft Game Studios made up of the same creative minds that made *Flight Simulator*.

MOST CRITICALLY ACCLAIMED PURE FLIGHT SIMULATOR

Holder: *Microsoft Flight Simulator 2002* (ACES Game Studio, 2001)

The *Microsoft Flight Simulator* franchise dominated the flight sim genre throughout its run from 1982 to 2006. The highest-rated title is *Microsoft Flight Simulator 2002*, which has an average review score of 90% on Metacritic. The 2002 edition introduced interactive air-traffic control and artificial-intelligence aircraft, which enable users to fly alongside computer-controlled aeroplanes and to communicate with airports.

/// "A PERSISTENT, UNSHARDED GAME WORLD, FULLY CUSTOMIZABLE MECHS AND ROBOTS WITH HUNDREDS OF EQUIPMENT ITEMS" ///

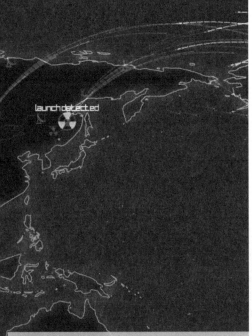

launch detected

TOP 10 MOST CRITICALLY ACCLAIMED COMBAT AND FLIGHT SIMULATORS

GAME	SCORE*	RELEASE DATE
FreeSpace 2	91%	30 September 1999
IL-2 Sturmovik	91%	18 November 2001
Flight Simulator 2002	90%	19 October 2001
Falcon 4.0: Allied Force	90%	28 June 2005
Star Wars Rogue Leader: Rogue Squadron II	90%	9 November 2001
Galaxy on Fire 2	90%	27 October 2010
Ace Combat 4: Shattered Skies	89%	1 November 2001
Microsoft Flight Simulator 2004	88%	29 July 2003
FirePower for Microsoft Combat Flight Simulator 3	88%	11 June 2004
Crimson Skies: High Road to Revenge	88%	21 October 2003

Source: Metacritic.com   * Accurate at 5 August 2011

TRAUMA SURGEONS

Trauma Center (Atlus, 2005–present) is a futuristic Japanese fusion of simulation and visual novel that casts a player in the role of a surgeon at a fictional hospital. The Nintendo platform series makes use of motion and touch abilities to simulate surgery. The Wii games, for example, enable players to move the Wii controller as a scalpel, and to weave it as if stitching wounds. It's not for the squeamish!

MOST CRITICALLY ACCLAIMED SPACE-COMBAT SIMULATOR

Holder: *FreeSpace 2* **(Volition, 1999)**
With an average review score of 91% on Metacritic, *FreeSpace 2* is the highest-rated space-combat simulation game. Developer Volition's sequel to 1998's *Descent: FreeSpace – The Great War* is considered by some to be the definitive simulation game. Players assume the role of pilots, flying starfighters for a galactic government in order to fight nefarious aliens and defend the human race.

FIRST STREET-CLEANING SIMULATOR

Holder: *Street Cleaning Simulator* **(Astragon/TML Studios, 2011)**
The appropriately named *Street Cleaning Simulator* is one for fans of the quirkier sims games. Players own and operate a small firm specializing in keeping the town's roads free from leaves and dirt. The street-cleaning machine has three brushes and high-powered jets, much needed to get rid of irksome street dirt. The game was released for the PC, and the same developers also created *Garbage Truck Simulator* and *Farming Simulator*.

LIFE SIMULATORS

THE SIMS (MAXIS, 2000), THE BEST-SELLING TITLE IN THE SERIES TO DATE, HAD

FASTEST-GROWING ONLINE PET SIM

Holder: *Moshi Monsters*
(Mind Candy, 2008)

Browser gamers have taken to pet simulation in a big way. The most recent success story is kids' site *Moshi Monsters*, which announced in June 2011 that it had exceeded 50 million registered user accounts. That works out at an average of 43,029 users joining every single day – enough to fill 103 Jumbo Jets.

Moshi Monsters has been particularly successful in the UK, where over half of all children aged between six and 12 have logged on and adopted a colourful creature.

/// "A MYSTERIOUS JESTER. A FORBIDDEN SCEPTRE. A FIENDISH CURSE" ///

SOLD MORE THAN 16 MILLION COPIES WORLDWIDE AS OF AUGUST 2011 ▶

MOST CRITICALLY ACCLAIMED LIFE SIM

Holder: *The Sims* **(Maxis, 2000)**
The highest-rated life simulator is the very first *The Sims* game, which has an average review score of 92% according to Metacritic. American creator Will Wright's masterpiece popularized the life-simulation genre and, in doing so, influenced a host of PC games. *The Sims Deluxe* (Maxis, 2002) also scores 92% on Metacritic, but it is essentially a re-release of *The Sims* combined with the popular expansion pack *Livin' Large* (Maxis, 2000).

TOP 10 MOST CRITICALLY ACCLAIMED MAXIS-CREATED GAMES

GAME	REVIEW SCORE	RELEASE DATE
The Sims	92%	31 January 2000
The Sims Deluxe	92%	15 September 2002
The Sims 2	90%	14 September 2004
The Sims: Hot Date	85%	12 November 2001
Spore	84%	7 September 2008
SimCity 4	84%	12 January 2003
The Sims: Livin' Large	82%	27 August 2000
The Sims: Bustin' Out	81%	15 December 2003
The Sims 2: University	81%	28 February 2005
The Sims: Makin' Magic	80%	28 October 2003

Source: Metacritic.com   Accurate at 4 August 2011

THE WRIGHT STUFF

The Sims creator Will Wright (USA) is working on a game inspired by sci-fi author Bruce Sterling's short story *Maneki Neko*. Will describes his new project as being about "a karmic computer that keeps a balance of payments between different people, causing them to interact with each other in interesting ways to improve their lives". The plan is to release the game on social networks, tablets and smartphones.

FIRST LIFE SIMULATOR IN GLASSES-FREE 3D

Holder: *nintendogs + cats* **(Nintendo EAD, 2011)**
The first life sim to appear in 3D – and therefore not require the player to wear 3D glasses – is the latest in the *nintendogs* series. The 3DS's inner camera helps the virtual puppy recognize the player's face, and dogs can even follow a player's head movements. The pop-up pooches appear to leap out of the screen to lick their "owner". As the name of the game suggests, cats now also appear in the series.

BEST-SELLING PC SERIES

Holder: *The Sims* **(Maxis, 2000–present; The Sims Studio, 2008–present)**
In March 2011, EA announced that combined sales of *The Sims* series had totalled over 125 million in the 11 years since its launch. The new figure solidifies the simulation game's position as the best-selling PC series to date. It is now translated into over 20 different languages and sold in at least 60 countries. What's more, with an incredible 250 million downloads of user-generated content (UGC), *The Sims 3* (The Sims Studio, 2009) holds the record for the **highest number of downloads of** **UGC for a simulation game**. The content created by *Sims* aficionados includes characters, houses and stories. The figure beats the 154 million UGC items uploaded to the Sporepedia, where users of *Spore* (Maxis, 2008) share their creations.

FIRST DATING SIMULATOR

Holder: *Girl's Garden* **(Sega, 1984)**
The first romantically themed simulator was *Sonic the Hedgehog* creator Yuji Naka's debut, *Girl's Garden*. The 8-bit title was released exclusively in Japan for Sega's own SG-1000 console. The plot involves a pink-haired country girl named Papri collecting 10 different flowers, and evading several bears, in order to prevent her boyfriend, Minto, from falling for another girl.

INSTANT GAMING

OVERVIEW

Instant games are straightforward enough to be played immediately, without the need for manuals or complex explanations. Easily playable, they are instant by their very nature. Mobile phones and handheld consoles have made gaming a portable experience, and there are still plenty of arcades providing instant gaming at the drop of a coin. Installed in cinemas, bowling alleys, restaurants and bars as well as specialist videogame arcades, non-home arcade games have long been enjoyed by gamers. While arcades are not as popular outside of Japan as they once were, coin-ops are still viable crowd-pullers with new machines produced each year. But that's not all. Since 2001, there has been a rise in the popularity of alternate reality games, which gather people together online and take puzzle-solving into the real world.

BIOGRAPHY

Having written for *Amstrad Action* and *Amiga Format* in the 1990s, David Crookes now pens articles for several gaming magazines, including the award-winning *GamesTM* and *Retro Gamer*. He also writes for *The Independent* and has a games column which appears in several UK regional newspapers. He is the curator of *Videogame Nation*, which ran for much of 2011 in the north-east of England, having made its debut in 2009.

CONTENTS

CRITICAL HIT!: *DONKEY KONG*   174
CLASSIC ARCADE   176
MODERN ARCADE   178
ALTERNATE REALITY GAMES   180

PAC-MAN TM&(C)NAMCO BANDAI Games Inc.

LARGEST *PAC-MAN* VIDEOGAME

Holder: *The World's Biggest PAC-MAN* **(Soap Creative, 2011)**

Measured by its total number of pixels, the largest PAC-MAN game is *The World's Biggest PAC-MAN*, with a total of 4,014,144,000 pixels across 62,721 mazes. The game, playable online at worldsbiggestpacman.com, went live on 12 April 2011 and was developed by Australia's Soap Creative agency to celebrate 30 years since the original arcade release by Namco. As well as letting Facebook users play against each other, the game allows fans to design and share their own levels. Based on the total number of PAC-Dots eaten as of 27 September 2011, the USA ranks highest (with 531,665,193), followed by Brazil (with 157,076,610) and then Argentina (with 89,163,674).

DONKEY KONG

DONKEY KONG, WHICH CELEBRATED ITS 30TH BIRTHDAY IN 2011, FEATURED THE

LARGEST *DONKEY KONG* HIGH-SCORE COMPETITION

Holder: The Kong Off

Hosted by Richie Knucklez Arcade Games in Flemington, New Jersey, USA, on 19–20 March 2011, The Kong Off pitted 32 entrants, including 12 established *Donkey Kong* players, in a contest to see who could amass the highest score. Seasoned gamer Hank Chien (USA) won the two-day contest with a score of 994,400 points, far short of his own record.

2,000 The number of *Donkey Kong* arcade cabinets made in the machine's original manufacturing run. The game proved so popular that it completely sold out.

TOP 10 SCORES ON *DONKEY KONG JR* (ARCADE CABINET)

RANK	SCORE	PLAYER	DATE
1	1,307,500	Mark L Kiehl (USA)	19 Jul 2010
2	1,270,900	Billy L Mitchell (USA)	31 Jul 2010
3	1,190,400	Steve J Wiebe (USA)	11 Feb 2010
4	1,033,000	Ike Hall (USA)	10 Aug 2008
5	953,500	Antonio Medina (USA)	6 Feb 1983
6	951,100	Matt Brass (USA)	20 Jan 1983
7	948,000	Kent Farries (Canada)	6 Nov 1982
8	885,200	John Bishop (USA)	11 Jan 1983
9	873,700	Bill Newshan (USA)	11 Jan 1983
10	870,400	Victor HugoFalbo (USA)	1 Dec 1983

Source: TwinGalaxies.com

HIGHEST SCORE ON *DONKEY KONG*

Holder: Hank Chien (USA)
On 27 February 2011, Hank Chien claimed the highest score on the arcade cabinet version of *Donkey Kong* with a total of 1,090,400 points. Chien's score trumped those of rivals Steve Wiebe and Billy Mitchell (both USA), whose long-running battle for the highest score on the game formed the basis of documentary film *The King of Kong* (USA, 2007). The previous record of 1,064,500 points was set by Wiebe on 30 August 2010 while Mitchell's best score is the 1,062,800 points he recorded on 31 July 2010.

WONKY WRONG?

In his guise as clueless gamer Keith Apicary, actor/comedian Nathan Barnatt (USA) has laid claim to the spurious "record" for the lowest ever *Donkey Kong Jr* score. The impressively low score of -400 was supposed to be due to Apicary's incredibly poor gaming skills.

Barnatt even appeared in character to discuss his "achievement" in an interview on the twingalaxies.com video podcast. Many gamers missed the joke and were completely fooled!

MOST EXPENSIVE *DONKEY KONG* CARTRIDGE

Holder: *Donkey Kong Country* Competition Cartridge (Nintendo, 1995)
In terms of physical game cartridges, the *Donkey Kong* title that has fetched the highest price is the *Donkey Kong Country* Competition Cartridge. The game was produced for the Blockbuster World Videogame Championship II in 1995 and just 2,500 copies were made. Now a collector's item, copies have since sold for as much as $1,000 (£625).

SMALLEST *DONKEY KONG* CABINET

Holder: Sean "Bender" Beavers (USA)
Shrinking things down considerably, seasoned modifier of gaming tech, Sean "Bender" Beavers, managed to manufacture a tiny *Donkey Kong* arcade cabinet measuring just 21 cm (8.25 in) tall, making it 512 times smaller than the full-size games cabinet, by volume. Sean's machine was powered by a modified version of the open-source handheld GamePark GP2X, and featured tinted glass to make it look like the full-scale cabinet.

FIRST USE OF A D-PAD IN A GAMING SYSTEM

Holder: *Donkey Kong* Game & Watch handheld (Nintendo, 1982)
The first gaming machine to have a modern cross-design directional pad was the 1982 Game & Watch conversion of the original *Donkey Kong* arcade game. Strangely, the later Game & Watch version of *Donkey Kong Jr* had a directional controller made up of four separate round buttons. The D-pad was the innovation that paved the way for portable, pocket-friendly handheld gaming, and its folding "clamshell" design proved both popular and influential.

> "One thing I can say is I am constantly thinking."
>
> SHIGERU MIYAMOTO, CREATOR OF *DONKEY KONG*

MOST *DONKEY KONG 3* RECORDS

Holder: George Riley (USA)
Donkey Kong 3 fan George Riley holds four high scores for the game on marathon and tournament settings for both the arcade cabinet and the Multiple Arcade Machine Emulator (MAME) versions. On arcade, George hit 3,087,100 points for the marathon record and 857,200 points under tournament conditions. On the MAME, he scored 3,676,000 points for the marathon record and amassed 806,500 points in tournament mode.

STUBBORN GORILLA

According to his oft-repeated story, gaming guru and *Donkey Kong* creator Shigeru Miyamoto came up with the English name for his game by looking up alternative words for the descriptors "stubborn" and "gorilla" in a dictionary.

CLASSIC ARCADE

FIRST 3D ARCADE GAME

Holder: *SubRoc-3D* (Sega, 1982)

The first arcade game to offer players a 3D gaming experience was the FPS *SubRoc-3D*. The game used a special 3D viewer to send slightly different images to both of the player's eyes, enabling him or her to perceive a stereoscopic 3D image. The cabinet used simple technology in comparison to today's 3D machines – the goggles contained spinning discs that alternated the images that the player's eyes could see.

MOST PROFITABLE ARCADE RELEASE

Holder: *Space Invaders* (Taito, 1978)

Designed by Japan's Tomohiro Nishikado, the iconic *Space Invaders* generated more than $500 million (£309 million) for developer Taito from sales of 360,000 arcade units manufactured during the title's production run up to 1983. This figure places it ahead of *PAC-Man* (Namco, 1980), which sold 350,000 units.

ADAPTED AS A BOARD GAME BY MILTON BRADLEY (USA) ▶

MOST PROLIFIC VIDEOGAME GRAFFITI ARTIST

Holder: Invader

A French street artist who goes by the name of Invader has produced more than 1,000 mosaics of classic arcade sprites. In June 2011, he created his 1,000th example in Paris, the city in which he put up his first mosaic in 1998. The artist claims his idea is to "bring the virtual into reality" and his mosaics can now be seen in 22 cities across Europe as well as Tokyo, New York and Mombasa. He even placed one on the Hollywood sign in Los Angeles.

TOP 10 HIGHEST SCORES ON *ASTEROIDS* (ATARI, 1979)

RANK	SCORE	PLAYER	DATE
1	41,838,740	John P McAllister (USA)	5 Apr 2010
2	41,336,440	Scott Safran (USA)	13 Nov 1982
3	40,101,910	Leo P Daniels (USA)	6 Feb 1982
4	30,100,100	Dennis Hernandez (USA)	12 Jan 1982
5	30,000,000	Lonnie J Cancienne (USA)	20 Nov 1981
6	25,932,800	Jay Howell (USA)	5 Nov 1981
7	25,930,690	Wayne MacLemore (USA)	5 Jul 1981
8	23,274,970	Rick V Scott (USA)	23 Jun 1981
9	20,832,560	Douglas J Ede (USA)	16 May 1981
10	20,307,890	Mike Titus (USA)	12 Mar 1982

Source: TwinGalaxies.com

HIGHEST SCORE ON *BUBBLE BOBBLE*

Holder: Olly J Cotton (UK)
On 23 February 2011, gamer Olly J Cotton popped his way to a score of 6,060,730 on *Bubble Bobble* (Taito, 1986).

FIRST ARCADE GAME BOSS

Holder: *Phoenix* (Amstar Electronics, 1980)
A key innovation in the world of shoot-'em-up games, Taito's space-themed shooter *Phoenix* featured the first extra-strong end-of-level enemy after five rounds of regular enemies had been vanquished.

LEGS PLAY!

Centipede (Atari, 1980) was the **first arcade game co-developed by a woman**. It was produced by Ed Logg and Dona Bailey, who was the only female software engineer employed by Atari at the time. Bailey went on to teach at the University of Arkansas.

"Studies have shown that games are one of the best ways for people to learn."

NOLAN BUSHNELL, CREATOR OF *PONG* (ATARI, 1972)

FIRST ARCADE GAME TO USE A MICROPROCESSOR
Holder: *Gun Fight* (Midway, 1975)
Before the release of *Gun Fight*, early arcade machines used simple logic-gate circuits to create the games they displayed. The original *Gun Fight* arcade machines designed by Taito for the Japanese and European markets used this technology. When Midway acquired the rights to publish the game in the USA, they completely redesigned the machine to incorporate the cheaper Intel 8080 microprocessor.

MOST PLAYERS SUPPORTED ON A *PAC-MAN* ARCADE GAME

Holder: *PAC-Man Battle Royale* (Namco Bandai Games, 2011)
Enabling up to four-way play, the *PAC-Man Battle Royale* cabinet was released in January 2011 in the wake of the 30th anniversary of *PAC-Man*. Requiring at least two players, *Battle Royale* is a more adversarial version of the game than the original, which pitted the player against computer-controlled ghosts. In this game, each player gains the ability to gobble their opponents when they consume a power pellet. As well as displaying scores, the game also collects other stats such as the player who won most rounds or ate the most *PAC-Man* characters.

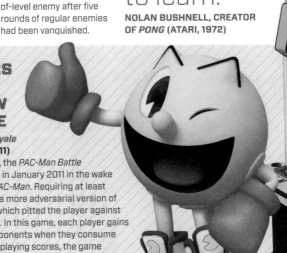

MODERN ARCADE

TERMINATOR SALVATION (RAW THRILLS, 2010) IS ONE OF THE FASTEST-SELLING

Shown with iPhones for scale

SMALLEST MAME CABINET

Holder: Pixelbox (Vance Fry, 2007)
The smallest functional MAME (Multiple Arcade Machine Emulator) cabinet in the world is Pixelbox, a project launched by gaming enthusiast Vance Fry (USA). Pixelbox has almost all of the capabilities of a full-sized arcade cabinet, yet its acrylic box is just 33 cm (13 in) in height and 25 cm (10 in) in width. It has a single-player control panel and a trackball measuring 3.8 cm (1.5 in). The cabinet is powered by a 2GHz Pentium M processor with a gigabyte of RAM, and it consists of a one-player control panel with Sanwa arcade parts and a trackball.

MOST VERSATILE ARCADE EMULATOR

Holder: MAME
An arcade emulator replicates the behaviour of hardware in original arcade machines. The most widely used arcade game emulator is the MAME, which was released on 5 February 1997 and has the ability to emulate a large number of central processing units. Developed by Italian Nicola Salmoria as a not-for-profit project, this open-source emulator has gone on to support more than 5,000 different games.

/// "THE GAME THAT STARTED IT ALL IS ABOUT TO START AGAIN" ///

40,000 yen The price Japanese gamers paid for a rare subspecies of stag beetle following the huge success of *Mushiking: King of the Beetles* (Sega, 2003).

RECENT ARCADE GAMES, PUSHING 1,000 UNITS IN LESS THAN 30 DAYS ▶

LARGEST CLAW MACHINE

Holder: The Santa Claw (Real Art Design, 2011)

At 5.1 m (17 ft) x 2.4 m (8 ft) x 3.6 m (12 ft), the epic Santa Claw holds the record for the largest claw machine. Allowing gamers to remotely control it over the internet, the game started on 3 January 2011 and ended in May 2011, with 100,000 gamers having tried their luck. Online gamers could use their keyboard arrow keys or mouse to control the giant claw, watching as two cameras located within the machine broadcast live online at thesantaclaw.com. More than 4,000 prizes were grabbed, each of them posted out to the winners.

TOP 10 FASTEST BEGINNER LAP TIMES ON *DAYTONA USA* (MULTIPLE MODES)

RANK	TIME	PLAYER	MODE
1	17.190 seconds	Jeffrey D Lowe, Jr (USA)	Traffic
2	17.320 seconds	Brian Ho (USA)	Traffic
3	17.450 seconds	Brian Ho (USA)	Time Attack
4	17.590 seconds	Jeffrey D Lowe, Jr (USA)	Time Attack
5	17.760 seconds	Mr Kelly R Flewin (Canada)	Time Attack
6	17.980 seconds	Patrick Scott Patterson (USA)	Time Attack
7	18.000 seconds	Nicole S Ashdown (Canada)	Traffic
8	18.100 seconds	David R Archey (USA)	Traffic
9=	18.120 seconds	Rusty Nunnelee (USA)	Time Attack
9=	18.120 seconds	David C Hernly (USA)	Traffic

Source: TwinGalaxies.com

FIRST ARCADE GAME TO USE A "KEY" AS A NET ENTRY SERVICE
Holder: *Battle Gear 3* (Taito, 2002)

Japanese racing game *Battle Gear 3* enables its players to use a "net entry key" to unlock additional features and register their rankings online. The PS2 release of the game offers a secure personal code that can be used on the arcade cabinet in game centres. It allows players to upload their Best Time records and unlock certain features such as new cars and parts, as well as providing exclusive access to online gameplay.

FIRST ARCADE GAME TO INTEGRATE TWITTER
Holder: *Virtua Fighter 5 Final Showdown* (Sega, 2010)

Virtua Fighter 5 Final Showdown is the first arcade game to allow players to link together their Virtua Fighter and Twitter accounts. This means players can follow each other's fortunes (or otherwise) while they punch and kick their way through bouts. Impressive combat moves are posted automatically on to the fast-growing social network. According to Sega, 16% of Japanese internet users have Twitter accounts.

FIRST NON-GLASSES 3D ARCADE CABINET
Holder: *Disney 3D Ping Pong* (3D Group, 2010)

The first arcade cabinet to allow gamers to play in 3D without the use of glasses was *Disney 3D Ping Pong*. Although the Nintendo 3DS was the first handheld to offer glasses-free 3D gaming, *Disney 3D Ping Pong* pipped it to the post. Released in China, Hong Kong, Macau and Taiwan, it stars three legendary Disney characters – Mickey Mouse, Minnie Mouse and Donald Duck. The ping-pong balls they strike appear to whizz out of the screen.

MOST PROLIFIC COIN-OPERATED VIDEOGAME FRANCHISE
Holder: *Golden Tee Golf* (Incredible Technologies, 1989–present)

As of September 2011, the arcade golf videogame franchise *Golden Tee Golf* has had 27 versions produced – more than any other coin-operated arcade. *Golden Tee 2010* (Incredible Technologies, 2009) is the **first arcade game to allow players to upload their best shots to YouTube**. The series has been played by approximately 1 billion people in 12 countries. The very first game appeared in 1989 as a 2D, 18-hole golfing experience.

ALTERNATE REALITY GAMES

ILOVEBEES WAS THE FIRST ALTERNATE REALITY GAME TO WIN ITSELF A GAME

WHAT IS AN ARG?

Strictly speaking, alternate reality games (ARGs) are not so much "games" as interactive stories that the reader or "player" engages with via websites, telephone messages, e-mails and various other elements set up specifically for the "game".

Used mainly as a marketing tool to promote a film, product or event, ARGs blur the boundaries between virtual and real life, They frequently involve puzzles that can be solved by people from around the world collaborating to uncover the next part of the story, online or in person.

Follow our investigation as we piece together the evidence for world records in this genre of gaming...

David is 11 years old,
He weighs 60 pounds,
He is 4 feet, 6 inches tall.
He has brown hair.
His love is real.
But he is not.

A.I.
A STEVEN SPIELBERG FILM
ARTIFICIAL INTELLIGENCE

SUMMER 2001

FIRST COMMERCIAL ARG

The Beast (Microsoft) was an ARG that ran for 12 weeks in 2001 to help promote the film *A.I.: Artificial Intelligence* (2001). The first clue most players came across was a mysterious credit on the film's poster for a "Jeanine Salla", a "Sentient Machine Therapist". Googling her name led the curious to a series of websites set in the film's world that told the story of a murder mystery.

Who is Jeanine Salla? Sentient Machine Therapist?

Longest-running ARG website

• Founded in 2001 by American ARG enthusiast Steve Peters, ARGN.com is a large news blog covering the latest developments in the world of alternate reality gaming.

• The site's player forums have been active since 2002 and its oldest news article dates from October of that year.

ARGNet
Alternate Reality Gaming Network

Most languages associated with an ARG

Created by the interactive marketing agency AKQA and American games designer Jane McGonigal (left), *The Lost Ring* was an ARG that ran during the Beijing Olympics in 2008. It was based on the idea that an Olympic sport called "labyrinth running" had been lost to history 2,000 years ago, but that five labyrinth runners had recently turned up across the world. To make the game accessible to a global audience, its websites were translated into eight languages. In total, more than 2.5 million users participated in the game.

Find out more about Labyrinth Running

DEVELOPERS' CONFERENCE INNOVATION AWARD ▶

Largest cash prize for an ARG

The goal of the ARG *Perplex City* (Mind Candy, 2005) was to find and recover the Receda Cube (right), a mysterious object stolen from the fictional city. The puzzle-based treasure hunt involved collecting trading cards and meeting other players to solve puzzles. Andy Darley (UK, below) eventually unearthed the cube, buried in Wakerley Great Wood, UK. He won the game's £100,000 ($172,000) cash prize for his efforts.

NB: These games often include objects placed in the real world!

Dave Szulborski: Mr Big of the ARG world

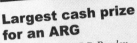

THE COLLECTIBLE PUZZLE CARD GAME

PERPLEXCITY
WWW.PERPLEXCITY.COM

"THE PUZZLE ... NG UP TO BECOME THE
INTERAC... ...N OF THE YEAR"

937 3486723 30573 8 782301   • 2 FEB 2007

Obituary   24 April 2009

Dave Szulborski, Most prolific ARG developer

Between 2001 and 2008, pioneering American game designer Dave Szulborski (1957–2009) worked on a total of 13 major ARGs, starting with "Majestic", EA's attempt to create an immersive, persistent government-conspiracy-themed game. He went on to become the first professional independent ARG developer and wrote a number of books about how to make and play them.

continues to redefine ... games can and should be though th... ...breaking.

Videogame attracts +10 million players

Why So Serious? was an ARG created by 42 Entertainment as part of a viral marketing campaign tied to the release of the movie *The Dark Knight* (2008). The game, which played out over 14 months and recruited more than 10 million players, encouraged gamers to dress up as The Joker and become involved in a fictional election campaign for the film's District Attorney, Harvey Dent.

MOST PLAYERS OF AN ARG   **Daily Record** 42

Search the web:
gothamcabs
thegothamtimes
whysoserious

GOTHAM POLICE DEPARTMENT
UPDATE: "JOKER" ELIMINATED – ALL FORCES STAND DOWN

Do Not Disseminate
Police Department Use ONLY

/// "LATELY, ITS OUTPUT HAS BEEN LESS THAN SATISFACTORY" ///

TOP 50 GAME ENDINGS

OVERVIEW

The readers have spoken! Welcome to *Gamer's Edition 2012*'s greatest 50 videogame endings, as voted for by you, the readers. Those of you who logged on to **www.guinnessworldrecords.com/gamers** had the chance to cast a vote from 25 February to 15 August 2011. During this time, an amazing 13,519 dedicated *Gamer's Edition* readers used the online poll to register their love for a whole host of game endings across several different genres. From sandbox titles to shooters, this top 50 offers a definitive list of great endings, and while there are bound to be plenty of your favourites in there, it'll also remind you of some classics you'd forgotten all about.

/// SPOILER

WARNING!

Everyone has an opinion on how to end a game, whether it's an epic boss fight, a clever plot twist or a 90-minute movie. We've got all that and more on the pages that follow. But a word of warning: as this year's vote is dedicated to game endings, it is absolutely full of spoilers about plots, characters and gameplay. If you don't want to know how these games end, you should stop reading now and turn to page 192. If you just can't wait to find out what happens, read on and prepare to be amazed!

ALERT!!!

50. RESIDENT EVIL 4
(Capcom, 2005)
Special agent Leon S Kennedy's final confrontation with the cult leader Osmund Saddler stays true to the classic *Resident Evil* series tradition of providing the player with a rocket launcher, just when it seems as if all is lost.

49. STAR WARS: KNIGHTS OF THE OLD REPUBLIC
(BioWare, 2003)
In a shocking, unexpected plot twist, the player character, who is forced to choose between the paths of good or evil, is revealed to be the missing Sith Lord, Darth Revan!

48. RATCHET & CLANK FUTURE: A CRACK IN TIME
(Insomniac, 2009)
After a showdown with Alister, a Lombax who wants to see his species repopulate the dimension, Ratchet and Clank (right) depart for the stars once more. Their foe, Captain Qwark, is left stranded on an asteroid with a hungry WarGrok...

47. CRYSIS 2
(Crytek, 2011)
Our hero, the protagonist Alcatraz (right) puts an end to the invading Ceph aliens by turning their own bioweapons against them. This neatly removes the need for the human resistance to nuke New York. Too bad that Alcatraz is then assimilated by a consciousness stored in his own Nanosuit...

46. THE ELDER SCROLLS IV: OBLIVION
(Bethesda Softworks, 2006)
With the help of the player, Martin Septim, the heir to an empire, transforms into a godly dragon and banishes the army of Daedra creatures back through the "oblivion gate" from whence they came. While the dragon turns to stone, the player is rewarded with the title "Champion of Cyrodiil" and some nifty new armour.

45. CALL OF DUTY: WORLD AT WAR
(Treyarch, 2008)
Our hero, the Soviet soldier Private Dimitri Petrenko, is shot up in a hail of bullets from a dying Nazi soldier. But his wounds don't stop him from planting the Soviet Flag above the Reichstag, signalling an end to World War II in Europe.

44. STAR WARS: THE FORCE UNLEASHED II
(LucasArts, 2010)
Our ending here "depends greatly on our own point of view," as a certain Jedi might say. If you choose the light side you end the game flying off into space with your love interest, pursued by Boba Fett. If you choose the dark side you are killed by an even more evil clone of your character.

43. HALF-LIFE 2: EPISODE TWO
(Valve, 2007)
After braving countless antlions (below) and headcrabs, our hero Gordon Freeman successfully repels an assault from the forces of the Combine and is reunited with his friends, Alyx and Eli Vance. Then, two monstrous Combine "Advisors" appear and brutally murder Eli. What a downer!

42. SUPER METROID
(Nintendo, 1994)
Our heroine Samus Aran (above) locates the terrifying Mother Brain and is almost killed, only to be saved by the Metroid Larva, a "baby" that had mistaken poor Samus for its mother. The baby sacrifices itself to save our heroine. Ultimately Samus uses the last of her strength to destroy Mother Brain and escape to her space ship as the Space Pirates' hideout explodes around her. Epic stuff.

40. NEW SUPER MARIO BROS. Wii
(Nintendo, 2009)
After travelling through various worlds, Mario is again forced to fight Bowser, first at his natural size, then as an angry giant. The massive Koopa is able to destroy all platforms, so it is much easier for Mario to defeat him (and rescue Princess Peach) if equipped with the propeller suit (left).

41. THE LEGEND OF ZELDA: TWILIGHT PRINCESS
(Nintendo, 2006)
As with most *Zelda* games, the final battle is between the hero Link and his recurring foe Ganondorf. Once Link defeats him, peace is returned to Hyrule, but Midna (above) is revealed as the Twilight Princess and is forced to return to rule her realm.

39. inFAMOUS
(Sucker Punch, 2009)
Our protagonist Cole MacGrath learns the terrible truth about his "nemesis", Kessler. The apparently evil mastermind is actually none other than MacGrath himself, returned from the future to turn his past self into the perfect superhero.

38. FALLOUT 3
(Bethesda, 2008)
The actions of the Lone Wanderer invoke many different outcomes. If you follow the path of good karma, you sacrifice yourself in the irradiated control room to allow water to flow into the Capital wasteland.

36. GEARS OF WAR 2
(Epic, 2008)
Baird (below) and his fellow Gears are successful in sinking Jacinto, the last human city. This act floods the underground tunnels of the planet Sera with energy-rich emulsion fluid that mutates the Locusts into "lambents". Was this part of someone's secret plan all along?

37. GRAND THEFT AUTO: SAN ANDREAS
(Rockstar, 2004)
As he finally reaches the pinnacle of the life that crime has brought him, Carl "CJ" Johnson (above) is finally able to take his revenge on Sergeant Frank Tenpenny. As riots rage throughout Los Santos in response to the corrupt law enforcer's acquittal, Tenpenny attempts to escape the city in a fire truck. In the daring final chase he crashes off the bridge overlooking CJ's old neighbourhood. A fitting end for a great villain.

32. METAL GEAR SOLID 3: SNAKE EATER
(Konami, 2004)
Snake engages "The Boss" in close combat, killing her for apparently defecting to the Soviet Union and inheriting the title of "Boss" himself.

34. STARCRAFT II: WINGS OF LIBERTY
(Blizzard, 2010)
Marshall Jim Raynor activates an ancient Xel'Naga artefact on the planet Char, routing the Zerg invaders and transforming their mutated general, the Queen of Blades, back into the Terran Sarah Kerrigan (above). Raynor then shoots his former comrade Tychus to prevent him from killing Kerrigan.

35. BIOSHOCK
(2K Boston, 2007)
The final fight is a showdown between the player and a super-powered gangster, Frank Fontaine, who has become deformed from using the "ADAM" stem cells. Depending on whether the player has saved the Little Sisters (girls with mutant sea slugs in their guts) or harvested them for "ADAM", the final scenes are either the girls growing up or some mutants seizing a nuke.

33. SONIC ADVENTURE 2
(SEGA, 2001)
Sonic and Shadow work together, using the Chaos Emeralds to become their golden "Super" selves. They heroically defeat the Biolizard and prevent the ARK space colony from colliding with the Earth.

30. MASS EFFECT
(BioWare, 2007)
The heroic Commander Shepard arrives back at the Citadel just in time to witness a Geth invasion force led by the sentient machine known as Sovereign. The choices made throughout the game determine humanity's position in the galaxy and the direction of future games in the series. Many gamers have replayed it several times in preparation for its sequel.

29. SUPER MARIO GALAXY
(Nintendo, 2007)
This showdown with Bowser in his star reactor is an epic multi-stage battle that tests even the most accomplished Mario veterans. Once defeated, the King of the Koopas looks on in horror as his hopes of empire are sucked into a black hole. It's a stellar victory for Mario!

31. KINGDOM HEARTS II
(Square Enix, 2005)
Our heroes Sora (above) and Riku take down the evil Xemnas at the top of the Castle That Never Was and escape back to the Destiny Islands, where they are reunited with the Disney characters Mickey and Donald.

28. SONIC THE HEDGEHOG
(SEGA, 1991)
After destroying the evil Dr. Eggman's machines of destruction, Sonic (above) returns to the Green Hill Zone where he is greeted by all the animals he has freed on his quest, with squirrels, pigs, penguins and otters all invited to the party.

27. METAL GEAR SOLID
(Konami, 1998)
Our protagonist, Solid Snake, discovers that his radio contact and mentor, Master Miller, was actually his evil clone, Liquid. After disarming the fearsome foe, Snake and Liquid battle it out. Although Solid survives, he learns that eventually he too will be killed by the FOXDIE nanovirus.

26. ASSASSIN'S CREED II
(Ubisoft, 2009)
The assassin Ezio (right) infiltrates the Vatican and carries out a successful, if long-winded, assassination attempt on the Pope, Rodrigo Borgia.

25. ASSASSIN'S CREED (Ubisoft, 2007)

Desmond (pictured left), the protagonist of the series, narrowly avoids a death sentence imposed by his captors, and finishes the game with the realization that he has acquired his ancestors' "Eagle vision" power.

24. SHADOW OF THE COLOSSUS (Team Ico, 2005)

Our hero Wander returns from destroying the final colossus to be confronted by the revelation that the 16 giant monsters he was ordered to kill were, in fact, keeping the world safe. By slaying them he has resurrected the evil god Dormin. Wander is attacked by Lord Emon and his guards, transforming into a horned, shadowy form as he attempts to destroy them. Emon casts a spell that sucks Dormin into a pool of light. Wander's dead love, Mono, miraculously awakens on the dais to find a tiny horned baby in the spot where Wander had disappeared.

23. CALL OF DUTY 4: MODERN WARFARE (Infinity Ward, 2007)

After a daring escape through the Russian countryside, Captain Price's unit is finally cornered by the nefarious arms dealer Zakhaev on a bridge, and the troops prepare to meet their end. As his comrades lie injured on the road, Price slides his M1911 pistol to the main character, Sergeant John "Soap" MacTavish, who kills Zakhaev and buys enough time for the unit to escape to safety.

22. KINGDOM HEARTS (Square, 2002)

Disney crossover game *Kingdom Hearts* (right) combines a number of *Disney* and *Final Fantasy* characters and locations. Main character Sora is on a mission to find his friends. Along with Donald and Goofy, he faces off with the imposter Ansem, who opens the door to Kingdom Hearts expecting to find darkness within to augment his power. Instead, light sprays out of the door, banishing Ansem.

21. UNCHARTED 2: AMONG THIEVES (Naughty Dog, 2009)

After setting off the explosive blue resin in the tree of life, Nathan Drake leaves the evil Lazarevic to a gruesome fate at the hands of the guardians of Shambhala. Drake escapes with Elena and Chloe as the mythical city collapses around them. Chloe asks Drake if he loves Elena, and Drake does not respond. Safely away from the carnage, Elena and Drake kiss as they watch the sun set behind a dramatic mountain range...

20. SUPER MARIO GALAXY 2 (Nintendo, 2010)

Mario returns for more intergalactic adventures as he cheerfully pursues arch-nemesis Bowser through outer space. Following another explosive battle, the fearless Mario dispatches Bowser into a black hole. He denies Bowser the huge cake he craved, and rescues Princess Peach. Again.

19. MASS EFFECT 2 (BioWare, 2010)

In the second of the RPG *Mass Effect* trilogy, Commander Shepard (left) is brought back to life by a shadowy organization. Under his legendary leadership, the crew of the *Normandy* carry out a "suicide mission" into the uncharted Omega 4 Relay. All survive to thwart the next stage in the evil Reapers' invasion plan. Once destroyed, the crew escapes back through the relay, having attracted the full attention of the Reapers, and having made humanity their new primary target.

18. GRAND THEFT AUTO IV (Rockstar, 2008)

There are two possible endings in the fourth *Grand Theft Auto* instalment, leaving Niko Bellic (above) with a dilemma in the game's closing moments: both of his potential choices will result in the murder of someone close to him. Either his brother, Roman Bellic, or his love interest, Kate McReary, will die.

17. PORTAL 2
(Valve, 2011)

In puzzle platformer *Portal 2* (right), players take on the character of Chell, who must teleport between portals in order to overcome a number of conundrums. Chell is desperate to escape the clutches of artificially intelligent computer system GLaDOS. She uses everything at her disposal in the final showdown with *Portal 2*'s misguided boss, creating a portal on the moon to suck the hapless AI into space, where she can float for eternity.

15. PRINCE OF PERSIA: THE SANDS OF TIME
(Ubisoft, 2003)

Having told Princess Farah his incredible story, the Prince (below right) is interrupted by the arrival of the Vizier, who fears his treachery has been uncovered. After killing the Vizier in single combat, the Prince realizes that the future he had shared with Farah will never happen and he returns the dagger of time to her. Not to be discouraged in his pursuit of the beautiful girl, he recalls a secret name she once told him and mentions it as proof that he knows her. The Prince then vanishes from her balcony, leaving Farah fascinated by this very mysterious man...

16. ASSASSIN'S CREED: BROTHERHOOD
(Ubisoft, 2010)

Ezio Auditore da Firenze (below) single-handedly cuts his way through most of Rodrigo Borgia's army, finally killing the man himself. Meanwhile, Desmond discovers the Temple of Juno underneath the Basilica of Santa Maria. There he finds the Apple of Eden. As he holds it, the Apple takes control and forces him to kill his friend Lucy Stillman.

14. HALO: COMBAT EVOLVED
(Bungie, 2001)

The Master Chief (below) and Cortana successfully activate the self-destruct sequence on the crashed starship *Pillar of Autumn*. They manage to escape in time to watch the enormous Halo ring shatter into burning shards.

13. HALO 3
(Bungie, 2007)

After activating the second Halo, destroying it and the Ark that created it in the process, the Master Chief (right) and the Arbiter escape into a slipspace portal back to Earth. However, the portal closes, cutting the ship in half and leaving the Master Chief and Cortana stranded in a distant part of space. The Chief goes into cryonic sleep, demanding only to be woken when Cortana needs him.

12. POKÉMON BLACK AND WHITE
(Game Freak, 2010)

The player makes their way to the Pokémon League, where Pokémon trainers must gather to challenge and defeat "N", the mysterious leader of Team Plasma, and then his mentor, Ghetsis. After beating them, a new Pokémon League champion is crowned and they all live happily ever after...

11. SUPER MARIO BROS.
(Nintendo, 1985)

In the sequel to the seminal *Mario Bros.*, courageous plumbers Mario and Luigi must make their way through the Mushroom Kingdom, avoiding evil Bowser's cohorts and rescuing Princess Peach. After making his way through seven suspiciously similar-looking fortresses, Mario finally beats the odds: for once, the peachy Princess is not in another castle!

TOP 50 GAME ENDINGS 10-4

10. *HEAVY RAIN*
(Quantic Dream, 2010)
The multiple paths of *Heavy Rain* (pictured below) allow for a huge range of outcomes to the Origami Killer case, from an all-round happy ending in which Shaun is found safely, to the deaths of most of the game's major characters. The various possible endings add to the excitement of this film noir-esque action thriller.

8. *METAL GEAR SOLID 4*
(Konami, 2008)
His body wracked with the effects of his premature ageing, protagonist Solid Snake (below, right) resolves to end his own life. He puts his pistol in his mouth but the suicide attempt is interrupted by his genetic father, Big Boss (below, left), who finally explains how the Military Industrial Complex was created.

9. *FINAL FANTASY VII*
(Square, 1997)
The seventh *Final Fantasy* title (above) concludes with an epic, almost apocalyptic finale. Cloud and Sephiroth face off inside the Lifestream, allowing Aeris' Holy spell to deflect the meteor on to a collision course with the Planet. Although they are too late to save the city of Midgar, the Planet itself is saved.

7. *PORTAL*
(Valve, 2007)
After final boss GLaDOS is dismantled piece by piece, she appears to have been destroyed. However, in a break with gaming tradition, the ending of *Portal* (left) involves GLaDOS performing a musical number. Titled "Still Alive", the song was written by American nerd-folk artist Jonathan Coulton and became something of a cult hit – it has since been immortalized in several online tributes.

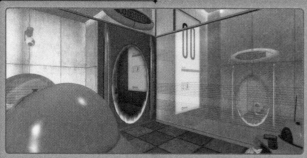

/// "FEEL THE BEAT. MOVE YOUR FEET" ///

6. RED DEAD REDEMPTION
(Rockstar, 2010)

Just like so many of the classic Western films that inspired its creation, Rockstar's mega-hit *Red Dead Redemption* finishes with retribution, revenge and bloodshed. After being reunited with his wife Abigail and son Jack, John Marston (left) resumes a simple life of ranching cattle, only to be betrayed and murdered by the federal agent he worked for. Three years after the bloodbath at the Marston Ranch in Beecher's Hope, John's son, now 19 years old, embarks on a mission to avenge his father's death, tracking down Edgar Ross (right) and laying his father's legacy to rest in a pool of blood.

5. GOD OF WAR
(SCE Studios Santa Monica, 2005)

Having achieved the impossible and slain the god Ares, who had betrayed him, Kratos (left and below) asks Athena to save him from his guilt-ridden nightmares, but she refuses. Kratos climbs to the summit of Mount Olympus and throws himself off, in the suicide scene that is shown at the very start of the game. But the Gods have other plans: with Ares' throne empty, the mortal who had defeated him will take his place as the new God of War.

4. CALL OF DUTY: MODERN WARFARE 2
(Infinity Ward, 2009)

In the sixth *Call of Duty* title (right and below), Soap and Price track down Lieutenant General Shepherd to the cave system code-named "Site Hotel Bravo", chasing him through the Afghan mountains before finally confronting and killing him in a deadly knife fight.

3. THE LEGEND OF ZELDA: OCARINA OF TIME

(Nintendo, 1998)
Following Link's epic encounters with a dragon (below) and other beasts, the story of this "Hero of Time" reaches a fitting conclusion. Our hero awakens the six sages and uses their power to break the seals barring entry to the villainous Ganondorf's castle. Link beats his nemesis, frees Princess Zelda and escapes – only to be forced to confront Ganondorf again, this time in the guise of a giant man-pig. After emerging victorious, Link decides to return to the past, safe in the knowledge that he will be reunited with Princess Zelda.

A TIMELY WISH

In *Ocarina of Time*, players can visit the final Great Fairy's Fountain by exiting Ganondorf's castle as soon as they have acquired the "Gold Gauntlets".

The fairy there gives the player a very powerful protection spell, effectively doubling the amount of damage Link can take in the final fight against Ganondorf. If only the Great Fairy had given gamers this endurance from the start...

HALO AGAIN

Observant players will be able to spot a brief cameo appearance by the Master Chief, in a cryogenic sleep unit on the right-hand side of the cargo bay in the *Pillar of Autumn*. These events lead directly into the start of the first game, *Halo: Combat Evolved* (Bungie, 2001), as the *Pillar* discovers the alien ringworld that gives this game series its title.

2. HALO: REACH

(Bungie, 2010)
As the human colony of Reach finally falls to Covenant forces, the remaining two members of Noble Team succeed in their mission to bring the Artificial Intelligence Cortana to the *Pillar of Autumn*. At the launch pad, the two Spartans defend the starship as it prepares to leave the planet. Noble Six (right), the last man standing, watches as the ship departs, and prepares to make his final stand against impossible odds. Although he is eventually overwhelmed, his sacrifice ensures that the Master Chief survives.

1. CALL OF DUTY: BLACK OPS
(Treyarch, 2010)

Set in the Cold War era (1946–91), *Black Ops* follows the hidden story of American soldier Alex Mason, who is captured in Cuba after an attempt to assassinate Fidel Castro goes wrong.

Alex ends up in the brutal Soviet prison of Vorkuta alongside the Russian soldier Viktor Reznov, last seen in *Call of Duty: World at War* (Treyarch, 2008). While it seems as though the pair have escaped, it is later revealed that Reznov died in Vorkuta and subsequently appeared to Mason as part of a delusion inspired by the conditioning he received in prison.

Mason is apprehended by his former colleague, Special Agent Hudson, who helps Mason break his conditioning and remember a code that enables the pair to prevent a cell of sleeper agents from attacking the USA.

In a final shoot-out inside a submarine, Mason drowns Nikita Dragovich, the man responsible for imprisoning him and Reznov. This gives his Russian friend the vengeance denied to him in life. However, in the closing sequence it is implied that one of Dragovich's sleeper agents was responsible for assassinating President John F Kennedy – a new twist on the classic conspiracy theory.

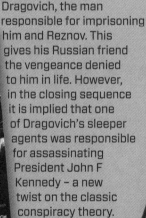

CODE OF DUTY
According to YouTube user 01Maverick10, *Call of Duty: Black Ops* contains a secret code message hidden in its mission briefings (seen on screen at the start of each mission). 01Maverick10 claims that this code can be deciphered to read: "Reznov is dead, or is he dead? There was no body, is he who he says he is?"

Did the Russian soldier really die while trying to escape from Vorkuta? We may need to wait for a future *Call of Duty* game to find out…

GAME OVER!

WHO ARE TWIN GALAXIES?

Twin Galaxies International has been a world authority on videogame scores, statistics, tournament results and player rankings for 31 years. Their records go back even further, with comprehensive gaming facts dating back to the 1970s, when gaming took off. Today, they keep track of all the stats for arcades, new and classic home consoles, PC games and pinball machines, as well as handheld and portable consoles. Twin Galaxies cover the videogame spectrum as thoroughly as *Gamer's* does, so we are delighted to include material from TG's extensive database in this book. You will already have seen Twin Galaxies facts and figures in some of our Top 10s. To find out more about their work, log on to **www.TwinGalaxies.com**.

HOW TO USE THIS SECTION

Over the next 14 pages, you'll find a selection of the latest Twin Galaxies world record scoreboards. We've split the records into five categories:
• Nintendo
• Sony
• Microsoft
• Old School Console
• Arcade.
And within each scoreboard, you will see six columns:
• game name
• game platform
• setting used for each record
• record-breaking score
• name (and country) of each record-holder
• date each record was set.
Enjoy the stats!

SCOREBOARDS

THE *MEGA MAN* VIDEOGAME FRANCHISE STARTED ON THE NES IN 1987 AND NOW

BEASTLY BOY

Originally an arcade title from the late 1980s, beat-'em-up *Altered Beast* (pictured above) was ported to the Wii Virtual Console in 2009. Prolific American gamer Matthew N Runnels holds the highest-score record using the settings for the Sega Genesis/Mega Drive, which were the first home consoles to feature the game.

DONKEY KONG GAME & WATCH

(Nintendo, 1982)
Oil Panic (pictured below) appeared as a title on the *Game & Watch* handheld system in 1982. The *Donkey Kong Game & Watch*, released earlier that same year, became the **first two-screen handheld**. Although very basic, the device was hugely influential and paved the way for modern consoles, in particular the Game Boy and DS.

NINTENDO

A–N

GAME	PLATFORM	SETTINGS	RECORD	PLAYER (COUNTRY)	DATE
Altered Beast	Wii Virtual Console	Sega Genesis/ Mega Drive	439,400	Matthew N Runnels (USA)	24-May-2011
Bejeweled 2	WiiWare	Action; High Score	518,950	Lance M Eustache (USA)	21-Jul-2011
Bejeweled 2	WiiWare	Classic; High Score	312,376	Lance M Eustache (USA)	5-Sep-2010
Bejeweled Twist	DS	Blitz Mode	231,500	Lance M Eustache (USA)	23-Nov-2010
Bubble Bobble	Wii Virtual Console	NES	3,676,940	Michael H Brady (USA)	22-Feb-2011
Bubble Bobble Plus!	WiiWare	Arrange; 1-player	1,097,730	Brian Mundo (USA)	19-Jan-2011
Bubble Bobble Plus!	WiiWare	Super Arrange; 1-player	1,186,150	Brian Mundo (USA)	1-May-2011
Bubble Bobble Plus!	WiiWare	Expert-1; 1-player	276,360	Michael E Sroka (USA)	13-Apr-2011
Bubble Bobble Plus!	WiiWare	Expert-2; 1-player	627,740	Michael E Sroka (USA)	13-Apr-2011
Bubble Bobble Plus!	WiiWare	Standard; 1-player	1,510,460	Michael E Sroka (USA)	18-Apr-2011
Castlevania III: Dracula's Curse	Wii Virtual Console	NES	999,999	Andrew D Furrer (USA)	4-Jun-2011
Contra: ReBirth	WiiWare	Points	136,390	John A Pompa (USA)	4-Sep-2010
Donkey Kong 3	Wii Virtual Console	NES	6,454,200	Andrew D Furrer (USA)	31-Dec-2010
Elevator Action	Wii Virtual Console	NES	54,800	Matthew N Runnels (USA)	14-May-2011
Game & Watch Collection	DS	*Oil Panic*; High Score	292	John M Brissie (USA)	6-Jul-2011
Game & Watch Collection 2	DS	*Parachute X Octopus*	158	John A Pompa (USA)	20-Apr-2011
Ghost Squad	Wii	Training Mode; Shooting Match	9,033	Michael E Estep (USA)	17-Nov-2010
Gradius III	SNES	Points	2,943,000	Tanner J Saylor (USA)	11-Jul-2011
Gradius ReBirth	WiiWare	Normal Game	66,540	John A Pompa (USA)	21-Nov-2010
Gradius ReBirth	WiiWare	Score Attack	79,480	John A Pompa (USA)	21-Nov-2010

10 billion The number of times it is estimated *PAC-Man* was played on arcade machines in the 20th century. It now features in *Namco Museum* on the DS.

NUMBERS OVER 50 TITLES, INCLUDING 10 IN THE MAIN SERIES

GAME	PLATFORM	SETTINGS	RECORD	PLAYER (COUNTRY)	DATE
Just Dance	Wii	The Trashmen, "Surfin' Bird"	21,529	Laura Sroka (USA)	8-Apr-2011
Just Dance 2	Wii	Boney M, "Rasputin"	8,796	Elizabeth Bolinger (USA)	29-Jan-2011
Just Dance 2	Wii	Franz Ferdinand, "Take Me Out"	10,012	Elizabeth Bolinger (USA)	29-Jan-2011
Just Dance 2	Wii	Katy Perry, "Firework"	9,282	Elizabeth Bolinger (USA)	29-Jan-2011
Just Dance 2	Wii	OutKast, "Hey Ya!"	10,055	Elizabeth Bolinger (USA)	29-Jan-2011
Just Dance 2	Wii	Quickplay: Katy Perry, "Hot N Cold" (Chick Version)	16,498	Elizabeth Bolinger (USA)	2-Dec-2010
Just Dance 2	Wii	Quickplay: Spice Girls, "Wannabe"	17,842	Elizabeth Bolinger (USA)	4-Dec-2010
Just Dance 2	Wii	The Jackson 5, "I Want You Back"	11,115	Elizabeth Bolinger (USA)	29-Jan-2011
Mario Bros.	Wii Virtual Console	NES; One Player Only	12,373,830	Timothy V Hykes (USA)	31-May-2011
Mario Kart DS	DS	Cheep Cheep Beach; Best Lap	32.043 sec	David H Klingler (USA)	16-Jun-2011
Mario Kart DS	DS	Cheep Cheep Beach; Best Time	1 min 37.540 sec	David H Klingler (USA)	16-Jun-2011
Mario Kart DS	DS	Luigi's Mansion; Best Lap	34.471 sec	David H Klingler (USA)	16-Jun-2011
Mario Kart DS	DS	Luigi's Mansion; Best Time	1 min 45.229 sec	David H Klingler (USA)	16-Jun-2011
Mario Strikers Charged	Wii	Domination Mode; Biggest Blowout	133	Fred Bugmann (Brazil)	19-Mar-2010
Mega Man 10	Wii Virtual Console	Fastest Completion; Mega Man	37 min 14 sec	Richard Gibson (Canada)	24-Jan-2011
Mega Man 9	Wii Virtual Console	Fastest Completion; Mega Man	21 min 28 sec	Richard Gibson (Canada)	14-May-2011
Mega Man 9	Wii Virtual Console	Fastest Completion; Proto Man	19 min 25 sec	Richard Gibson (Canada)	10-Jul-2011
Namco Museum DS	DS	*PAC-Man*	26,460	John M Brissie (USA)	8-Jul-2011
NBA Jam	Wii	Play Now Mode; Biggest Blowout; Single Player Only	69	Daniel Lee Strickland Perea (USA)	23-Jul-2011
New Super Mario Bros.	DS	Danger, Bob-omb, Danger	5,215	Brandon Y LeCroy (USA)	7-May-2011

JUST DANCE 2
(Ubisoft Paris, 2010)
The sequel to smash Wii hit *Just Dance* has sold 8.03 million copies as of August 2011, easily surpassing the 5.95 million sold by the first game in the series. This makes Ubisoft's *Just Dance 2* the **best-selling third-party Wii game**. Nintendo develop most of their own games for the Wii, making Ubisoft's *Just Dance* sales figures all the more impressive.

JAMMY
Under the creative leadership of Mark Turmell, developers Midway debuted basketball game *NBA Jam* on arcades in 1993, before porting it on to home consoles such as the SNES and Genesis. The NBA series was taken over by EA Sports, who brought Turmell back to assist in the development of the 2010 incarnation of *NBA Jam*.

SCOREBOARDS

RESIDENT EVIL 4 (CAPCOM, 2005) WAS AN INCREDIBLE SIX YEARS IN THE MAKING,

NINJA GAIDEN
(Tecmo, 1988)
Ninja Gaiden is a particularly tough game to complete, with the player taking on the role of a revenge-hungry ninja. Expert Juan M Castellanos (Mexico) holds the **highest score for all games in the Ninja Gaiden trilogy**; his impressive score on the first *Ninja Gaiden* (above) was followed by an even better total for sequel *The Dark Sword of Chaos.*

KO, OK?!!
Punch-Out!! began life as an arcade game in 1984, making its debut on the NES in 1987. Sequel *Super Punch-Out!!* hit the arcades in 1985, before a SNES release in 1994. These popular boxing games found a new audience with an updated release on the Nintendo Wii in 2009 (below). The punches now fly in 3D, and there is even a cameo appearance by the legendary Donkey Kong!

NINTENDO

N-T

GAME	PLATFORM	SETTINGS	RECORD	PLAYER (COUNTRY)	DATE
New Super Mario Bros.	DS	Whack-a-Monty	93	Daniel M Phillips (USA)	22-Jun-2011
Ninja Gaiden	NES	Points	2,610,800	Juan M Castellanos (Mexico)	20-Jun-2011
Ninja Gaiden II: The Dark Sword of Chaos	NES	Points	3,127,800	Juan M Castellanos (Mexico)	20-Jun-2011
Ninja Gaiden III: The Ancient Ship of Doom	NES	Points	1,090,000	Juan M Castellanos (Mexico)	9-Feb-2011
Planet Puzzle League	DS	Endless; High Score	227,646	Jeffrey D Lowe, Jr (USA)	11-Jan-2011
Punch-Out!!	Wii	Fastest KO/TKO of Von Kaiser #1	20.49 sec	Chris A Helmin (USA)	28-Nov-2009
Punch-Out!!	Wii	Fastest KO/TKO of Von Kaiser #1	20.49 sec	David R Archey (USA)	6-Jun-2009
Punch-Out!!	Wii	Fastest KO/TKO of Von Kaiser #1	20.49 sec	Jeffrey D Lowe, Jr (USA)	6-Jun-2009
Punch-Out!!	Wii	Fastest KO/TKO of Von Kaiser #1	20.49 sec	Zachary C Allard (USA)	29-Jun-2009
Resident Evil 4	GameCube	Fastest Completion [New Round]	2 hr 43 min 30 sec	Ben Scott (USA)	23-Mar-2011
Resident Evil: The Darkside Chronicles	Wii	Points [Single Player Only, Game of Oblivion; Chapter 1]	54,060	Daniel Lee Strickland Perea (USA)	22-Jul-2011
Resident Evil: The Darkside Chronicles	Wii	Points [Single Player Only, Operation Javier; Chapter 1]	39,010	Daniel Lee Strickland Perea (USA)	22-Jul-2011
Resident Evil: The Darkside Chronicles	Wii	Points [Single Player Only, Operation Javier; Chapter 2]	43,370	Daniel Lee Strickland Perea (USA)	22-Jul-2011
Retro Atari Classics	DS	*Centipede*; Marathon	955,031	John M Brissie (USA)	27-Jun-2011
Sonic & Knuckles & Sonic the Hedgehog 3	Wii Virtual Console	Sega Genesis/ Mega Drive; Fastest Full Completion; Knuckles Alone	1 hr 30 min 11 sec	Charles K Ziese (USA)	5-Mar-2011

WITH FOUR DIFFERENT VERSIONS DEVELOPED PRIOR TO RELEASE

GAME	PLATFORM	SETTINGS	RECORD	PLAYER (COUNTRY)	DATE
Sonic & Knuckles & Sonic the Hedgehog 3 *(see panel, right)*	Wii Virtual Console	Sega Genesis/ Mega Drive; Points	4,255,210	Charles K Ziese (USA)	12-Jul-2011
Sonic the Hedgehog	Wii Virtual Console	Sega Genesis/ Mega Drive; Points	1,060,450	Charles K Ziese (USA)	13-Jul-2011
Space Invaders Extreme 2	DS	Score Attack	10,802,360	John M Brissie (USA)	24-Jul-2011
Super Mario 64	Nintendo 64	Fastest Minimalist Completion [70–119 Stars Required]	1 hr 28 min 22 sec	Andrew W Riley (USA)	17-Sep-2010
Super Mario Bros.	Wii Virtual Console	NES	1,267,350	John J Lundrigan (USA)	23-Dec-2010
Super Punch-Out!!	Wii Virtual Console	SNES; Major Circuit	245,980	Matthew N Runnels (USA)	14-Jul-2011
Super Punch-Out!!	Wii Virtual Console	SNES; Special Circuit	272,340	Matthew N Runnels (USA)	16-Jul-2011
Super Punch-Out!!	Wii Virtual Console	SNES; World Circuit	199,530	Matthew N Runnels (USA)	14-Jul-2011
Super Smash Bros. Brawl	Wii	Stadium; Multi-Man Brawl; 100-Man Brawl; Fastest Time	2 min 11.58 sec	Andrew D Furrer (USA)	30-May-2011
Super Smash Bros. Brawl	Wii	Stadium; Multi-Man Brawl; 15-Minute Brawl; Kills	602	Andrew D Furrer (USA)	30-May-2011
Super Smash Bros. Brawl	Wii	Stadium; Multi-Man Brawl; Endless Brawl; Kills	342	Andrew D Furrer (USA)	5-Mar-2011
Super Smash Bros. Brawl	Wii	Stadium; Multi-Man Brawl; 10-Man Brawl; Fastest Time	11.96 sec	Lance M Eustache (USA)	21-Sep-2010
Tatsunoko vs. Capcom: Ultimate All-Stars	Wii	Points; Tournament Settings	1,922,268,000	Jeffrey D Lowe, Jr (USA)	20-Sep-2010
Tatsunoko vs. Capcom: Ultimate All-Stars	Wii	Time Attack Mode; Fastest Completion	3 min 53.58 sec	Jeffrey D Lowe, Jr (USA)	29-Sep-2010

KNUCKLE LOCK

The *Sonic & Knuckles & Sonic the Hedgehog 3* game listed here is the Wii version of the original Mega Drive/ Genesis game. *Sonic & Knuckles* (above) was a stand-alone game, but it also served as a useful expansion pack for *Sonic 3*, as well as other games on the Mega Drive/Genesis. It provided exciting new bonus levels and features by using "lock-on" technology: gamers opened the lid on the *Knuckles* cartridge and slotted in another title.

SUPER SMASH BROS. BRAWL

(Nintendo, 2008) Nintendo's crossover fighting hit *Super Smash Bros.* has spawned three games so far, and holds the record for the **best-selling fighting series on a Nintendo console** with sales of 23.1 million as of August 2011. Future titles for the 3DS and Wii U were announced at E3 2011. *Brawl* (below) is the third in the series, and features gaming stars such as Donkey Kong, Mario and *Pokémon*'s Jigglypuff.

TETRIS DS FEATURES NUMEROUS PLAY MODES BASED ON

TEENAGE MUTANT NINJA TURTLES
(Konami, 1989)
The heroes in a half-shell made their videogame debut on the NES in the late 1980s. Canadian gamer Kelsy Polnik holds the record for the **fastest completion of Teenage Mutant Ninja Turtles** in a lightning-quick 20 min 21 sec. Cowabunga, dude!

TETRIS & DR. MARIO
(Nintendo, 1994)
This release for the SNES was, as the box above shows, "2 games in one", neatly packaged for fans of block puzzlers. *Dr. Mario* was released on the back of the phenomenal success of *Tetris*, which holds a host of world records, including being the **first videogame shown to improve brain functioning and efficiency**. Tests conducted at the University of California proved *Tetris* players became sharper after long playing sessions.

NINTENDO
T–Z

GAME	PLATFORM	SETTINGS	RECORD	PLAYER (COUNTRY)	DATE
Teenage Mutant Ninja Turtles	NES	Fastest Completion	20 min 21 sec	Kelsy J Polnik (Canada)	18-Dec-2010
Teenage Mutant Ninja Turtles	NES	Points	559,100	Kelsy J Polnik (Canada)	19-Dec-2010
Tetris & Dr. Mario	SNES	*Tetris*	292 lines	Kevin M LaLonde (USA)	13-May-2009
Tetris & Dr. Mario	SNES	*Tetris*	292 lines	Patrick Scott Patterson (USA)	21-Jun-2011
Tetris & Dr. Mario	SNES	*Tetris*	435,904	Patrick Scott Patterson (USA)	21-Jun-2011
Tetris 2	NES	Points	999,990	Daryl Kiddey (USA)	19-May-2011
Tetris DS	DS	Points [Standard; Marathon]	1,492,000	Isaiah M Johnson (USA)	10-Feb-2011
Tetris DS	DS	Mission; Time Trail; Level 1	55.610 sec	Samantha Hancock (USA)	11-Feb-2011
Tetris DS	DS	Points [Standard; Line Clear]	200,000	Samantha Hancock (USA)	11-Feb-2011
Tetris Party	WiiWare	Beginner's Tetris; Marathon; 150 Lines	416,896	Sean M Sandefer (USA)	17-Jan-2011
Tetris Party Deluxe	Wii	Marathon Mode, Endless; Points	15,327,688	Jeffrey D Lowe, Jr (USA)	13-Oct-2010
Tiger Woods PGA Tour 10	Wii	Pebble Beach Golf Links; Least Amount of Strokes	64	Matthew N Runnels (USA)	22-Jul-2011
Tiger Woods PGA Tour 10	Wii	Torrey Pines GC; Least Amount of Strokes	67	Matthew N Runnels (USA)	23-Jul-2011
Wii Party	Wii	Minigames; Rope Sling; Yards	178	Jeff H Anson (USA)	24-Apr-2011
Wii Party	Wii	Challenge; Marching Orders	12,087	William Willemstyn III (USA)	31-Oct-2010
Wii Sports	Wii	Bowling	300	Brent T Dolan (USA)	7-Jul-2008
Wii Sports	Wii	Bowling	300	Carl Aspinwall (USA)	26-Apr-2007
Wii Sports	Wii	Bowling	300	Kimberley L Sanders (USA)	31-Jul-2009
Wii Sports	Wii	Bowling	300	Marc Cohen (USA)	11-Jun-2008

CLASSIC NINTENDO GAMES, INCLUDING *MARIO* AND *ZELDA*

GAME	PLATFORM	SETTINGS	RECORD	PLAYER (COUNTRY)	DATE
Wii Sports	Wii	Training; Baseball; Hitting Home Runs	6,041	Craig Rout Gallant (Canada)	20-Jun-2010
Wii Sports	Wii	Training; Golf; Hitting the Green	5.3	Stanley Lauskey (USA)	12-Apr-2011
Wii Sports Resort	Wii	Table Tennis; Return Challenge	999	Andrew Pete Mee (UK)	19-Oct-2009
Wii Sports Resort	Wii	Table Tennis; Return Challenge	999	Brandon M Skar (USA)	12-Aug-2009
Wii Sports Resort	Wii	Bowling; Regular Game	300	Brent T Dolan (USA)	9-Dec-2009
Wii Sports Resort	Wii	Table Tennis; Match	1,484	Kristian W Farnan (UK)	19-Jan-2010
Wii Sports Resort	Wii	Swordplay; Showdown	961	Marc Cohen (USA)	19-Feb-2010
Wii Sports Resort	Wii	Air Sports; Skydiving	241	Pekka H Luodeslampi (Finland)	24-Mar-2010
Zombie Panic in Wonderland	WiiWare	Arcade Mode; High Score	106,160	Ginger Stowe (USA)	5-Dec-2010

Wii SPORTS RESORT

(Nintendo EAD, 2009) Nintendo's follow-up to the hugely successful *Wii Sports* may not have sold as many copies as the original, but it did bring in a raft of innovations. Set on a charming beach retreat, *Wii Sports Resort* features 12 games, including table tennis, swordplay and bowling. It holds the record for being the **first Wii MotionPlus game**, utilizing the device's advanced movement sensors to full effect. Along with *Wii Fit*, the game now comes with a seal of approval from the American Heart Association.

SKY'S THE LIMIT

Wii Sports Resort was an attempt to build on the foundations of *Wii Sports*, both in terms of the technology used and the sports that were included. In the sequel, Nintendo added seven further games and a category named AirSports. This includes *Island Flyover*, in which gamers pilot a biplane over the game's resort. *Skydiving* (above) is the introductory game that automatically opens *Wii Sports Resort*. Players try to link up with other characters to form a group of five skydivers who can then pose, in various elaborate diving moves, for points-winning photos.

LOS ZOMBIES

Aside from having one of the more eccentric game titles of 2010, third-person shooter *Zombie Panic in Wonderland* (right) is also the first game developed by Spanish company Akaoni Studio. The Valencia-based outfit is hugely influenced by Japanese gaming and culture in general, as highlighted by the fact that the protagonist of their game is named after a Japanese folk hero. Momotaro, the star of the story, is a boy whose goal is to save his friends from the "amorous zombies" that are infecting Wonderland.

SCOREBOARDS

IN *NINJA GOLF* (BLUESKY SOFTWARE, 1990) PLAYERS HAD TO FIGHT ENEMIES

OLD SCHOOL CONSOLE

A-S

GAME	PLATFORM	SETTINGS	RECORD	PLAYER (COUNTRY)	DATE
Aero Blasters	TurboGrafx-16	Single Player	41,780,000	Ryan W Genno (Canada)	12-Jun-2011
Atari Anniversary Edition	Sega Dreamcast	*Tempest*	83,351	Meg Hurley (USA)	14-Jun-2011
Battletoads & Double Dragon	Sega Genesis/ Mega Drive	Points	999,999	Rudy J Ferretti (USA)	19-Jun-2011
Bomberman	TurboGrafx-16	Default Settings	21,741,110	Ryan W Genno (Canada)	3-Jun-2011
Bomberman '93	TurboGrafx-16	Points	63,800	Ryan W Genno (Canada)	18-Jun-2011
Bravoman	TurboGrafx-16	Points	28,400	Ryan W Genno (Canada)	7-Jun-2011
Brett Hull Hockey 95	Sega Genesis/ Mega Drive	Biggest Blowout	10	John Balawejder (USA)	9-May-2011
Chew Man Fu	TurboGrafx-16	Single Player	573,720	Ryan W Genno (Canada)	2-Jun-2011
Dead Moon	TurboGrafx-16	Points	3,319,900	Ryan W Genno (Canada)	7-Jun-2011
Donkey Kong	MAME	Points	1,153,000	Dean Saglio (USA)	2-Apr-2011
Golden Axe	Sega Genesis/ Mega Drive	The Duel; Fastest Completion	5 min 32 sec	Daniel Lee Strickland Perea (USA)	17-Apr-2011
Hit the Ice	Sega Genesis/ Mega Drive	Biggest Blowout	43	John Balawejder (USA)	9-May-2011
Karous	Sega Dreamcast	Points	48,740,490	George Figueiras (USA)	19-May-2011
Klax	Atari Lynx	Points	2,247,465	Roger L Gray (USA)	19-Jun-2011
Klax	Sega Genesis/ Mega Drive	Points	2,359,198	Roger L Gray (USA)	31-May-2011
Legend of Hero Tonma	TurboGrafx-16	Points	69,600	Ryan W Genno (Canada)	7-Jun-2011
Magical Chase	TurboGrafx-16	Points	2,912,730	Ryan W Genno (Canada)	1-Jun-2011
Mario Bros.	MAME	Hard No POW Challenge	785,240	Stephen K Boyer (USA)	27-Mar-2011
Mario Bros. Japan	MAME	Points	2,500,000	Stephen K Boyer (USA)	26-May-2011

MEGA DRIVE TO SUCCEED

Known as the Genesis in North America, Sega's third console was better known as the Mega Drive around the rest of the world. *Sonic the Hedgehog* (Sega, 1991) made its debut on the platform and the title's success led to multiple sequels. The game's blue blur of a hero was eventually adopted by the company as its official mascot, and became a great rival to Nintendo's Mario.

KAROUS

(Milestone Inc., 2007) Sega's last home console, the Dreamcast, ceased production in March 2001. However, many developers continued to support the platform for years afterwards, especially in Japan. The title for the **last official Dreamcast game** goes to the 2D shooter *Karous*, released in March 2007. Despite this, some die-hard indie developers continue to make Dreamcast games to this day.

WHILE PLAYING GOLF. THERE WERE EVEN SHARKS AT THE WATER HAZARDS! ▶

GAME	PLATFORM	SETTINGS	RECORD	PLAYER (COUNTRY)	DATE
Mr. Driller	Sega Dreamcast	Arcade Mode; 2,500 ft Challenge	336,385	Meg Hurley (USA)	24-May-2011
Ms. PAC-Man	Sega Genesis/ Mega Drive	Turbo Mode	179,060	Marc Cohen (USA)	20-Jan-2011
NBA Jam	Sega Genesis/ Mega Drive	Biggest Blowout	52	John Baker (Canada)	10-Jul-2011
NFL 2K	Sega Dreamcast	Biggest Blowout	116	Jeffrey M Widzinski (USA)	12-May-2011
NHL '94	Sega CD	Biggest Blowout	33	John Balawejder (USA)	9-May-2011
NHL '94	Sega Genesis/ Mega Drive	Biggest Blowout	47	Jeff Hinish (USA)	11-Jul-2011
Ninja Golf	Atari 7800	Points	168,560	Mark A Stacy (USA)	21-Jun-2011
Ordyne	TurboGrafx-16	Points	374,340	Ryan W Genno (Canada)	10-Jun-2011
Psychosis	TurboGrafx-16	Points	606,300	Ryan W Genno (Canada)	1-Jun-2011
Raiden	TurboGrafx-16	Points	874,650	Ryan W Genno (Canada)	31-May-2011
Road Rash	Panasonic 3DO	Napa Vally; Fastest Race	3 min 4.33 sec	Jeffrey M Widzinski (USA)	19-Jul-2011
RoadBlasters	Sega Genesis/ Mega Drive	Points	711,220	Ryan Sullivan (USA)	21-May-2010
Samurai Ghost	TurboGrafx-16	Points	31,600	Ryan W Genno (Canada)	7-Jun-2011
Satan's Hollow	MAME	Points	4,198,465	Donald Hayes (USA)	20-Feb-2011
Sega Ages Vol. 1	Sega Saturn	*Space Harrier*	30,001,940	Stu R Rankin (UK)	26-May-2011
Sega Bass Fishing	Sega Dreamcast	Cape; Heaviest Fish	18.63 lb	Meg Hurley (USA)	14-Jun-2011
Sega Bass Fishing	Sega Dreamcast	Cave; Heaviest Fish	18.44 lb	Meg Hurley (USA)	14-Jun-2011
Sega Marine Fishing	Sega Dreamcast	Arcade; Shallow; Tarpon; Heaviest Fish	250.63 lb	Meg Hurley (USA)	24-May-2011
Sega Marine Fishing	Sega Dreamcast	Mini Game; Lure Action Training	4,390 lb	Meg Hurley (USA)	24-May-2011
Sega Marine Fishing	Sega Dreamcast	Mini Game; Total Weight Training; Coral Reef	1,089.63 lb	Meg Hurley (USA)	24-May-2011

NHL
(EA, 1991–present)
Developer EA has established a formidable reputation in the field of officially licenced sports games, and boasts the record for the **longest-running ice hockey series**. Starting in 1991 with *NHL Hockey*, the franchise has embraced 18 different platforms, including the short-lived Sega CD, for which *NHL '94* (above) was the only compatible title in the whole series.

HAVING A BLAST
A decade before *Grand Theft Auto* (Rockstar, 1997) made anti-social driving games popular, *RoadBlasters* (Atari, 1987) gave players a chance to shoot cars and bikes off the road with reckless abandon. Although such behaviour added to the player's tally – and a score multiplier rewarded accurate shooting – the real aim of the game was to complete a 50-stage rally without running out of fuel.

SCOREBOARDS

IN THE SPACE-THEMED SHOOTER *GORF* (MIDWAY, 1981), THE

OLD-SCHOOL CONSOLE

S-Z

GAME	PLATFORM	SETTINGS	RECORD	PLAYER (COUNTRY)	DATE
Sega Marine Fishing	Sega Dreamcast	Mini Game; Total Weight Training; Fishing Port	1,585.56 lb	Meg Hurley (USA)	24-May-2011
Sega Marine Fishing	Sega Dreamcast	Mini Game; Total Weight Training; Shallow	1,351.19 lb	Meg Hurley (USA)	24-May-2011
Sega Marine Fishing	Sega Dreamcast	Mini Game; Total Weight Training; The Offing	1,343.44 lb	Meg Hurley (USA)	24-May-2011
Sinistron	TurboGrafx-16	Points	288,800	Ryan W Genno (Canada)	17-Jun-2011
Soldier Blade	TurboGrafx-16	Normal Mode	1,628,700	Ryan W Genno (Canada)	4-Jun-2011
Sonic the Hedgehog	Sega Genesis/ Mega Drive	Points	812,140	Michael E Sroka (USA)	15-May-2011
Splatterhouse 2	Sega Genesis/ Mega Drive	Fastest Completion	19 min 12 sec	Andrew D Furrer (USA)	17-May-2011
Splatterhouse 2	Sega Genesis/ Mega Drive	Points	381,413	Andrew D Furrer (USA)	17-May-2011
Tron: Deadly Discs	Intellivision	15-minute limit	1,050,700	Matthew S Miller (USA)	17-Jun-2011
WWF Super WrestleMania	Sega Genesis/ Mega Drive	Fastest One-On-One Match	1 min 15 sec	Daniel Lee Strickland Perea (USA)	17-Apr-2011
WWF Super WrestleMania	TurboGrafx-16	Points	31,600	Ryan W Genno (Canada)	7-Jun-2011

SEGA MARINE FISHING

(Wow Entertainment, 1999)

Sega Bass Fishing made a huge splash with fans and critics alike when it made its debut in the arcades in 1997, as did sequel *Sega Marine Fishing* (above).

Yet it was the home console version for the Dreamcast that reeled in the record for the **most critically acclaimed fishing game**, with a score of 79% on the reviews site Metacritic.

A decisive feature that gave the game an edge against its competition was its specially adapted fishing-rod-style controller.

WRESTLE-MANIA

(Rare, 1988)

The World Wrestling Federation (later renamed World Wrestling Entertainment) served as the inspiration for the **first wrestling videogame** with *WWF: Wrestlemania* on the NES in 1988.

The global wrestling brand has since spawned more than 50 videogames, but it's the *SmackDown!* series (known as *SmackDown! vs RAW* since 2004) that commands the title for the **best-selling wrestling franchise**, pile-driving more than 42.5 million copies worldwide as of August 2011.

TRON AND ON AND ON

At the height of the early 1980s games boom, Disney released the highly anticipated videogame-themed movie *Tron* (USA, 1982). Hype for the film led to five tie-in games, with three for Mattel's Intellivision console alone, including *Tron: Deadly Discs* (above left). In the arcades, Bally and Midway wowed the crowds with *Tron* (above right), a cabinet containing four mini games, and the sequel *Discs of Tron* in 1983, by which time the film had flopped and the videogame industry was undergoing its first lull in sales.

26,000 The production run of the original upright *Joust* arcade cabinet in 1982. The company also produced a smaller "cocktail table" version.

GAME'S TITLE IS AN ACRONYM FOR "GALACTIC ORBITING ROBOT FORCE" ▶

ARCADE

A-Z

GAME	PLATFORM	SETTINGS	RECORD	PLAYER (COUNTRY)	DATE
Black Tiger	Arcade	Points	2,634,300	Isaiah M Johnson (USA)	5-Jun-2011
Dig Dug	Arcade	Marathon	5,142,500	Donald Hayes (USA)	24-Mar-2011
Dig Dug	Arcade	Tournament Settings	3,750,300	Donald Hayes (USA)	3-Jul-2011
Donkey Kong	Arcade	3 Lives	1,090,400	Hank S Chien (USA)	27-Feb-2011
Donkey Kong 3	Arcade	Marathon	3,538,000	George Riley (USA)	3-Jun-2011
Elevator Action	Arcade	Normal Difficulty	149,350	Steve Wagner (USA)	24-Aug-2010
Galaga	Arcade	Tournament Settings	4,525,150	Andrew B Laidlaw (USA)	15-Dec-2010
Gauntlet	Arcade	Single Player	4,458,580	Dwayne Richard (Canada)	18-Sep-2010
Gauntlet II	Arcade	Single Player	104,398	Ron Corcoran (USA)	19-May-2003
Gorf	Arcade	3 Lives	1,129,660	Keith R Swanson (USA)	17-Jul-2011
Indiana Jones and the Temple of Doom	Arcade	3 Lives; Easy	800,000	Cliff Reese (USA)	13-May-2011
Joust	Arcade	Marathon; Single Player	107,301,150	John P McAllister (USA)	3-Nov-2010
Klax	Arcade	Standard	386,430	Brian T Cady (USA)	12-Apr-2010
Metal Slug: Super Vehicle-001	Arcade	Points	2,683,030	Cliff Reese (USA)	8-Mar-2011
Phoenix	Arcade	Points	1,007,115	Richie Knucklez (USA)	7-May-2011
Space Invaders	Arcade	Points	55,160	Donald Hayes (USA)	7-Jun-2003
The Real Ghostbusters	Arcade	Single Player	425,900	Lance M Eustache (USA)	4-Jun-2011
Tron	Arcade	Points	11,125,999	David Cruz (USA)	19-Dec-2010
Vs. Dr. Mario	Arcade	Tournament Settings	977,000	Patrick Stanley (USA)	4-Mar-2010
Vs. Super Mario Bros.	Arcade	Tournament Settings	3,054,150	Isaiah M Johnson (USA)	7-May-2011
Zoo Keeper	Arcade	Points	38,248,380	Jason Cram (USA)	18-Nov-2010

CAN I *DIG* IT?
(Namco, 1982)
In *Dig Dug*, the main character was originally known in the West as "Dig Dug". Today the character is better known as Taizo Hori, the father of Susumu Hori, the main character in *Mr. Driller* (Namco, 1999). *Mr. Driller* started development as "Dig Dug 3" before becoming a separate game franchise in its own right.

JOUST DO IT
An arcade classic, *Joust* featured players as knights perched on top of flying ostriches. In 2007, a company called CP Productions acquired the rights to make a *Joust* movie, described as "*Gladiator* meets *Mad Max*". As of August 2011, *Joust* is still listed as being "in production"…

SCOREBOARDS

ACCORDING TO PINBALL LOCATOR WEBSITE *PINFORMER*, THERE

SPACE INVADERS

(Bally, 1979)
The success of arcade smash *Space Invaders* (Taito, 1978) spawned the massively popular pinball version (above). The original game holds the record for the **first videogame to feature animated aliens**, as well as the **first arcade game debated in Parliament**. In 1981, a British MP tried to have the game banned, believing it caused child "deviancy". He failed.

GREEN WITH ENVY

The *Rock Band* title featuring American punkers Green Day (below) has sold 870,000 copies to date, while the only other game in the series to revolve around a band, 2009's *The Beatles: Rock Band*, has shifted over 3.7 million copies.

PINBALL

A-Z

GAME	PLATFORM	SETTINGS	RECORD	PLAYER (COUNTRY)	DATE
Cirqus Voltaire	Pinball	Factory Default; Three Ball	41,148,360	Keith Nelson (USA)	26-Sep-2009
Firepower II	Pinball	Factory Default; Three Ball	7,332,420	Raymond Davidson (USA)	18-Dec-2010
The Lord of the Rings	Pinball	Factory Default; Three Ball; Extra Balls Allowed	46,162,720	Keith Nelson (USA)	26-Sep-2009
Medieval Madness	Pinball	Factory Default; Three Ball	102,504,420	Mike Lorrain (USA)	31-Jul-2011
NBA Fastbreak	Pinball	Factory Default; Three Ball	141	Byron K Raynz (USA)	31-Jul-2011
Space Invaders	Pinball	Tournament Settings	1,721,050	Sanjay Shah (USA)	4-Jun-2011
Supersonic	Pinball	Tournament Settings	639,440	Keith Elwin (USA)	4-Jun-2011
The Simpsons Pinball Party	Pinball	Factory Default; Three Ball; Extra Balls Allowed	45,518,940	Todd MacCulloch (USA)	17-Apr-2010
Tron: Legacy Limited Edition	Pinball	Factory Default; Three Ball	48,634,410	Mike Lorrain (USA)	31-Jul-2011
World Poker Tour	Pinball	Tournament Settings	55,677,140	Zach Sharpe (USA)	4-Jun-2011

SONY

A-S

GAME	PLATFORM	SETTINGS	RECORD	PLAYER (COUNTRY)	DATE
Green Day: Rock Band	PlayStation 3	Single Player; Vocals	118,000	Jackie M Bartlett (USA)	16-Sep-2010
Marvel Pinball	PlayStation Network	*Blade*	17,977,500	Marc Cohen (USA)	31-Jan-2011
Marvel Pinball	PlayStation Network	*Iron Man*	32,664,000	Marc Cohen (USA)	14-Jan-2011
Marvel Pinball	PlayStation Network	*Spider-Man*	90,368,846	Marc Cohen (USA)	18-Jan-2011
Marvel Pinball	PlayStation Network	*Wolverine*	66,860,900	Marc Cohen (USA)	16-Jan-2011

4 ×   6 ×

ARE ONLY 712 PUBLIC PINBALL MACHINES IN THE UK AS OF AUGUST 2011 ▶

GAME	PLATFORM	SETTINGS	RECORD	PLAYER (COUNTRY)	DATE
Midway Arcade Treasures	PlayStation 2	*Joust*; 1-Player; Marathon	98,950	Jeremy N Woodworth (USA)	28-Feb-2011
Midway Arcade Treasures	PlayStation 2	*Rampart*	17,761	Jeremy N Woodworth (USA)	28-Feb-2011
Midway Arcade Treasures	PlayStation 2	*Smash TV*; 1-Player	917,530	Jeremy N Woodworth (USA)	28-Feb-2011
Midway Arcade Treasures	PlayStation 2	*Klax*	1,875,145	Roger L Gray (USA)	21-Mar-2011
Namco Museum Battle Collection	PSP	*Galaga*	206,750	Michael E Sroka (USA)	30-May-2011
PAC-Man Championship Edition DX	PlayStation Network	Championship I; Score Attack; 5 Minutes	453,820	Marc Cohen (USA)	5-Feb-2011
Pinball Hall of Fame: The Williams Collection	PlayStation 3	*Funhouse*	282,746,680	Gregrey S Hall (USA)	7-May-2011
Pinball Hall of Fame: The Williams Collection	PlayStation 3	*Whirlwind*	72,134,780	Gregrey S Hall (USA)	16-Apr-2011
Pinball Hall of Fame: The Williams Collection	PlayStation 3	*Pin*Bot*	5,390,140	Gregrey S Hall (USA)	9-May-2011
Pinball Hall of Fame: The Williams Collection	PlayStation 3	Williams Challenge	319	Gregrey S Hall (USA)	16-Apr-2011
Pinball Hall of Fame: The Williams Collection	PlayStation 3	*Sorcerer*	4,308,110	Marc Cohen (USA)	9-Feb-2011
Pinball Hall of Fame: The Williams Collection	PlayStation 3	*Space Shuttle*	7,723,780	Marc Cohen (USA)	11-Feb-2011
Pinball Hall of Fame: The Williams Collection	PlayStation 3	*Taxi*	18,185,970	Marc Cohen (USA)	8-Feb-2011
Sega Genesis Collection	PSP	*Flicky*	140,290	Jeremy N Woodworth (USA)	24-Feb-2011
SoulCalibur III	PlayStation 2	Soul Arena; Turntable; Hard [Fastest Completion]	2 min 32.28 sec	Christopher C Meeker (USA)	20-Mar-2011

AT THE MUSEUM

Namco Museum Battle Collection (Namco Tales Studio, 2005) brings together 21 classic Namco games ported to the PSP, including four new arrangements of retro games (above) that are exclusive to the Sony handheld. Gamers can enjoy titles such as *PAC-Man*, *Galaga* and *Dig Dug*.

SOUL-CALIBUR III

(Project Soul, 2005) A PS2 exclusive, the third *SoulCalibur* (below) scored an impressive 86% on Metacritic. But the first game in the series, *SoulCalibur*, remains the **most critically acclaimed fighting game** with a huge 98% Metacritic average.

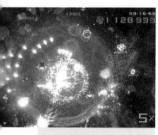

SHOOT THE MOON!

Everything is a target in the space shooter *Super Stardust HD* (Housemarque, 2007), as players are tasked with destroying everything on the screen. The game traces its lineage back to the original *Stardust* (Bloodhouse, 1993) but draws its main influence from the legendary arcade game *Asteroids* (Atari, 1979).

SONY
S-Z

GAME	PLATFORM	SETTINGS	RECORD	PLAYER (COUNTRY)	DATE
SoulCalibur IV	PlayStation 3	Arcade Mode – Fastest Completion	4 min 51.6 sec	Jeremy Florence (USA)	16-Jan-2011
SoulCalibur IV	PlayStation 3	Arcade Mode	404,620	Jeremy Florence (USA)	16-Jan-2011
Super Stardust HD	PlayStation Network	Arcade Mode	10,984,920	John A Pompa (USA)	14-Jun-2011
Super Stardust HD	PlayStation Network	Planet Mode; Coventina	6,435,705	John A Pompa (USA)	16-Jun-2011
Super Stardust HD	PlayStation Network	Planet Mode; Lave	4,594,955	John A Pompa (USA)	15-Jun-2011
Super Stardust HD	PlayStation Network	Planet Mode; Nemain	7,386,025	John A Pompa (USA)	16-Jun-2011
Super Stardust HD	PlayStation Network	Planet Mode; Segomo	7,633,530	John A Pompa (USA)	16-Jun-2011
Super Stardust HD	PlayStation Network	Planet Mode; Taravis	5,063,805	John A Pompa (USA)	16-Jun-2011
Super Street Fighter IV	PlayStation 3	Arcade Mode; Tournament Settings	2,587,000	Rob Seymour (UK)	5-Dec-2010
Taito Legends Power-Up	PSP	Cameltry; Expert Course	176,500	Kevin S Brisley (Canada)	22-Jan-2011
Taito Legends Power-Up	PSP	Elevator Action	64,250	Kevin S Brisley (Canada)	4-Mar-2011
We Love Katamari	PlayStation 2	"As Large As Possible", Level Five; Diameter	3,634.268 m	Rachel L Beaver (USA)	20-Apr-2011

WE LOVE KATAMARI
(Namco/NOW Production, 2005)

After the Prince (far left) recreated all the stars destroyed by his father, the "King of All Cosmos", in *Katamari Damacy* (Namco/NOW, 2004), the pair won lots of fans.

In the game's sequel, the Prince attempts to fulfil his fans' requests, again using his Katamari, a little ball of stuff that grows larger by adding smaller items to its mass. *We Love Katamari* scooped the Best Puzzle Game award at the E3 convention in 2005, as well as an impressive 86% average score on Metacritic, as of September 2011. See page 131 for details of another *Katamari* world record.

TAITO RECALL

Taito Legends (Taito, 2006) for the PSP allowed older players to revisit the games of their youth, while offering younger players the chance to enjoy games made before they were born. The title featured a collection of 26 games from Taito's back catalogue that players could share wirelessly with friends for a limited time.

AND AN EXCLUSIVE *SOULCALIBUR* T-SHIRT

MICROSOFT

A-Z

GAME	PLATFORM	SETTINGS	RECORD	PLAYER (COUNTRY)	DATE
Metal Slug XX	XBLA	Main Mission	2,965,090	Danny L Michael (USA)	29-Sep-2010
Midway Arcade Treasures	Xbox	*Klax*	2,052,921	Roger L Gray (USA)	14-May-2011
PAC-Man Championship Edition	XBLA	Challenge Mode 1	509,970	Michael E Sroka (USA)	18-Jul-2010
PAC-Man Championship Edition DX	XBLA	*Championship II*; Score Attack	1,913,540	Charlie D Wehner (USA)	29-Jan-2011
PAC-Man Championship Edition DX	XBLA	Dungeon; Score Attack; Five Minutes	1,953,770	Charlie D Wehner (USA)	22-Jan-2011
Pinball FX	XBLA	Agents Table	23,737,000	John A Pompa (USA)	7-Aug-2010
Portal: Still Alive	XBLA	Play Now Mode; Fastest Completion	44 min 28 sec	Chris Artrip (USA)	10-Jan-2011
SoulCalibur IV	Xbox 360	Arcade Mode; Fastest Completion	3 min 45.81 sec	Jeremy Florence (USA)	16-Jan-2011
SoulCalibur IV	Xbox 360	Arcade Mode	577,520	Jeremy Florence (USA)	16-Jan-2011
UFC Undisputed 2010	Xbox 360	Exhibition Mode; Fastest Victory	6 sec	T J Wilt (USA)	8-Aug-2010

PORTAL: STILL ALIVE
(Valve, 2007)
Available exclusively on Xbox Live Arcade, *Portal: Still Alive* was a downloadable version of the physics puzzle game *Portal* that included extra challenges, achievements and maps. Like the original *Portal*, it ended with the musical number "Still Alive", in which the malevolent AI GLaDOS announces to the world that she has survived the game's final scenes. The music is also the **first Western piece of music played at the "Press Start Symphony of Games"**, Japan's festival of videogame music.

UFC UNDISPUTED 2010
(Yuke's, 2010)
The Mixed Martial Arts (MMA) game *UFC Undisputed 2010* features a roster of 88 playable characters, including former basketball star Shaquille O'Neal, the **most playable characters in an MMA game**. The next game in the series is due in early 2012. Will the roster of fighters in *UFC Undisputed 3* enable it to claim the record?

eSPORTS LEAGUE TABLES

IN 2011, PLAYERS FROM THE GLOBAL *STARCRAFT II* LEAGUE (GSL) BEGAN

IT'S BEEN ANOTHER BUSY YEAR IN THE WORLD OF eSPORTS, PACKED WITH PLENTY OF SURPRISES. MANY COMPETITION FAVOURITES FAILED TO TAKE THE TOP SPOTS IN THEIR CHOSEN EVENTS, WHILE LOTS OF NEW BLOOD TRIUMPHED!

MULTIPLAY i42

Multiplay is the UK's premier local area network (LAN) event – and as its name suggests, it is a venue for multiplayer game competitions. Battling teams, such as Infused.TT (above), can walk off with a cash prize. Featured games included *Call of Duty 4* (Infinity Ward, 2007).

CALL OF DUTY 4

RANK	GAMER TEAM
1	#blight
2	YYT
3	Infused.TT

TEAM FORTRESS 2

RANK	GAMER TEAM
1	Infused.TT
2	Team Thermaltake
3	Children of Poop

STARCRAFT II

RANK	GAMER
1	SeleCT (South Korea)
2	BlinG (UK)
3	Lau (UK)

MAJOR LEAGUE GAMING (MLG) GRAND FINAL 2010

MLG is the most prominent eSports organization in North America, hosting monthly tournaments. The grand final of the 2010 season took place in Dallas, Texas, USA, and saw talented gamers take home some impressive cash prizes.

STARCRAFT II 1V1

RANK	GAMER (COUNTRY)	RACE
1	Liquid`Jinro (Sweden)	Terran
2	FnaticMSITT1 (Canada)	Protoss
3	Pain.User (USA)	Terran
4	Liquid`Tyler (USA)	Protoss

CALL OF DUTY: MODERN WARFARE 2 4V4 (PS3) (BELOW LEFT)

RANK	GAMER TEAM (COUNTRY)
1	Influence (USA)
2	Victory Without Sacrifice (USA)
3	HSG Xtravagant (USA)
4	OpTic Gaming (USA)

HALO: REACH 4V4

RANK	GAMER TEAM (COUNTRY)
1	UoR SyA (USA, below)
2	Hot Shots (USA)
3	UoR Victorious Secret (USA)
4	Darkest Hour (USA)

/// "WELCOME TO THE MAD HOUSE" ///

44 The number of different nationalities that made it to the 2011 Evolution Championship Series World Finals in Las Vegas, USA.

COMPETING IN MAJOR LEAGUE GAMING (MLG) EVENTS ▶

GLOBAL *STARCRAFT II* LEAGUE (GSL) 2010 OPEN SEASON 3

GSL is a series of competitions broadcast over the internet by GOMTV (South Korea). In the last 2010 Open Tournament, Chil "oGsMC" Jan Min won the top prize of 100 million Won ($89,000; £57,000)!

RANK	GAMER (COUNTRY)	RACE
1	oGsMC (South Korea)	Protoss
2	TSL_Rain (South Korea)	Terran
3	HongUnPrime (South Korea)	Protoss
4	Liquid`Jinro (Sweden)	Terran

EVOLUTION CHAMPIONSHIP SERIES (EVO) 2011

Evo is widely considered the most prestigious fighting game competition in the world. The big shock this year came when relative newcomer Fuudo (left) took the top prize in the *Super Street Fighter IV* (Capcom, 2010) competition ahead of the regular title favourite Daigo Umehara.

SUPER STREET FIGHTER IV ARCADE EDITION

RANK	GAMER (COUNTRY)	CHARACTER
1	Fuudo (Japan)	Fei Long
2	Latif (USA)	C Viper
3	Poongko (South Korea)	Seth
4	Daigo Umehara (Japan)	Yun

MARVEL vs. CAPCOM 3 (RIGHT)

RANK	GAMER (COUNTRY)	CHARACTER
1	Viscant (USA)	Wesker, Haggar, Phoenix
2	PR Balrog (Puerto Rico)	Dante, Wolverine, Tron
3	Justin Wong (USA)	She-Hulk, Wolverine, Akuma
4	Combofiend (USA)	She-Hulk, Taskmaster, Spencer

MORTAL KOMBAT

RANK	GAMER (COUNTRY)	CHARACTER
1	Perfect Legend (USA)	Kung Lao
2	REO (USA)	Mileena
3	JOP (USA)	Johnny Cage, Raiden
4	ChrisGNY (USA)	Reptile

FIFA INTERACTIVE WORLD CUP

This year's final of the **biggest videogame tournament** saw the best and brightest of the world's virtual soccer stars competing in Los Angeles, USA. Turn to page 58 for full details on this awesome event.

RANK	GAMER (COUNTRY)	TEAM
1	Francisco Cruz (Portugal, above right with US soccer player Eric Wynalda)	Chelsea
2	Javier Muñoz (Colombia)	Real Madrid
3	Mark Azzi (Australia)	Chelsea
4	Adam Winster (UK)	Chelsea

Bold entries in the index indicate a main entry on a topic, and entries in **BOLD CAPITALS** indicate an entire chapter.

2D Fighters 116–117, 120
2D Platformers 106–107
2D Shooters 46–47
2D/3D hybrid games 131
3D gaming:
  arcade 176, 179;
  Nintendo 3DS 32–33, 87, 94, 100, 135;
  remakes 94, 100;
  simulations 171;
  social gaming 48;
  sports games 60;
  stealth games 103;
  stereoscopic 62, 108;
  strategy 166
3D Fighters 118–119
3D Platformers 108–109
5th Cell 124
720° 65
1080° Snowboarding 57

A
Acaba, Daniel 71
Academy of Interactive Arts & Sciences 57, 101
Accept the Challenge 20–21
Ace Combat 4 169
ACES Game Studio 168
ACTION-ADVENTURE GAMES 94–111
Action RPGs 142–143
Activision 37, 38, 89
Addictive Games 59
Advance Wars 148
advertising 46, 85, 127
Aero Blasters 200
Aion 155
Akaoni Studio 199
Albrigtsen, Eirik 133
Alien Sidestep 92
Alienware M11x 30
Allen, Ben 6, 22
Allied Leisure Industries 59
Alpha Protocol 103
Altered Beast 194
alternalw 143
Alternate Reality Games 172, **180–181**
Amaya, Daisuke 29
American football 60
American Sports 60–61
Amery, Mark 103

Amnesia: The Dark Descent 11, 15, 31
Baldur's Gate 146
Amstar Electronics 177
AMY 105
Angry Birds 16, 20, 35, **126–127**
APB 156
Apple 34, 356; App Store 126, 132; *see also* iPad; iPhone
AR.Drone 86
AR Games 33
arcade emulators 178
arcade games 137, 172;
  Classic 176–177;
  Modern 178–179;
  Racing 74–75;
  scoreboard 203
Archetype 49
ARGN.com 180
Armadillo Run 133
Arnold, David 143
Arnold family 139
ARQuake 86
Art of Balance 133
Art of Fighting 3 117
Art Style: Cubello 129
Asheron's Call 2 156
Assassin's Creed 95, **96–97**, 101, 185, 186;
  Brotherhood 11, 97, 187;
  Revelations 97
Asteroids 177
Astron Belt 50
Atari 64, 92, 177
Atari Anniversary Edition 200
Auf Wiedersehen, Pet 93
Augmented Reality 32, 33, **86–87**
Auto Assault 156
avatars 42, 43
awards 19;
  AIAS 57, 101;
  BAFTAs 11, 82, 97, 101, 132;
  Develop 10;
  Game Critics Best of E3 10, 59;
  Game Developers Choice 11, 181;
  Gamer's 12–15;
  Golden Joystick 15;
  Grammy Awards 164;
  Independent Games Festival 11;
  Ivor Novello 165;
  Round-up 10–11

B
Bach, Patrick 41
Back to the Future: The Game 14, 111
BAFTA awards 11, 82, 97, 101, 132

Bailey, Dona 177
Baldur's Gate 146
Bandai Power Pad 63
Bangs, Michael 51
Barravento 92
baseball 61
basketball 60
Bastion 10, 25
Batchelor, Tom 131
Bates, John 7
Batman: Arkham Asylum 101;
  Arkham City 13, 15
Battlefield 10, 12, **40–41**
Battle Gear 3 179
Battle Mii 28
Battletoads & Double Dragon 200
Batty, Todd 57
Bayonetta 121
The Beast 180
Beat-'em-Ups 120–121
Beavers, Sean 175
Bedard, Martin 75
BeFreak 70
Bejeweled 128, 159, 194
Bell, Timothy 43
Bend Studios 26
Bentley, Edward 107
Berry, Dan Bunten 166
Best of Mobile 34–35
Best of PC 30–31
Best of PlayStation 26–27
Best of Wii 28–29
Best of Xbox 24–25
beta-testing 52
Bethesda Softworks 19
Big Brain Academy 135
BioShock 185;
  Infinite 10, 18, 43
BioWare 17, 136, 147
BIT.TRIP RUNNER 11
Bizarre Creations 74, 75
Black Tiger 203
Blazing Souls Accelate 149
Bleach: Shattered Blade 119
Bleszinski, Cliff 53
Blizzard 143, 162, 163
Block Puzzles 128–129
Blu-Ray 37
Blue Dragon 145
blur 74, 75
Blystad, Tore 103
boardcross 56
Bogost, Ian 159
Bolinger, Elizabeth 91
Bomberman 200
Borderlands 43
boxing 123
Braid 131
Bravoman 200

Brett Hull Hockey 95, 200
Brink 43
Broken Sword 3 111
Bubble Bobble 177, 194
Bulletstorm 43, 44
Burnout Paradise 76, 77
Bushnell, Nolan 177

C
CaféWorld 159
Call of Duty 40, 208;
  Black Ops 16, 37, 38, 43, 191;
  Modern Warfare 12, 38, 42, 43, 186, 189, 208;
  World at War 184
camouflage 102
Capcom 104, 105, 142, 143
Capcom Crossovers 114–115
Capcom vs. SNK 2 114, 115
Capybara Games 101
cartridges 135, 175
Castellanos, Juan M 196
Castle Crashers 121
Castlevania 100, 194
Cave 47
Cave Story 29
Cecil, Charles 103
cel-shading 65
Centipede 177
Cetin, Sami 6, 68
character customization 43
Charlie's Angels 93
Chase Mii 29
Chew Man Fu 200
Chien, Hank 175
Child of Eden 25, 51, 129
Chillingo 16
Chime 129
Chimes, Carl 162
Chronicles of Spellborn 156
Chrono Trigger 144
City of Heroes and Villains 155, 156–157;
CityVille 158, 159
Civilization 160, 164, 165
Classic Arcade 176–177
claw machines 179
Clone Wars Adventures 150
Codemasters 72, 73
Codename Eagle 40
Cologne Gamescom 19
combat crossovers 114–115
combat simulators 169

Combat Sports 122–123
comic books 101
Command & Conquer 166
Company of Heroes 166
Condemned: Criminal Origins 105
Contra: Rebirth 194
controllers:
  D-pad 175;
  guitar 89;
  Kinect 16, 17, **82–83**, 89, 91;
  largest 22–23
  Move 111;
  Wii U 28
controversial games 19
Cosmic Shock Absorber 92
Cotton, Olly J 177
Count Duckula 2 93
Counter-Strike 48, 49, 67
Country Dance 91
cover-based shooters 45
Cow Clicker 159
Cranberryzero 87
Crash Bandicoot 109
Crash Nitro Kart 79
Crash Team Racing 79
The Creative Assembly 165
Crimson Skies 169
Critter Crunch 133
crossover characters 78
cross-platform gaming 48, 49
Crush 131
Cruz, Francisco 59
Crysis 2 44, 184
Crytek 10
Cuisset, Paul 105
Culley, Benjamin 146
Cutler, Matthew 76
cutscenes 65
Cut the Rope 11, 132
Cytron Masters 166

D
D-pad 175
Dance Central 80, 82, 89, 90, 91
Dance Dance Revolution 90
dance mats 83, 90
Dancing 82, **90–91**
danmaku shooters 46, 47
Darkfall 155
Dark Souls 13
Darkstalkers 115
Data East 114
David Beckham Soccer 59
Daytona USA 115, 179
DC Universe Online 150, 157
Dead Island 98, 99

Dead Moon 200
Dead or Alive 118, 119
Dead Space 15, 51, 104, 105
Deadly Premonition 105
Deathsmiles 47
Def Jam: Icon 119
Defcon 168
Defender 46
Demon's Souls 143
Descent: FreeSpace 169
Desktop Dungeons 11
Desmet, Tony 97
Deus Ex: Human Revolution 14, 45
Develop Awards 10
Diablo 3 143
Diamond Dash 159
Dig Dug 203
DiRT 3 13, 72, 73
Disgaea 26, 138, 149
Disney 3D Ping Pong 179
Dissidia: Final Fantasy 119
DJ Atomika 57
djWHEAT 67
dnd 147
Dr. Kawashima's Body & Brain Exercises 134
Dr. Mario 129, 198
Doctor Who: The Adventure Games 103
Dofus 155
Donkey Kong 106, 109, **174–175**;
  scoreboard 194, 200, 203
Doom 19
Dota 2 19, 66
downloads 46, 83, 88, 89, 105, 171;
  illegal 163;
  post-release 165
Dragon Age 12, 17, 146
Dragon Quest 145
Dragon Slayer 142
DreamHack 49
Dreamworks Madagascar Kartz 79
DS; *see* Nintendo DS
Duke Nukem Forever 19, 168
Dungeon Fighter Online 120
Dungeon Siege 147
Dykstra, John 51
dynamic soundtrack 57

E
E3 18;
  Awards 10, 59
EA 16, 76;
  alternate reality 181;
  MMOs 152, 153, 157, 158;

real-time strategy 166;
simulations 168
EA Black Box 64, 65
EA Digital Illusions CE 40, 41
EA Sports 63, 201;
American football 60;
basketball 54, 195;
snowboarding 56–57;
soccer 58, 59
EA Sports Active 80, 84, 85
Earth and Beyond 156
Easter eggs 42, 119
Eat Sleep Play 45
echochrome 130, 131
Ecotopia 158
The Elder Scrolls 10, 12, 138, 146, 147, 184
Electronic Arts; *see* EA
Electronic Entertainment Expo; *see* E3
electronic sports; *see* eSports
Electronic Sports World Cup 67
Elemental: War of Magic 165
Elevator Action 194, 203
Elf Bowling 61
Elite IV 168
Empire: Total War 165
Empires & Allies 159
EmTenTeo 132
Enemy Zero 105
Eno, Kenji 105, 111
Enslaved 10
Entropia Universe 157
Epic Games 52, 53
Epic Mickey 108, 109
Ericsson Xperia 34, 35
eSports 163;
EVO 115, 116;
eSports League Tables 208–209;
Pro-gaming Review 66–67;
tournaments 41, 58, 60, 66, 67, 139, 167, 174;
World Cyber Games 65, 67
E.T. The Extra-Terrestrial 92
EteRNA 135
Eternal Ring 143
European Sports 62–63
Eve Online 155, 157
Everquest 150
Every Extend Extra 129
Evolution Championship Series (EVO) 115, 116, 209

Extreme Sports 64–65
Eye of Judgment 87

F
F1 2010 10, 11, 72
F1GP 72
Fable 37, 143
Facebook 48, 123, 134, 158, 159, 164, 173
Face of Mankind 156
Face Raiders 33, 86
Fairy Trails 87
Falcon 4.0: Allied Force 169
Fallout 138, 146, 147, 185
Family Game Night 121
Family Trainer: Aerobics Studio 90
Famitsu magazine 121
Fan, George 167
Fantasy MMORPGs 154–155
Fantasy Westward Journey 155
FarmVille 158, 159
Fastlane Street Racing 77
Feiertag, Adrian 105
FIFA 43, 58, 59, 60;
Interactive World Cup 58, 59, 209
Fight Night 123
Fighter's History 114
Fighters Megamix 115
FIGHTING GAMES 112–123
Fighting Layer 119
Final Fantasy 37, 138, 144, 145;
Final Fantasy VII 188;
Final Fantasy XI 154, 155;
Final Fantasy Tactics: The War of the Lions 148, 149
Firaxis 164, 165
Fire Emblem 148
First-person Shooters 38, 40, 42–43;
social gaming 48, 49
fishing games 201, 202
Fist of the North Star 117
fitness games 84–85
Flees, Matt 130
flight simulators 168, 169
God of War 11, 37, 120, 121, 189
Golden Axe 200
Golden Joystick Awards 15
Golden Tee Golf 179
golf 62, 63, 179
Golf 62
Goodall, Richard 75
Gorf 202, 203
Gradius 194
graffiti 177
Graffiti Man 93
Grammy Awards 164
Gran Trak 10 68

FreeSpace 2 169
Frictional Games 31
From Software 143
FrontierVille 158, 159
Fry, Vance 178
Fulwood, Andy 85
Fury 156
Futant462 116
Fuudo 209

G
GagaVille 159
Galaga 47, 203
Galaxy on Fire 2 169
Galaxy S11 35
Gallant, Eric 97
Game & Watch 175, 194
Game Critics Best of E3 Awards 10
Game Dev Story 34
Game Developers Choice Awards 11, 181
game endings 182–191
Game Freak 140, 141
Game Informer 7
Gaming Awards Round-up 10–11
Gaming Fail 92–93
Gaming Round-up 16–19
Cammon, Jeffrey 97
Gangster Town 50
Gardens of Time 158, 159
Garrett, Terry 131
Garriott, Richard 146, 152, 153
Gauntlet 203
Gears of War 37, 38, 45, **52–53;**
Gears of War 2 185;
Gears of War 3 24
gekkanokihaku 119
Geometry Wars: Retro Evolved 2 46
Get Fit with Mel B 85
The Getaway 45, 111
Ghostrider 73
Ghost Squad 194
Ghost Trick 14
Girl's Garden 171
Global Starcraft II League 67, 163, 209
Gloyd, Christopher 43

Gran Turismo 17, 37, 70, 72, 73
Grand Theft Auto 7, 99, 143, 186;
Chinatown Wars 99;
San Andreas 185;
Grandia 143
Graphic Adventure 110–111
Grezzo 94, 100
Griesemer, Jamie 42
Groudon 141
Guilty Gear 116
guitar games 89
Guitar Hero 80, 89;
Legends of Rock 88
Gun Fight 177
Guy (Final Fight) 120
Gyromite 133
Gyruss 51

H
H, Philipp 167
hack and slash 121
hacking 150
Haemiont Games 24
HAL Laboratory 60
Hale, Jennifer 147
Half-Life 19, 184
Halo 37, 187;
Combat Evolved 42, 187;
Reach 43, 190, 208
HARDWARE 22–37
Harmonix 88, 89
Hart, Ryan 112
Hawk, Tony 65
HD 46, 72, 102, 104
Heavy Rain 11, 111, 188
Hed, Mikael 126, 127
Heide, Steven Ter 27
Helsing's Fire 11
Henson, Erica 129
Herrig, Felice 122, 123
HIGH SCORES 192–207;
action-adventure 97, 99, 103;
AR games 87;
dance games 91;
fitness games 85;
instant gaming 174, 175, 177, 179;
puzzle games 127, 128, 129, 130, 131, 132, 134, 135;
racing games 75;
shooters 43, 45, 46, 47, 51;
sports games 63, 65;
High Voltage 91
Hit the Ice 200
Hitman: Blood Money 103
Hjerpseth, Marius 58
Hoe, Chin Chun 128
hungryman88 121
Hunter 92, 98

I
ice hockey 61, 201

Ice-T 53
iFPS Online 49
IGN.com 7
Ignition Entertainment 130
IL-2 Sturmovik 169
ilovebees 180, 181
Impossible Game 107
Independent Games Festival Awards 11
Indiana Jones and the Temple of Doom 203
inFAMOUS 27, 99, 184
Infinity Blade 17, 34
inline skating 65
Insomniac Games 109
INSTANT GAMING 172–181
Instruments 88–89
Intel Extreme Masters 67
Intelligent Systems 148
Intergalactic Cage Match 92
internet memes 124
Invizimals 87
IO Interactive 103
iOS 17, 34, 35, 47, 132, 147
iPad 16, 21, 34
iPhone 35, 49, 86, 87, 155
iPod Touch 49
Irrational Games 18
Island Run 85
Ivor Novello Awards 165
Iwata, Satoru 29, 87

J
Jack LaLanne's Physical Conditioning 85
Jackson, Richard 75
Jae Ho, Jang 167
Japanese RPGs 144–145
Jarniou, Alain 77
Jarvis, Eugene 46
Jeanne D'Arc 149
Jet Set Radio 65
John Madden Football 55
Joltik 141
Jones, Cameron 21
Joust 203
Jump Ultimate Stars 115
Junction Point Studios 108, 109
Just Dance 16, 83, 90, 91, 195

K
Kaga, Shouzou 148
karaoke 83, 88, 89
Karate Champ 123
Karnov 114
Karous 200

Kart Racing 78–79
Kessler, Scott 130
Kiazyk, Stephen 148
Kikai, Mutsugu 9
kill screens 92–93
Kill Switch 45
Killzone 27, 37, 42–43
Kim Won-Gi 163
Kinect 10, 16, 17, 24, 37, 51, 71, **82–83,** 89, 91
Kinect Sports 11, 81, 82
King of Fighters 117
King of Kong (movie) 175
Kingdom Hearts 143, 185, 186
Kirby 21, 29
Kish, Stephen 20, 85
Kitase, Yoshinori 145
Klax 129, 200, 203
Kojima, Hideo 102
Konami 90
Konno, Hideki 32
Kovacs, Steven 74

L
L.A. Noire 14, 110, 111
Lady Gaga 159
Laidlaw, Andrew 47
LAN parties 49
Langrisser III 149
LaserDisc 50
The Last Remnant 145
Lawson, Gerald A 135
League of Legends 66
Left 4 Dead 2 49
Legend of Hero Tonma 200
The Legend of Zelda 18, 29, 101;
Ocarina of Time 13, 32, 94, 100, 190;
Skyward Sword 10, 29;
Twilight Princess 184
Lego Star Wars 136, 137
Lenart, Dennis 111
Level-5 149
Lexis Numerique 105
Life Simulators 170–171
Lifestyle & Fitness 84–85
light guns 50
Limbo 10, 11, 107
Lineage 155
Lips 88
LittleBigPlanet 27, 37, 99, 106, 107
Little League 114–115
Livingstone, Ian 10
Logg, Ed 177
Logic Puzzles 134–135
Long, Jordan Wayne 155
The Longest Journey 111

Lord British 152, 153
Lord of the Rings 149;
  Online 155;
  pinball 204;
  Lost Odyssey 145;
  The Lost Ring 180
LucasArts 57, 136
Lumines 25, 129

M
Machinarium 111
Madden Bowl 60
Madden NFL 60, 61
Magic: The Gathering 155
Magical Chase 200
Mahjong Trails 134
Major League Gaming 66, 67, 208
MAME cabinets 178
manga 115, 117
marathons 7, 9, 27, 38, 43, 97, 117;
  relays 145
Marble Madness 130
Mario 9, 63, 140, 174
Mario & Sonic at the Olympic Games 63
Mario Bros. 195, 200
Mario Kart 6, 68, 78, 79, 133, 195
Mario Strikers Charged 195
martial arts 122, 123
Martin, Hector 16
Marvel Pinball 204
Marvel vs. Capcom 13, 114, 115, 209
Mass Effect 11, 18, 146, 147, 185, 186
mass participation 127
Massively Multiplayer Online; *see* MMO
Mattel 85
Maxis 171
Maze 135
McFarlane, Todd 118
McNab, Andy 40
McNamara, Brendan 111
mdkrafis 123
Meat Boy 106
Medal of Honor 40
Media Molecule 10
Mega Man 194, 195
Meguro, Shoji 145
memorabilia 9
Menounos, Maria 60
Mercury Meltdown Revolution 130
MercurySteam 100
Meridian 59 153
Messi, Lionel 59
Metal Gear 97, 103
Metal Gear Solid 103, 185, 188;
  Guns of the Patriots 103;
  Snake Eater 102, 185;
  Metal Slug 203, 207
Metroid 106
Mikami, Shinji 45
microphones 88
microprocessor 177

Microsoft 83;
  Flight Simulator 160, 168, 169;
  scoreboard 207;
  see also Kinect;
  Xbox
Microvision 134
Midway 115, 177, 195
Midway Arcade Treasures 205, 206
Mii characters 86, 87
Milton Bradley 134, 177
MindArk 157
Mindbuster 134
Minecraft 10, 11, 98, 99, 106
mini-games 33
Mirren, Helen 85
Misadventures of P.B. Winterbottom 133
Mitchell, Billy 175
Miyamoto, Shigeru 107, 175
Mizuguchi, Tetsuya 25, 51, 129
MLB 2K11 61
MMO GAMES 150-159
  beat-'em-ups 120;
  conventions 152;
  social networking 158-159
MMORPGs 31, 136, 144;
  fantasy 154-155;
  sci-fi 156-157
mobile gaming 86, 126-127, 172;
  Best of Mobile 34-35
Mobsters 158
Modern Arcade 178-179
ModNation Racers 79
Moerkerk, Jesse 9
Mojang 10, 98, 99
Molyneux, Peter 11, 83
Monkey Island 2 57, 111
Monster Galaxy 159
Monster Hunter 142, 143
Moore, Peter 83
Morasky, Mike 48
Mortal Kombat 15, 116, 117, 119, 209
Mortal Kombat vs DC Universe 115
Moshi Monsters 170
motion capture 110
MotionScan 110
motocross 65, 74
MotoGP 73
motor racing 70-73
motorcycle racing 73, 75, 76
MotorStorm: Apocalypse 13, 17, 26
movies 104, 135, 141, 175
Mr. Driller 201, 203
Ms. PAC-Man 201
Mullen, Ben 129
Multiplay i42 208

Mushiking: King of the Beetles 179
music 18, 159, 207;
  awards 164, 165;
  dynamic soundtrack 57;
  Instruments 88-89;
  karaoke 88, 89;
  soundtracks 48, 56, 100, 101, 130, 145, 165;
  theme songs 164
Muzyka, Ray 147
MX vs ATV: Alive 74
My Empire 11

N
Naka, Yuji 171
Namco Bandai 47, 177
Namco Museum 195, 205
Nancy Drew 111
Napoleon: Total War 165
Narrative Adventure 100-101
Naruto 119
NASCAR Kart Racing 79
Naughty Dog 26, 101
NBA: Elite 11 54;
  Jam 60, 195;
  pinball 204
NCAA Basketball 60
NCAA Football 11 60, 61
NCsoft 157
Need for Speed 11, 72, 77
Neo Geo 117
NES; *see* Nintendo NES
net entry key 179
Never Dead 15
Neversoft 88
Neverwinter Nights 147, 153
New Super Mario Bros. 106, 107, 108, 184, 195, 196
Newtoy 159
Nexon 120
NFL 2K 201
NHL 61, 201
Nichols, Will P 129
Nidhogg 11
Ninja Gaiden 196
Ninja Golf 200, 201
Nintendo 18, 32, 90, 133;
  scoreboard 194-199;
  see also Wii
Nintendo 3DS 16, 141;
  3DS 32, 33, 87, 94, 100, 135;
  Best of 3DS and DS 32-33;
  scoreboard 194-198
Nintendo GameBoy 129
Nintendo NES 196, 198, 201;
  controller 6, 22
nintendogs + cats 32, 171
Nishikado, Tomohiro 59, 176
Nishitani, Aya 145
Nonaka, Ryutaro 149

Norindr, Marie-Laure 7, 112
North, Nolan 101, 147
Norval, Victoria 134
N.O.V.A. 2: The Hero Rises Again 35, 49
Nvidia 35

O
Obsidian 103, 147
Oddworld: Abe's Exoddus 131
Old Time Baseball 61
Olympic Games 62, 63
Olympic Gold 62
OMM (Online Multiplayer Mode) 38, 105
ondra123 63
O'Neill, Gerard 44-45
Online Racing Association 72
Online Shooters 48-49
open-world games 98, 99, 106
Order & Chaos 155
Ordoñez, Lucas 73
Ordyne 201
Out Run 75

P
PAC-Man 173, 195, 205, 207;
  Battle Royale 177
Panzer Dragoon Orta 51
Papa Sangre 10
Papa-Wheelie 45
Parachute Ninja 133
Paradise Paintball 48
parallax barrier 32
Parallel Kingdom 87
PARTY GAMES 80-91
Patapon 166
PC gaming 30-31
Peggle 133
Perplex City 181
Persson, Markus 98
pet simulation 32, 170
Pet Society 158
Peto-Mad 21
Phantasy Star 145
Phantom Brave 149
Phoenix 177, 203
Physics-based Puzzles 132-133
Piepho, Blake 163
pinball 204, 205, 207
Pincus, Mark 159
Pixelbox 178
Planet Puzzle League 196
Plants vs. Zombies 167
Platformers 27;
  2D 106-107;
  3D 108-109
Playdom 158
Playfish 158
PlayStation 16, 45;
  Best of PlayStation 26-27;
  Eye Camera 87;
  games 79;
  Move Controller 37, 111
PlayStation 2 27, 57, 149

PlayStation 3 101;
  games 37, 43, 54, 120;
  Xbox 360 vs. PSP 36-37
PlayStation Network 17
PlayStation Portable 45, 129, 149
PlayStation Vita 10, 26, 79
Pokémon 139, **140-141**;
  Black/White 33, 141, 187;
  Mystery Dungeon 143;
  Red/Green/Blue 33, 140, 141;
  Stadium 141
Polnik, Kelsy 198
polygons 70
Polyphony Digital 17
Pong 55, 177
Popcap 16, 128
PoPoLoCrois 149
Portal 188;
  Portal 2 15, 17, 106, 132, 133, 187;
  Still Alive 207
Power Gig: Rise of the SixString 89
Prince 117
Prince of Persia: The Sands of Time 141, 187
Pro Evolution Soccer 59
pro-gaming 112, 163;
  Pro-gaming Review 66-67
Professor Layton 135
Project Gotham Racing 46
PS2; *see* PlayStation 2
PS3; *see* PlayStation 3
PSP; *see* PlayStation Portable
Psychosis 201
Punch-Out!! 123, 196
PUZZLE GAMES 124-135
Pye, Mason 21

Q
Q Entertainment 129
Quake 48, 49, 86

R
RACING GAMES 25, 26, **68-79**
Radiant Silvergun 46
Raiden 201
Rail Shooters 50-51
Rail Simulator 168
rally driving 73
Ramjagsingh, Sean 61
Rare 81, 82, 109
Ratchet & Clank 109, 184
Rayman 3D 108
Ray-O-Light 50
Ready 2 Rumble Boxing 123
Real Ghostbusters 203
Real Sound: Kaze no Regret 111
Real-time Strategy 166-167

Realtime Worlds 156
Rebmann, Jesse 97
Rechtschaffner, Steve 56
Red Dead Redemption 11, 45, 189
Red Faction: Armageddon 45
Resident Evil 104, 105, 184, 196
Retro Atari Classics 196
Reutersvärd, Oscar 131
Rez 25, 51, 129
rhythm games:
  Dancing 90-91;
  Instruments 88-89
Rift 31
Riley, George 175
Riven 111
Riviera: The Promised Land 149
RoadBlasters 201
Road Rash 201
ROB (Robotic Operating Buddy) 133
Robotron 2084 47
Rock Band 80, 88, 89, 204
rocket sliding 44
Rockstar 99
Rodriguez, Hector T 65
Roguelikes 147
ROLE-PLAYING GAMES 25, 30, 34, **138-149**;
  action 142-143;
  Japanese 33, **144-145;**
  strategy 148-149;
  western 146-147
Rollercoaster Tycoon 169
Rosenkilde, Juri 167
Rovio 10, 16, 126, 127
Runescape 155
Runnels, Matthew N 194

S
Sakamoto, Hideki 130
Salmoria, Nicola 178
Sam & Max 111
Samsung 35
Samurai Ghost 201
Samurai Shodown II 117
Samurai Spirits 117
Sandbox 98-99
Sandnes, Sean 123
Santa Claw 179
Satan's Hollow 201
Sci-Fi MMORPGs 156-157
Scott Pilgrim vs. The World: The Game 120, 121
Sculptured Software 60
SEE Virtual Worlds 157
SEED 156
Sega 46, 145, 201-202;
  Dreamcast 143, 200;
  Light Phaser 50;

Mega Drive 200;
Saturn 118
Sega Ages 201
Sega Genesis
Collection 205
Seven45 Studios 89
Sewer Shark 51
Seymour, Rob 117
Shadow of the
Colossus 186
Shadowrun 49
Shin Megami Tensei
144;
Persona 4 145
Shining Force 148
SHOOTING GAMES
24, 25, 27, 38-53
side-scrolling 46
sigRSW 47
SimCity 4 171
The Sims 160, 162,
170, 171
Simulation Racing
72-73
Simulation Round-up
168-169
SingStar 80, 89
Sinistron 202
Siren: Blood Curse 105
Skate 60, 64, 65
skateboarding 64, 65
Sled Storm 75
Sly Collection 108
smartphone gaming
34, 35
Smilebit 65
snowboarding 56-57
snowmobile racing 75
Soap Creative 173
Soccer 58-59
Soccer 59
Social Network
Gaming 48, 150,
158-159
SOCOM: Special
Forces 45
Soldier Blade 202
Solomon's Key 131
Sonic 63, 117
Sonic Adventure 2 185
Sonic & Knuckles &
Sonic the Hedgehog
196, 197
Sonic and the Secret
Rings 109
Sonic the Hedgehog
185, 197, 200, 202
Sony 17, 89, 130;
Online Entertainment
150;
scoreboard
204-206
SoulBlade 119
SoulCalibur 118, 119,
205-206, 207
Sound Shapes 10
Space Invaders 176,
197, 203;
pinball 204
space simulator 168
Spatial Puzzles
130-131
Spector, Warren 108,
109
The SpeedGamers 145
Spider-Man 7
Splatterhouse 2 202
Splinter Cell; see Tom
Clancy

'Splosion Man 106
Spore 171
SPORTS 54-65;
Combat Sports
122-123
SQIJ! 93
Square Enix 37, 144
SSX 56-57
Stadium Events 63
StarCraft 66, 143,
160, 162-163, 208,
209;
Brood War 163;
Wings of Liberty
162, 163, 185
Stardock 165
Star Fox 18, 50, 51
Star Wars 136-137;
The Force Unleashed
137, 184;
Knights of the Old
Republic 137, 146,
147, 184;
The Old Republic
136, 157;
Rogue Leader 169;
Star Wars Galaxies
136, 156
Stealth 96-97,
102-103
Steam 48
stereoscopy 62, 108
STRATEGY &
SIMULATION
160-171
Strategy RPGs
148-149
Street Cleaning
Simulator 169
Street Fighter 7, 66,
112, 114, 117;
Street Fighter III: 3rd
Strike 116;
Street Fighter X
Tekken 10;
Street Fighter Alpha
120
StreetPass Quest 33
Street Racing 76-77
Strong Bad's Cool
Game for Attractive
People 111
SubRoc-3D 176
Sucker Punch 27, 99
Sumo Digital 103
Superbrothers: Sword
and Sworcery EP 101
Super-Heros 64
Superman 115
Super Mario 7, 109,
197
Super Mario Bros. 187,
197
Super Mario Galaxy
108, 109, 185, 186
Super Mario Kart 68,
79
Super Mario Strikers
58-59
Super Mario Sunshine
109
Super Meat Boy 106
Super Metroid 184
SuperNemesis001 77
Super Paper Mario 131
Super Punch Out!! 196,
197
Super Scribblenauts
124

Super Smash Bros.
Brawl 117, 197
Super Soccer 59
Super Stardust HD 46,
206
Super Street Fighter
33, 116, 117, 120,
206, 209
Supremacy MMA 122,
123
Surf Ninjas 93
Survival Horror
104-105
Suzuki, Yu 11
SVT Merc 52
SwaggaLykUs 52
Sword of the Fargoal
147
Syberia 111
synaesthetic games
25
Syphon Filter 45, 53
Szulborski, Dave 181

T
Tabula Rasa 156
Tactics Ogre 149
Taito 176, 177
Taito Legends 206
Tajiri, Satoshi 141
Takahashi, Keita 130
Tatsunoko vs. Capcom
115, 197
Team Bondi 110
Team Fortress 2 48,
49, 208
Team Legends 41
Team Meat 106
Team Need for Speed
76
Team Shift n Drift 71
Techland 98
Teenage Mutant Ninja
Turtles 198, 199
Tegra Zone 35
Tekken 119
television 46, 141, 149
Telltale Games 111
tennis 62, 63
Terminator Salvation
178
Terraria 106
Test Drive 77
Tetris 128, 129, 198
Tetsujin 28-go 86
Texas Hold'Em Poker
159
TheChrisDood 72
theme park simulator
169
Thief: The Dark Project
103
Third-person Shooters
44-45, 53
Tiger Woods PGA Tour
62, 63, 198
Time Crisis 45
Time Gentlemen,
Please! 111
Time of Defiance 156
Tiny Wings 35
Tom Clancy 38, 96,
102
Tony Hawk 65
Too Human 142
Top 50 Game
Endings 182-191
Top Gear 71
Top Spin 4 62

Toro Station 9
Total Annihilation 166
Total War 31, 165
tournaments; see
eSports
Towell, Justin 73
Toyama, Keiichiro 105
Track & Field 62, 63
trading card games
87
trailers 98, 99, 119
Treyarch 16
Trials HD 75
Trine 133
Trion Worlds 31
Tron 202, 203;
pinball 204
Tropico 4 24
Tsujimoto, Ryozo
143
TurboGrafx-16 200,
201, 202
Turbo Out Run 75
Turn 10 70, 71
Turn-based Strategy
164-165
Turnell, Mark 195
TWIN GALAXIES
SCOREBOARDS
192-207
Twisted Metal 45
Twitter 101, 179

U
UberStrike 48
Ubisoft: action-
adventures 96-97;
dance games 90,
195;
fitness games 84;
Uplay 97
UFC Undisputed 123,
207
Ultima 146
Ultima Online
152-153
Ultimate Fighting
Championship 122
Ultimate Mortal
Kombat 117
Umehara, Daigo 116
Uncharted 26, 37, 101,
186
Unreal Tournament
48
UnspokenSix8 47
USB devices 160
user-generated
content 79, 99, 171

V
Valcalda, Dustin 65
Valkyria Chronicles
148, 149
Valve 10, 17, 19, 133
Vanguard 150
Vanquish 44
Victory Games 166
Virtua Fighter 115, 118,
119, 179
voice actors 57, 101, 111,
136, 146, 147, 157
Volition 169
Votava, Tom 131
Vs. Dr. Mario 203
Vs. Excitebike 65
Vs. Super Mario Bros.
203
Vulgus 115

W
Walker, Robin 49
Walt Disney Company
158
Warcraft III 167
Wardell, Brad 165
wargames simulator
168
Warhammer 40,000
166
WarioWare: Smooth
Moves 133
We Love Katamari 131,
206
websites 7
Western RPGs
146-147
Westmount Secondary
School, Ontario 83
Whisenhunt, Gary 147
Why So Serious? 181
Wiebe, Steve 175
Wii: Balance Board 84;
Best of Wii 28-29;
games 28, 29, 63,
90, 109, 130, 135,
142;
MotionPlus 199;
scoreboard 194-199;
Wheel 79
Wii Fit 80, 84, 85
Wii Party 198
Wii Sports 7, 63, 198,
199
Wii Sports Resort 63,
199
Wii U 18, 22, 28, 29
Wild Arms 149
Willemstyn, William 129
Wilson, Bryan 163
Wilson, Gareth 75
Windows Live 49
WinslowLee420 41
The Witcher 2:
Assassins of Kings
30, 106
Wong, Justin 115
Wood, Ray 147
World Cyber Games 65,
67
World of Goo 133
World of Warcraft 154,
155
wrestling 122, 123, 202
Wright, Edgar 121
Wright, Will 171
WWE Smackdown! 122
WWE Smackdown! vs.
Raw 123
WWF Super
WrestleMania
202
WWF War Zone 123

X
Xbox 51:
Best of
Xbox 24-25;
games 24-25;
see also Kinect
Xbox 360 24;
controllers 37;
games 24, 25, 37,
41, 53, 70, 71, 83,
104, 121, 133, 145;
Xbox vs PS3 36-37
Xbox Live: avatars 42;
games 25, 41, 75,
99, 107;

users 81
Xbox Live Arcade 121
Xbox Nations Free
Live Weekend 81

Y
Yoostar 2 82, 83
Your Shape 84
YouTube 58, 73, 126,
171, 179

Z
Zada, Mathew 135
Zaxxon 46
Zelda; see The Legend
of Zelda
Zeptolab 132
Zhang, Derek 164
Zidane_shinigami 114
Zoë Mode 131
Zombie Panic in
Wonderland 199
Zoo Keeper 203
Zynga 158, 159

TAGLINE QUIZ ANSWERS

THE *GAMER'S EDITION 2012* TAGLINE QUIZ
BEGAN ON PAGE 7. HOW MANY TAGLINES
DID YOU MATCH TO GAMES? NOW'S
THE TIME TO CHECK YOUR ANSWERS
AND FIND OUT THE NAME OF THE GAME.
THE TITLES ARE LISTED BENEATH THE
APPROPRIATE PAGE NUMBER.

Page 7
Little Big Planet 2

Page 8
Halo: Reach

Page 9
*Prince of Persia:
The Forgotten Sands*

Page 10
Deathsmiles

Page 11
Kinect Adventures

Page 12
*Dr Kawashima's
Brain Training*

Page 13
Rock Band

Page 14
Apache: Air Assault

Page 15
Fight Night Champion

Page 16
Ms. PAC-Man

Page 17
F.E.A.R. 3

Page 18
Guitar Hero: On Tour

Page 20
*Xenoblade
Chronicles*

Page 21
Prince of Persia

Page 24
*Harry Potter and the
Deathly Hallows*

Page 25
Wii Play

Page 26
Halo Wars

Page 27
Just Dance 2

Page 28
Dust 514

Page 29
*Need for Speed:
The Run*

Page 30
*Guitar Hero III:
Legends of Rock*

Page 31
*Transformers:
Dark of the Moon*

Page 32
Clock Tower 2

Page 34
inFAMOUS 2

Page 35
*Sonic and SEGA
All-Stars Racing
for iPad*

Page 36
Dragon Quest IX

Page 37
*StarCraft II:
Wings of Liberty*

Page 40
FIFA 12

Page 41
*Dreamworks
Madagascar Kartz*

Page 42
Def Jam: Fight for NY

Page 43
Kingdom Hearts

Page 44
*Haunted House
(1982)*

Page 45
Super Mario World

Page 46
*Dragon Ball Z:
Burst Limit*

Page 47
*Sonic the
Hedgehog 2*

Page 48
*Call of Duty:
World at War*

Page 49
*Warhammer 40,000:
Dawn of War*

Page 50
Kirby's Epic Yarn

Page 51
Metroid Prime

Page 52
Wii Fit

Page 53
*The Legend of Zelda:
Ocarina of Time*

Page 56
Assassin's Creed

Page 57
Dead Space 2

Page 58
*Battlefield:
Bad Company 2*

Page 59
Tekken 6

Page 60
SoulCalibur V

Page 61
Yakuza 4

Page 62
*Power Gig:
Rise of the SixString*

Page 63
Killer Instinct

Page 64
*The Misadventures
of P.B. Winterbottom*

Page 65
StarCraft

Page 66
*Dungeons & Dragons
Online*

Page 67
*Left 4 Dead 2:
The Passing*

Page 70
Dead Rising 2

Page 71
*Mortal Kombat vs
DC Universe*

Page 72
Fairy Trails

Page 73
*Metal Gear Solid 4:
Guns of the Patriots*

Page 74
BioShock

Page 75
Metal Gear Solid

Page 76
*Dead Space:
Extraction*

Page 77
Sonic Unleashed

Page 78
*Command &
Conquer: Red Alert 3*

Page 79
*Shogun:
Total War 2*

Page 82
Destroy All Humans!

Page 83
*Monkey Island 2:
LeChuck's
Revenge*

Page 84
blur

Page 85
Spore

Page 86
Mass Effect 2

Page 87
*Tiger Woods PGA
Tour 12: The Masters*

Page 88
*SOCOM:
Special Forces*

Page 89
Bayonetta

Page 90
Gears of War

Page 91
*Scott Pilgrim vs. the
World: The Game*

Page 92
Gears of War 3

Page 93
NBA Jam 2010

Page 96
Forza Motorsport 2

Page 97
Kinect Sports

Page 98
Forza Motorsport 3

Page 99
WipEout HD

Page 100
*Midnight Club:
Los Angeles*

Page 101
Skate 3

Page 102
Donkey Kong

Page 103
Monster Hunter Tri

Page 104
*World of Warcraft:
Cataclysm*

Page 105
Donkey Kong 3

Page 106
SSX 3

Page 107
Ultima Online

Page 108
Madden NFL 12

Page 109
Super Scribblenauts

Page 110
Top Spin 4

Page 111
Professor Layton

Page 114
Vanquish

Page 115
Final Fantasy XIII

Page 116
Pokémon

Page 117
Dragon Age: Legends

Page 118
Assassin's Creed II

Page 119
God of War II

Page 120
Final Fantasy Tactics: The War of the Lions

Page 121
Sega's company tagline in the 1980s

Page 122
Guitar Hero: Warriors of Rock

Page 123
Super Mario Bros.

Page 126
Bulletstorm

Page 127
AR.Drone

Page 128
Tom Clancy's Splinter Cell

Page 129
SSX (2012)

Page 130
Skull Girls

Page 131
Oblivion

Page 132
Marvel vs. Capcom 3

Page 133
Supremacy MMA

Page 134
The Sims

Page 135
God of War

Page 136
Heavy Rain

Page 137
The X Factor

Page 140
Call of Duty 3

Page 141
EA Sports Active

Page 142
Portal 2

Page 143
Empires & Allies

Page 144
Angry Birds

Page 145
Tony Hawk: Ride

Page 146
Cars 2

Page 147
The Sims 3

Page 148
Braid

Page 149
DEFCON

Page 152
Billy Hatcher and the Giant Egg

Page 153
Majestic

Page 154
Valkyria Chronicles

Page 155
Dr. Mario

Page 156
Yoshi's Cookie

Page 157
Civilization Revolution

Page 158
Borderlands

Page 159
Microsoft Flight Simulator 2004: A Century of Flight

Page 162
Band Hero

Page 163
Dead Space

Page 164
EVOKE

Page 165
Michael Jackson: The Experience

Page 166
Brütal Legend

Page 167
Eternal Darkness: Sanity's Requiem

Page 168
Perpetuum

Page 169
Street Fighter III: 3rd Strike

Page 170
Dragon Quest VIII: Journey of the Cursed King

Page 171
Crysis 2

Page 174
Child of Eden

Page 175
Geometry Wars: Retro Evolved 2

Page 176
Dreamfall: The Longest Journey

Page 177
Civilization

Page 178
Ultima Online: Kingdom Reborn

Page 179
Battlefield 3

Page 180
Command & Conquer

Page 181
World of Goo

Page 184
Red Faction: Guerrilla

Page 185
Assassin's Creed: Brotherhood

Page 186
Dungeon Siege III

Page 187
Gran Turismo 5

Page 188
Just Dance

Page 189
MAG

Page 190
Operation Flashpoint: Red River

Page 191
LEGO Batman: The Videogame

Page 194
Call of Juarez: The Cartel

Page 195
Killzone 2

Page 196
Assassin's Creed: Revelations

Page 197
De Blob 2

Page 198
Ratchet & Clank: A Crack in Time

Page 199
Red Faction: Armageddon

Page 200
Red Dead Redemption

Page 201
Truth or Lies

Page 202
Mindjack

Page 203
Prototype

Page 204
Kane & Lynch 2: Dog Days

Page 205
Mortal Kombat

Page 206
Just Cause 2

Page 207
Little Big Planet

Page 208
Batman: Arkham Asylum

Page 209
Dragon Age II

FROM ZERO TO HERO

Give yourself a point for each tagline you matched correctly, then add up your tally and see below to find out which gaming legend you are. Have you become a popular hero, or a shady villain?

0:	Zombie from *Dead Rising*	**101-110:**	Sub-Zero
1-10:	Edgar Ross	**111-120:**	The Master Chief
11-20:	Andrew Ryan		
21-30:	Psycho Mantis	**121-130:**	John Marston
31-40:	GLaDOS	**131-140:**	Ezio Auditore da Firenze
41-50:	Bowser		
51-60:	Robert de Sablé	**141-150:**	Lara Croft
61-70:	Sephiroth	**151-160:**	Captain Alex Mason
71-80:	Luigi	**161-165:**	PAC-Man
81-90:	Yoshi	**166-170:**	Link
91-100:	Sonic the Hedgehog	**171+:**	Mario

p.4–5: Gary Lucken
p.6: Ranald Mackechnie/Guinness World Records
p.6: Richard Bradbury/Guinness World Records
p.7: Richard Bradbury/Guinness World Records
p.8–9: Shinsuke Kamioka/ Guinness World Records
p.10–11: David Fisher/Rex Features
p.16: Kinect Cracker
p.16: Emmanuel Dunand/Getty Images
p.18: Kevork Djansezian/Getty Images
p.19: Jason Sussman
p.22–23: Ranald Mackechnie/ Guinness World Records
p.36: istock
p.36: Darrin Klimek/Getty Images
p.60–61: Tom Pennington/ Getty Images
p.60–61: Jason DeCrow/PA Images

p.68–69: Richard Bradbury/ Guinness World Records
p.75: Arcade Flyer
p.88–89: Suzie Gibbons/Getty Images
p.101: Jason Merritt/Getty Images
p.112–113: Richard Bradbury/ Guinness World Records
p.126: Justin Sullivan/Getty Images
p.127: Martti Kainulainen/Getty Images
p.130–131: Hideki Sakamoto
p.138–139: Ryan Schude/ Guinness World Records
p.146–147: Christopher Polk/ Getty Images
p.165: Kevork Djansezian/Getty Images
p.174–175: Alamy
p.174–175: Francis Bijl
p.174–175: Arcade Flyer

p.176–177: T.Laquet/http://space.invaders. paris.free.fr
p.178: Real Art USA
p.180–181: Tim Hawley/Getty Images
p.180: Warner Bros.
p.180: Bart Nagel
p.192–193: ArcadeImages
p.193: Alamy
p.202: Arcade Flyer
p.203: Arcade Flyer
p.204: Arcade Flyer
p.204: Rick Colls/Rex Features
p.205: Elie Bernager/Getty Images
p.206: Keith Brofsky/Getty Images
p.207: David Oliver/Getty Images
p.208: Major League Gaming
p.214–215: Getty Images
p.216: Chris Ward

ACKNOWLEDGEMENTS

Guinness World Records would like to thank the following individuals, groups and websites for their help in the creation of this book:

Danitra Alomia, Richard Booth, Pete Bouvier, Lauren Bradley, Jonnie Bryant, Hugo Bustillos, Dominic Carey, Charles Cecil, Ian Chambers, Nikki Chavez, Sophie Choudry, Walter Day, Jesse Divinich, Nicola Duarte, Roxana Etemad, Eurogamer.net, Gamesindustry.biz, Gamespress.com, Gametrailers.com, Chris Glover, Will Guyatt, Daan Hendrikse, Chris Higgins, Clay Hillhouse, IGN.com, Seth Killian, Lee Kirton, Simeon Lansiquot, Ollie Macefield, Emma Munro-Smith, Michael O'Dell, Cathy Orr, Stefano Petrullo, Mark Robins, Matt Roche, Brian Rubin, Ryan Seabury, Kristen Sharbaugh, Dean Shaw, Greg Short, Alex Simmons, Iain Simons, Caroline Thea Smith, Simon Smith-Wright, Jennie Sue, Leo Tan, Norie Tomoka, Adam Tuckwell, Twin Galaxies International, Alex Verrey, VGChartz.com, Mark Ward, Ewan Wells, Ryan Whelan, Emily Wooliscroft and Geoff Zatkin.

STOP PRESS

HIGHEST SCORE ON *MEGA JUMP*

Holder: Philipp Schneckenburger (Switzerland)
On 3 October 2011, gamer Philipp Schneckenburger was recognized for his score of 6,133,889 points on the mobile phone game *Mega Jump*. Philipp achieved the record as part of a week-long competition organized by in-game advertising start-up company Kiip (USA). Kiip provide real-world rewards in the form of products and services from leading brands for a variety of gaming achievements on popular iOS and Android games.

LONGEST VIDEOGAME MARATHON PLAYING A FIRST-PERSON SHOOTER
Holder: Jeff Nation, JJ Locke, Casey Coffman and George Vogl (all USA)
Just as we were going to press, we received news that a team of four gamers at Montana State University College of Technology in Great Falls, Montana, USA, had played *Battlefield: Bad Company 2* (EA DICE, 2010) for 51 hr 21 min between 20 and 22 August 2011. This beats the previous record featured on page 43.

LARGEST HANDHELD GAME CONSOLE PARTY
A total of 1,019 Nintendo DS users took part in a gaming party organized by GameStop (USA) at the Mandalay Bay Hotel & Casino in Las Vegas, Nevada, USA, on 28 August 2011.

LONGEST-RUNNING COMMERCIAL GRAPHICAL MMORPG
Holder: *The Kingdom of the Winds* (Nexon, 1996)
The pay-to-play MMORPG *Nexus: The Kingdom of the Winds* has been operating continuously in its native South Korea for a total of 15 years 189 days as of 5 October 2011. The game depicts the atmosphere of ancient Korea in the age of the Goguryeo kingdom.

LARGEST EYE-CONTROLLED GAMING TOURNAMENT

One of the most popular gadgets at the Eurogamer Expo 2011, held in London, UK, between 23 and 25 September 2011, was a game control system based on eye movement developed by the videogames charity SpecialEffect. The controller uses a camera to determine what the player is looking at and moves a cursor on screen accordingly, to provide responsive controls for hands-free racing fans and the physically impaired. As part of the weekend festivities, a total of 341 players competed in a tournament on *TrackMania Nations Forever* (Nadeo, 2008) organized by the Director of SpecialEffect, Dr Mick Donegan (left), and Eurogamer's

Johnny Minkley (right). The tournament's winner was Marc Lye (UK), who beat off some tough competition to set the record for the **fastest completion of the track "AO3-Race" using an eye control**, with a time of 21.94 seconds.

MOST PERFECT GAMES ON *Wii SPORTS*: BOWLING
Holder: John Bates (USA)
A golden oldie, 85-year-old John Bates had scored 8,550 perfect games on the bowling challenge on *Wii Sports* (Nintendo, 2006) as of 3 September 2011.